Seeking Fair Treatment

Seeking
Fair
Treatment
From the AIDS Epidemic to
National Health Care Reform

NORMAN DANIELS

New York   Oxford
OXFORD UNIVERSITY PRESS
1995

136668

Oxford University Press

Oxford   New York
Athens   Auckland   Bangkok
Calcutta   Cape Town   Dar es Salaam   Delhi
Florence   Hong Kong   Istanbul   Karachi
Kuala Lumpur   Madras   Madrid   Melbourne
Mexico City   Nairobi   Paris   Singapore
Taipei   Tokyo   Toronto

and associated companies in
Berlin   Ibadan

Published by Oxford University Press, Inc.
200 Madison Avenue, New York, New York 10016

Oxford is a registered trademark of Oxford University Press, Inc.

Library of Congress Cataloging-in-Publication Data
Daniels, Norman, 1942–
Seeking fair treatment : from the AIDS epidemic to
national health care reform /
Norman Daniels.
p.   cm.
Includes bibliographical references and index.
ISBN 0-19-505712-0
1. AIDS (Disease)—Patients—Medical care—United States
—Moral and ethical aspects.
2. Health care reform—United States.
3. Right to health care—United States.
I. Title.
RA644.A25D345   1995
362.1'969792'00973—dc20   94-39966

2 4 6 8 9 7 5 3 2

Printed in the United States of America
on acid-free paper

For the women in my life
Anne, Ellen, and Evelyn

Preface

Although I was trained as a philosopher of science, I began writing about issues of justice and health care because I wanted my philosophical work to have a bearing on problems of the real world. I had come of professional age during the civil rights and anti-war activism of the 1960s and early 1970s, and I had felt the pull of the call to "relevance." My timing was not ideal, for I began working on ethics and health policy in 1978, the exact moment that the nation turned its back on the goal of universal health insurance and focused attention on cost-containment instead. Despite my intentions, the world resisted being relevant to my work.

The idea that gripped Washington for the next dozen years was that we could not attempt to provide universal access until we solved the problem of runaway health care costs. This was a tragic and foolish error. During the 1980s, the "insurance gap" between those with adequate coverage and those lacking it grew enormously. During the same period, we watched our health care costs soar. At the beginning of the Carter years, just after Canada introduced its national Medicare system, we spent nearly the same percentage of Gross National Product on health care. Now we spend 50 percent more than the Canadians—and have worse health outcomes. We tried nearly every trick in the bureaucratic book, introducing Diagnosis Related Groups (DRGs), forcing millions into managed-care arrangements that disrupted existing doctor-patient relationships, and hiring armies of claims processors responsible for micromanaging the decisions of clinicians. Blue Cross of Massachusetts, which has 2.7 million subscribers, employs more people (6,680) than the whole Canadian health care program, which covers 26 million people (Himmelstein and Woolhandler 1994). As costs rose, we raised eligibility requirements for public insurance and forced the elderly to pay more out of pocket. We never reduced costs, only shifted them from one group or one budget to another. We even allowed insurers to make a paradox out of health care coverage: The more people needed it, the less they could get it.

In the late 1980s—the darkest period of anti–health care reform— one group, the AIDS activists, effectively drew national attention with their demands for better treatment and access to care. The more I thought about the issues they raised, the more it seemed that their fight was not the fight of a desperate and isolated group but a fight for exactly the things all of us needed in this health care system. While many were inclined to think "their" problems are only special problems, not "ours," analyzing the issues they raised revealed a common cause. It was that idea that led me to conceive of this book. Somewhat ironically, in the current groundswell for national health care reform, it is unfashionable to link health care reform to the issues raised by AIDS activists. There is a fear of tainting the broad appeal of reform with an unsavory association with HIV.

This book bucks that fashion. It explores the issues of justice that underly central controversies about how we should treat one another in the HIV epidemic: about the duty of physicians and other health care workers to treat HIV patients, about the conflicting rights of patients and infected health care workers, about the insurability of those at high risk, about access to unproven drugs, about rationing expensive treatments for HIV patients, about sex education in the schools. A unified account of justice and health care connects each of these controversies to the central problems in national health care reform. The lessons of the AIDS epidemic are lessons we must all take to heart if we are to succeed in treating one another fairly through health care reform. We must take these lessons to heart whether we attempt comprehensive reform, of the sort that elevated the hopes of many in the last couple of years, or whether we attempt a series of incremental reforms, of the sort that seems politically more likely in the next few years.

I owe debts to institutions as well as individuals for the support they have given me over the years I worked on this book. I received generous support from the National Endowment for the Humanities and the National Library of Medicine during the years 1989–1992. During 1992–1993, I benefited from a Tufts sabbatical leave and a fellowship in the Harvard Program for Ethics and the Professions. My effort to complete the book in the spring of 1993 was interrupted by my participation in the Ethics Working Group of President Clinton's Health Care Task Force, but I learned about the details of national health care reform in ways that inform my discussion in Chapter 8.

Many individuals generously shared their time and knowledge with me. I would like to thank these people for helpful comments on particular chapters of the book: Arthur Applbaum, Robert Baker, Flavio Baronicelli, Les Boden, Troy Brennan, Deborah Cotton, Ezekial Emanuel, Lachlan Forrow, Leonard Glantz, Sherwood Gorbach, Michael Grodin, Al Jonsen, Sheldon Krimsky, Paul Menzel, E. Haavi Morreim, James Noble, Stephen Pauker, Diane Rugg, Dennis Thompson, and David Willis. I owe a special debt to these friends with whom I have discussed many ideas in the book over a period of years: John Arras, Ron Bayer, Dan Brock, Allan Buchanan, Joshua Cohen, Larry Gostin, Don Light, John Rawls, James Sabin, Stephen White, and Dan Wikler. I benefited from both their agreements and disagreements with my views.

I owe my single greatest debt to Constance Putnam for her help in completing this book. Her considerable editorial skills, insight into the issues, perseverence, ability to work with good spirits under pressure, and tact in delivering firm but constructive criticism enabled her to introduce far more unity and clarity than was contained in the draft I placed in her hands. Its shortcomings remain my own.

Finally, I want to acknowledge drawing on previously published work for several of the chapters. I wish to thank the relevant editors and publishers for permission to use material from the following articles:

"Insurability and the HIV Epidemic: Ethical Issues in Underwriting." *Milbank Quarterly* 68:4(199):497–526.

"Duty to Treat or Right to Refuse?" *Hasting Center Report* 21:2(March-April 1991):36–46.

"HIV-Infected Health Care Professionals: Public Threat or Public Sacrifice?" *Milbank Quarterly* 70:1(1992):3–42.

"HIV-Infected Professionals, Patient Rights, and the Switching Dilemma." *JAMA* 267:10(March 11, 1992):1368–71.

Contents

Seeking Fair Treatment

1

AIDS and the Moral Fabric of Society

Living with the HIV Epidemic

The Human Immunodeficiency Virus (HIV) hides itself in the ecstasy of bedrooms and brothels in Asia and Africa, California and Florida. It drifts unnoticed, on a high, through needles in New York and Amsterdam. In ten million morality plays, HIV casts pleasure as the instrument of death—and as we learned from the 1993 International AIDS Congress in Berlin, there is no deus ex machina in the wings. There is no technological fix in sight to rescue us from the myriad tragedies already under way.

Only recently we had been assured that Auto Immuno Deficiency Syndrome (AIDS), the advanced stages of HIV infection, was being tamed, converted into a chronic disease like the many others that we have learned to "manage" for years with poisonous drug therapies. That assurance now seems premature, despite some success treating the opportunistic infections typical of more advanced stages of HIV infection. AZT (azidothymidine, now called zidovudine), it now turns out, fails to extend life and is being withdrawn as the early treatment of choice for delaying the onset of AIDS. Other exotic treatments hailed during testing add toxic disappointment as they, too, fail to avert the denouement HIV always brings. Vaccines are years or decades away.

Without a magic bullet, our fate is in our own hands. To avoid

3

tragedy, we must change what we do, how we behave. We must rewrite the inexorable plot.

Alas, that is easier said than done. The behavior we must change is intimate and compelling. Cloaked in privacy, even secrecy, this is held fast by culture and tradition—fed by the desperation of ghetto life, the uprooted loneliness of peasants seeking jobs in cities, or the denial that comes with adolescent visions of invulnerability. Professional journals bring encouraging reports about the (modest) successes of needle exchange programs on the streets and sex education programs in schools. Yet moral zealots block those very programs in the United States, and latex condoms are unfamiliar and unaffordable in poor African and Asian societies. Prevention through behavioral change, at present our best and only hope, offers no sure salvation.

We will be living with the HIV epidemic throughout our lives; this book is about how we can treat one another fairly while we do. I use the word "treat" deliberately. Most of what I will be discussing concerns medical treatment, construed broadly to include preventive measures. But how we treat one another in the settings I discuss says a lot about how we treat one another more generally; thus I mean "fair treatment" to be understood figuratively, as well as literally.

AIDS tests the moral fabric of our society, not because it is punishment for the wages of sin, as a few self-righteous individuals would have it, but because it sharpens controversies about our rights and our responsibilities toward one another. These are not novel moral controversies, but HIV makes them salient and urgent, forcing us in some cases to face them for the first time. Because so many who are infected belong to groups that are traditionally discriminated against—gays, drug abusers, members of minority groups, and a rapidly growing number of women and children—HIV tempts us to think in terms of "us" versus "them." To do so, and to treat people with HIV accordingly, is to fail the moral test. This book is about how we can pass it.

Treating Fairly: The Division of Labor

What are the rights and responsibilities of patients, doctors and other providers, and society as a whole in the HIV epidemic? What does fair treatment require? These questions are deceptively easy. No simple list will suffice to tell us. Our rights to fair treatment conflict with and limit each other. We have responsibilities and obligations to parties who, with some justification, make incompatible demands. The need to act forces us to resolve these conflicting claims as they occur, as best we can given the ethical tools we have at hand. I will use tools derived from ethical theory in general and from my own work on justice and health care, but I will aim at providing practical guidance about what fair treatment requires in the controversies I discuss.

Controversy about fair treatment crystallizes around issues that lie at the heart of the relationship between doctors and their patients. From there—from these people with special relationships to each other—it spreads outward to envelop other providers, insurers, and (eventually) society as a whole. Controversy spreads from those who need treatment, to those at risk of needing it, to those who are uninfected but need protection. My discussion follows the same order, and thus I will focus first on what the risks of transmission in medical settings imply about fair treatment between patients and doctors.

What is fair treatment between doctors and patients in the HIV epidemic? In the late 1980s, some doctors vocally and visibly refused to treat HIV-infected patients. Many more refused quietly (and still do). Many continue to demand that patients be tested. Is it fair for doctors to refuse to treat, or to demand to know the HIV status of, their patients? The American Medical Association (AMA) ruled in 1987 that physicians must treat HIV patients "regardless of risk." Other specialty associations disagree or have remained silent on the issue; state medical boards have taken conflicting positions.

How do we decide what the limits of professional obligations are, especially when those obligations involve taking risks? Do physicians have obligations independent of the level of risk? Are these obligations determined by historical practice? or by the "nature" of the profession itself? or by decisions of the relevant professional organizations? Or are these obligations perhaps requirements of justice? For example, do physicians have obligations to treat despite the risks they face because there is a general requirement of justice that all who need treatment are entitled to receive it? Or is there an obligation of justice not to discriminate against the handicapped? (People with HIV infection count as "handicapped" according to the Americans with Disabilities Act [ADA] of 1990.) Is it discriminatory for physicians to protect themselves against risks by refusing treatment in certain cases? Have physicians voluntarily undertaken an obligation to face some standard level of risk when they enter the profession, and does this standard bind them to treating HIV patients? These are the questions I consider in Chapter 2.

Transmission during treatment is a two-way street. The risk of doctor-to-patient transmission exists. In 1993, a sixth patient believed to have been infected by one Florida dentist was identified. In Chapter 3, I will look at whether it is fair for infected physicians to treat patients. In 1988, the AMA called for infected physicians to withdraw from "invasive procedures" or to inform patients of their status, allowing the patient a chance to give informed consent to the risks involved. The Centers for Disease Control (CFC) guidelines (1991) also called for infected physicians to refrain from "exposure prone" procedures. Infected physicians have insisted they will not comply with these rules. They oppose the rules as an unfair restriction of their rights as "handicapped workers," insisting they impose minuscule risks on patients. But, unimpressed with this argument, patients still insist they have a right to know the HIV status of their physicians—even when the risks are minimal; reasonable people want to avoid even small risks of death if they can do so with little effort or cost. Whose rights take priority here?

What is fair treatment at the hands of an insurer? Is it fair to exclude those with HIV infection or even AIDS from insurance, or to provide them with less coverage at much higher cost? These are the questions I will explore in Chapter 4. Since we cannot buy fire insurance when the engines are rushing to our house, insurers insist we should not be able to buy health insurance when we are HIV infected. Allowing either purchase would encourage people not to buy insurance until they knew they needed it; insurance then becomes expensive and burdensome to those who are at low risk. As we will see, some insurers even say it is unfair to those at low risk to make them subsidize the costs to those at high risk. They protested against "AIDS exceptionalism" when some states tried to prohibit HIV screening for health insurance. It was unfair, they argued, to treat HIV differently from other high-risk conditions that preclude people from standard insurance coverage.

The insurers are right that it would be unfair to single out HIV infection in this way; it *would* be unjustifiable "AIDS exceptionalism." But they are wrong that it is fair to exclude anyone at high risk of needing medical services from standard coverage. Health insurance is different from fire insurance. Health insurance is not simply a prudent way to manage risks, though it is that; rather, it is a way to meet a social obligation. In fact, the view of justice on which I shall be relying throughout makes it *a requirement of justice* to assure people access to needed services. We all have an obligation to share the burden of meeting that requirement; those at low risk have an obligation to subsidize those at high risk. Insurers can make their argument because society has not met its obligation to assure people access to necessary services. Determining what fair treatment is at the hands of insurers requires clarity about what fair treatment is at the hands of society.

What kinds of insurance reform would ensure that HIV patients have the access to services that justice requires? A survey of the kinds of access problems facing such patients suggests that incremental reforms of the current system would eliminate some of the barriers. The fundamental problems faced by those infected with HIV, however, typify problems faced by others as well; once again, AIDS exceptionalism is not the issue.

Another question that needs to be answered has to do with what treatments we must make available to HIV patients. Is it fair to deny people with AIDS access to drugs whose efficacy and safety are not fully proven? Here, too, it is evident we have much to learn about rights and responsibilities in general from focusing on the particulars brought to the fore by the large number of patients with HIV in our midst. In a case involving another life-threatening disease, cancer, the Supreme Court gave the Food and Drug Administration (FDA) the power to prohibit access to Laetrile because it had not been proven effective or safe. People with AIDS fought such restrictions as paternalistic. Demanding rapid "therapeutic" access to drugs still being tested, whenever there was any preliminary evidence of effectiveness, they made impassioned pleas of the following sort: "Time is critical; we cannot wait for testing that takes years to complete. We'll die without it, and we'll take the chance it may make us die sooner or with more complications, since it is our best chance at living longer."

The FDA revised its policy, providing what is now known as "parallel track" access to drugs that were not fully tested, *provided* that this therapeutic release does not undermine ongoing clinical trials. In Chapter 5, I will explore some of the questions raised by that policy: Is the proviso justified? Is it fair to insist on even this restriction on access to these drugs? Does the proviso in effect coerce some people into clinical trials (because there will be no early, "therapeutic" release for anyone not in a trial, unless enough others take part in the trials)? Does it hold people with AIDS hostage to this effort to promote the long-term welfare of others by producing knowledge that will prove beneficial down the road?

In Chapter 6, I will turn to look at one small piece of the puzzle known as rationing. When is it fair to ration or restrict access to treatments or services that are of particular importance to AIDS patients? In particular, I shall look at an instance of rationing that might have a significant impact on HIV patients; it involves an emerging group of high-technology home care services such as infusion and respirator therapies. These services seem to be precisely the kind of high-cost, low-benefit, end-of-life interventions that many have said we should not provide. These anti–interventionists might even say, "What better place to draw the line than here? Nipping this technology in the bud will be easier than cutting it back later." But would it be *fair* in the sense I have been using that term to refuse insurance coverage for the broad category of such treatments? Answering this question requires specifying the conditions that must be met for any rationing decision to be fair. And here, too, there is really no reason to engage in AIDS exceptionalism; as noted above, we learn from thinking about the case of HIV what is fair for all of us under other conditions as well.

Fair treatment in the HIV epidemic must involve the vigorous pursuit of preventive measures and not simply access to medical treatments. Although everyone agrees to the fundamental importance of prevention, and though everyone agrees about the lives at stake if preventive measures are not effective, more smoke and fire has surrounded discussion of prevention than any other aspect of the HIV epidemic. Because HIV is spread primarily through behaviors that many people think are immoral (or illegal), such as needle sharing in drug use or pre- and extramarital sex, the debate about prevention has been permeated with demands that only "moral" means be advocated. Needle exchange programs have been difficult to introduce as a result; opponents fear they will encourage drug use or at least condone it. Even more volatile has been the issue of sex education in the public schools—hardly a new issue, of course, but for the first time one perceived to be a matter of life and death. Advocates in one school district after another have aggressively gone about trying to institute sex education programs in local schools. Here the debate focuses on "abstinence only" programs versus "comprehensive" sex education. Many parents feel their basic values are threatened by comprehensive sex education; some even fear their children will be at greater risk if they are exposed to comprehensive sex education than if they receive all their sex education at home. In Chapter 7, I will turn my attention to what happens when moral convictions and public policy come into conflict in our efforts to protect the uninfected.

Throughout the 1980s, many people became aware that the problems faced by HIV patients in our health care system were problems we all faced. HIV patients lost insurance when they became sick; so did patients with cancer. HIV patients increasingly were locked in to jobs because they feared losing insurance if they changed employment; so were diabetics and others with chronic or preexisting conditions. HIV patients found they could not obtain adequate home care and other social support services; so did the partially disabled elderly. In many ways, HIV patients were like canaries in the mine: Their plight warned us about our risks in a badly designed system.

It is ironic how quickly we forget the canary. To change the morbid metaphor, the HIV epidemic throughout the 1980s provided a lens through which we could study the shortcomings of our health care system. The lens has turned into a mirror: Nationally, we now see that we ourselves—and not only HIV patients—are on view. With major national health care reform being considered seriously in Washington, there is very little discussion of the lessons to be learned from the HIV epidemic for this reform. Indeed, there almost seems to be a reluctance to admit that major reform will vastly improve the lives of HIV patients—it is as if we must be undertaking reform for "us" and not "them." No one, I was cautioned when I talked to friends about emphasizing health care reform in a book about fair treatment for HIV patients, wants to mix up the two issues.

Fair treatment for HIV patients, however, ultimately requires that we all treat one another fairly in the health care system. We need a system that works for all of us, that gives us what we need, where and when we need it. We must share equitably the burdens of building such a system. And so I conclude this book with a discussion of the design features comprehensive reform must have if it is to ensure fair treatment. Will coverage be truly universal? Will no one be excluded? Will coverage be "portable," or will it trap people in jobs? Will a comprehensive array of services be provided, covering the range of needs patients have? Will some people have more effective or better quality care than others? Will limitations on care be determined democratically and in a principled way? Will insurance be "community rated," so that premiums do not reflect individual risk, and will the burden of financing the system be borne according to ability to pay? Will reforms be responsive to patient or consumer choice? Fair treatment for HIV patients requires a system that will provide fair treatment for everyone.

The world of HIV is a microcosm of a larger world. I have already suggested that HIV exceptionalism needs justification, and that there is little about HIV that is different enough to warrant treating people with it differently from others. My hope is that by examining closely several of the particular questions that have moved center stage as a result of the HIV epidemic, we can learn how to think more clearly about rights and responsibilities in the world beyond HIV as well. Fair treatment is something about which we need to be concerned at every level.

Fair Equality of Opportunity and Health Care

Before turning to the exploration of these separate aspects of the fairness issues raised by the HIV epidemic, a word is in order about what I mean by "fairness." I have so far spoken loosely (and mostly implicitly) about what "justice" requires; at many points in the following chapters I will again appeal to claims about the requirements of justice. To make the foundation on which I am relying more precisely understandable, I will here sketch briefly the account of justice in health care that I have developed in more detail elsewhere (Daniels, 1985, 1988).

Most of us believe that health care is "special." In societies in which we tolerate many inequalities, we take more serious steps to assure we are being egalitarian in our delivery of health care than we do with the distribution of many other goods and services. We believe we have obligations to provide medical assistance—to friends *or* strangers—while we see no such obligation to meet many other needs they have. Why is that? We might be tempted to think that health care is special because people need their health quite independent of whatever else they may want, or that health is a requirement for happiness or fulfillment. But, desirable though good health is, it is by no means essential either to happiness or to leading a satisfying life; people can (and often do) adjust remarkably well to disease and disability.

We find a better answer by thinking more about what the good health ideally achieved by adequate health care *does* for us. Of course it extends life and improves the quality of life. But it is the way it *improves our situation* that matters. A central, unifying purpose of health care is to maintain, restore, or prevent the loss of—in short, to *promote*—functioning that is typical or normal for our species. Reducing pain and suffering also helps sustain the possibility of peculiarly human interactions. Thus preventive, acute, long-term, and palliative services all "promote" normal functioning.

By impairing normal functioning, disease and disability shrink our shares of opportunity to something less than what is fair. Health care thus—much like education—protects equality of opportunity. For each of us, a fair share of the normal opportunity range is the array of life plans we may reasonably choose in our society, given our talents and skills. The normal range of such plans may vary from one society to another, and from one period in history to another. Health care lets people utilize those portions of the normal range to which their full spectrum of skills and talents would give them access (assuming these have not also been impaired by special social disadvantages).

Because in a just society we have general social obligations to assure people fair equality of opportunity, we have specific obligations to provide health care services that promote normal functioning.[1] There should be no financial, geographical, or discriminatory barriers to a level of care that promotes normal functioning, given reasonable or necessary limits on resources. Otherwise, we are allowing opportunity to depend on other differences among people that should not be permitted to have such significant effects. Thus our obligation to assure access to needed health care services is a special case of our obligation to protect equality of opportunity—a point I shall stress repeatedly.

This account of what is fair also has implications for what kinds of health care services we are obliged to provide people. Health care is not the only important good, and since resources will always be limited, we will always have to choose among the services we offer. (This point, too, will come up more than once.) We can guide hard public-policy choices about which services are the critical ones to provide by considering their relative impact on the normal opportunity range. Rights and entitlements to health care are thus *system relative:* Entitlements to services can be specified only within a system that works to protect opportunity as well as possible, given reasonable limits on resources.

Many kinds of health care systems are compatible with this fair-equality-of-opportunity account. For instance, at least in theory, it leaves room for "tiered" systems with public and private sectors: If we can characterize a basic tier of services that society is obliged to make available to everyone, because of its effects on opportunity, there is nothing in these principles that prohibits allowing individuals to purchase private insurance for more elaborate services—unless the higher tiers work to undermine the most basic one, or unless the tiering fails adequately to protect the opportunities of the worst-off groups. The concern that the opportunities of all be protected thus imposes serious constraints on the *structure of inequality* that results from tiering. (Consequently, one argument against tiering—the standard European one—focuses on the way tiers tend to undercut the solidarity needed to maintain the system.)

The arguments I develop in this book will not always turn on specific features of the fair-equality-of-opportunity account; they are compatible with views about justice and health care that establish in alternative ways some of the principles or other claims I rely on. But for the sake of consistency, and to show the implications of my own account, I will appeal to the fair-equality-of-opportunity account throughout.

2

The Duty to Treat and Access to Care

Duty to Treat or Right to Refuse?

Although the disease of AIDS is relatively novel, the moral problems it poses are not. One very old question in particular that the HIV epidemic forces us to reconsider is this: Do physicians and other health care workers have a moral duty to treat HIV patients despite the risk of contagion?

This question was thrust into public consciousness in the late 1980s, when a world-famous heart surgeon proclaimed that he would not operate on HIV positive patients and when Dr. Lorraine Day, an orthopedic surgeon in San Francisco, vigorously protested— in the newspapers and on TV—the risks she faced in treating HIV positive patients (Goodman, 1988). The question became real for me when a dinner I was enjoying with Peter, a surgeon friend, was inter- rupted by a phone call: Peter was being asked to operate on a patient with a fractured cheek. He inquired whether the patient—a transves- tite who had been assaulted after a pickup in a bar—would take an HIV test, and was told no. Peter then refused to operate and sug- gested that the patient be sent to a nearby public hospital, if no one else would take the case.

I asked Peter what would happen to the patient; he replied that a plastic surgery resident would get some practice he probably needed. When I asked why the resident should have to take the risk when he wouldn't, Peter said, "Because he can't get out of it, and I can."

Peter insisted that surgery of this sort—where bone chips and wiring are frequently involved—often produces cuts, and that there is no way to avoid them. Working as he did in a city with a high incidence of HIV, he believed that his cumulative risk of infection was high even if the risk in one operation was not. "Lots of surgeons carry antibodies for hepatitis B," he said; "that's a risk we all have taken. But I won't take the chance of bringing AIDS into my bed and killing my wife. Would you take that risk?"

I confessed I knew neither what the risks were nor how I would behave in his place. I then asked him whether he would still feel the risk was not worth taking if AIDS mainly affected pregnant women or young children—and he said *he* didn't know. In the end, a different surgeon in the same hospital took the case.

Did my friend have a moral duty to treat that patient? If so, did it derive from a professional oath or code, or from medical tradition? Or from the moral requirement to act in a nondiscriminatory manner? Or is such a moral duty—if it exists—a consequence of a social obligation to guarantee patients access to health care? Will the reluctance of physicians like my friend mean than many HIV patients go without treatment? What happens to our social obligations in this realm of activity if physicians deny they have a duty to treat or simply do not carry the duty out?

Professional Disagreements About Duties

Answers to these questions about a duty to treat remain controversial among physicians. Peter, for example, was sure he did not have a duty to accept patients when they put him at personal risk. He said he could refuse to accept patients for less important reasons, including that they could not pay him—so why not refuse when the patients threatened his or his family's health? Despite his firmness on this point, however, he was defensive about his refusal.

Nor is my friend alone in expressing such an attitude. In its August 1990 report to President Bush, the National Commission on AIDS remarked that "a shocking number of physicians are reluctant to take care of people living with HIV infection and AIDS" (National Commission, 1990:8). Only "10 percent of internal medicine residents have a strong commitment to the care of HIV infected people and are likely to include them in their post-training practice," it was noted, whereas "25 to 30 percent have a definite aversion to HIV work and are planning in their professional lives to avoid contact with these patients" (National Commission, 1990:9). The number of dentists who will treat people with HIV infection, the commission's report also points out, is "grossly inadequate and unacceptable" (National Commission, 1990:7).

Factors other than fear of contagion also contribute to this reluctance to treat. Some physicians and dentists express concern that their practices will be shunned by non-HIV patients if it is known that AIDS patients are being treated. Others insist they do not know enough about HIV infection and are too busy to learn. (This excuse drew a rebuke from the National Commission, which insisted that with more than one million HIV patients across the country, physicians "simply must acquire the expertise" [National Commission, 1990:9].) Still other providers clearly have antipathies to one or more of the groups at highest risk. Unlike fear of contagion, such reasons seem to be expressions of bias or capitulations to it rather than respectable grounds for denying that one has a duty to treat.

It is difficult to know merely from surveys of physician attitudes precisely what the effect of reluctance to treat is on HIV patients' access to care. The National Commission clearly believes these attitudes matter; even if they have no major impact on access—because enough other providers offer treatment, when and where it is needed, to take up the slack—the central question remains: What are the moral and professional duties of physicians in these cases?

State professional organizations and medical boards disagree about the duty to treat. In 1987, the Board of Medical Examiners in New Jersey proclaimed that, "A licensee of this Board may not categorically refuse to treat a patient who has AIDS or AIDS related complex, or an HIV positive blood test, when he or she possesses the skill and experience to treat the condition presented." A diametrically opposed position was taken by the Arizona Board of Medical Examiners (v. Annas, 1988:30). Medical boards specify the legal duties of physicians in both these states, but these divergent rulings probably reflect a difference in underlying beliefs about moral duties. James Mann, chairman of the Texas Medical Association's Board of Counselors, defended that board's decision that there is no moral or professional duty to treat as follows: "We didn't agree that a physician who diagnoses AIDS is mandated to treat the patient. I don't think it can be called discrimination when it's a matter of a guy [sic] laying his health and career on the line" (cited in Annas, 1988:30).

Disagreement exists at the national level as well. Nursing codes, not surprisingly, take a strong stand in support of a duty to treat: "In most instances, it would be considered morally obligatory for a nurse to give care to an AIDS patient. If the nurse is immunosuppressed, however, it could be reasonably argued that the nurse is not morally obligated to care for that patient . . . [and the nurse must then] . . . choose whether or not to go beyond the requirement of duty" (American Nursing Association Committee on Ethics, 1986, cited in Freedman, 1988). The distinction between normal and immunosuppressed nurses is important, for a nurse with a compromised immune system is more at risk of infection. So is the implication that the level of risk to the individual determines whether treatment is within or above the call of duty. (I will return to this point later.) In contrast, the 1986 national American Medical Association statement on the issue left a door wide open to refusals to treat: It allowed physicians who were "emotionally" unable to care for AIDS patients to refer such patients to others. Then, in late 1987, the AMA issued a new statement—which seems to close that very door:

> A physician may not ethically refuse to treat a patient whose condition is within the physician's current realm of competence solely because the patient is seropositive [tests positive for the antigens to HIV—a person who changes from seronegative to seropositive is said to "seroconvert"]. The tradition of the American Medical Association, since its organization in 1847, is that: "when an epidemic prevails, a physician must continue his labors without regard to the risk to his own health." . . . Physicians should respond to the best of their abilities in cases of emergency where first aid treatment is essential, and physicians should not abandon patients whose care they have undertaken (AMA, "Ethical Issues Involved in the Growing AIDS Crisis," cited in Freedman, 1988:24).

In contrast to the AMA, some professional organizations of surgeons—such as the American Academy of Orthopedic Surgeons (AAOS)—have not insisted that surgeons have a duty to treat HIV patients. The AAOS has said that access to good orthopedic care should be assured and that there is a moral and ethical responsibility to provide care to all patients, but it has not taken the explicit stand found in the 1987 AMA statement. In off-the-record conversations with those involved with the AAOS Task Force on AIDS, I was told that the organization was clearly split and the leadership did not want to go beyond where the membership was likely to follow.

Problems with the AMA Position

Why is there so much disagreement here? If we examine the AMA position, the sources of controversy become apparent. The 1987 statement takes the following stand:

> Principle VI of the 1980 Principles of Medical Ethics states that "A physician shall in the provision of appropriate patient care, except in emergencies, be free to choose whom to serve, with whom to associate and the environment in which to provide medical services." The Council has always interpreted this Principle as not supporting illegal or invidious discrimination. . . . Thus, it is the view of the Council that Principle VI does not permit categorical discrimination against a patient solely on his or her seropositivity.

This position is open to an obvious reply: Refusal to treat HIV patients (or those at high risk for HIV) is not invidious discrimination, but merely self-protection. Even if the effects of such choices fall most heavily on certain groups—such as gays—who are often the object of invidious discrimination, the intent here is not to discriminate, but to protect oneself. Exactly this line was taken in an article entitled "My Brother, the Doctor, Is in Danger," in the April 1989 issue of *The New York Doctor* (Charen, 1989). And indeed, as my friend Peter argued, if physicians can protect themselves against economic loss—for instance, by refusing to take Medicaid patients or those without insurance—then why should they not be able to protect themselves against risks to health? The AMA statement simply claims, without discussion, that categorically refusing to treat HIV positive patients is "invidious discrimination." Yet, at least on the surface, risk avoidance and discrimination reflect two very distinct intentions.

To save the AMA position, we might flesh out its implicit argument as follows:

Refusing to treat HIV positive patients is discriminatory, because physicians have a duty to face some standard level of risk associated with their profession.

The risks of HIV positive infection and its consequences do not exceed that level and are comparable to other risks physicians willingly take.

Consequently, appealing to self-protection in the case of patients with high risk for HIV is discriminatory.

Two challenges face this revised position. First, even if there is a duty to treat in the face of *some* level of personal risk, the risks of HIV infection might exceed that level for some or all practitioners. Then it would be supererogatory (i.e., beyond the call of duty) for such physicians to treat HIV patients. Second, some might deny that physicians have a duty to treat in the face of *any* significant levels of personal risk. To evaluate these challenges, we must consider the evidence about HIV risks to health care workers. Before doing so, however, I want to make a more basic point.

Consent and the Distribution of Risks

The general mechanism for distributing the benefits and burdens of risk-taking is, and should be, *consent*. If physicians have a duty or obligation to take certain risks, it must be the result of their *agreeing* to do so. This is my provisional hypothesis about the foundations for any duty to treat despite risks of contagion.

The centrality of consent to risk-taking in medical contexts should be obvious. In the past twenty years, medical providers have had to learn that they must obtain from patients informed consent to whatever risks are being imposed on them, even when clear benefits accompany the risks. But our society's reliance on the idea of consent is evident well beyond the medical setting. For example, hazard pay negotiations imply that persons have a limited right to sell, at its market value, their willingness to face risks. We become skeptical about this market for risk-taking when we realize that workers in some industries and contexts have little option but to consent to hazardous work. In such cases, we may insist on strict regulation of hazards because we believe the consent to face risks is not truly voluntary (v. Daniels, 1985:Ch.7). We take consent (with the control it involves) to be so important that we allow it to lead to what otherwise may look like inconsistent behavior. For instance, people who do not want a canning company to put additives in their food or farmers to use pesticides—even though these impose only a minute risk of death by cancer—may still smoke, eat fatty meats, and refuse to buckle their seat belts, or they may scuba dive or hang glide or live in Washington, D.C.; as a society, we are accustomed to accepting these idiosyncratic choices.

My provisional hypothesis is also consistent with our views about obligations to take risks in other dangerous occupations or professions. For example, firefighters or police officers are obliged to take risks that are greater than those in many other occupations; we assume that in choosing those careers, undergoing the training they involve, and agreeing to follow the codes and practices regulating members of fire and police departments, individuals have given consent to facing those risks. This may not mean that they can articulate the risks with statistical precision. But they are aware in a general way of the kinds of risks they will typically face, and can differentiate those typical risks from others that are exceptional. The distinction between these two classes of risks is clear. The standard level of risk that firefighters are obliged to face is already higher than the standard level for ordinary citizens; it is higher yet, when the lives of people (rather than when property preservation alone) are at issue. Undertaking *exceptional* risks, however, is still viewed as beyond the norm. The firefighter who truly risks life and limb is hailed as a hero, not merely as a competent doer-of-duty.

We often believe that people in risky occupations are self-selected for their daring. This presupposes that the risks are widely perceived and that people have real alternatives. Moreover, those who stay in risky occupations often participate in a subculture that supports their willingness to take risks. Sometimes the subculture has a "macho" tone, but—more generally—social support and rewards are exchanged in recognition of the daring required.

The parallels to medicine are strong. People who enter medical fields clearly had alternatives. Moreover, there is a general understanding among physicians and the lay public alike that physicians face an increased risk of contagion from disease (remember Peter's remark about hepatitis B [HBV] infection among surgeons), and this understanding is refined during schooling and training. For example, screening new house staff and nurses in medical centers to determine whether individuals face special risks of contagion (because of, say, immunosuppression or pregnancy) is common. Those determined to be at high risk may be asked to avoid certain treatment situations, materials, or hospital areas. Similarly, some Occupational Safety and Health Administration regulations aim at protecting "hypersensitive" individuals who cannot tolerate the standard level of risk (v. Daniels, 1985:Ch.8). Protecting immunosuppressed health care providers is reasonable "risk management," it might be argued, a measure taken to reduce bad outcomes. But such special protection supports a claim that only standard risks are included in the duty to treat, while—as the American Nursing Association code makes explicit—some nosocomial or treatment-related risks clearly range beyond what duty requires.

One dissimilarity between risky nonmedical occupations and medicine is worth noting. In recent years, no subculture of heroism surrounds health care workers, perhaps because the risks from infection have significantly diminished during the period of Pax antibiotica, in Arras's (1988) apt phrase. It has been remarked that during the period 1850 to 1950, physicians standardly cared for patients with infectious diseases, and their risk-taking was compensated for by the power, self-esteem, and admiration they derived from a cultural climate in which they were granted extensive paternalistic powers. Because such supports have largely eroded, "the first step in making physicians heroes is unequivocal support, emotional and financial, for any one who seroconverts in the line of duty" (Flegenheimer et al., 1989:960).

Consent and the AMA Statement Qualified

As we have seen, the 1987 AMA claims that physicians are expected to treat "*without regard to the risk to [their] own health*" (emphasis added). This claim cannot be taken at face value, however, for it implies that physicians have consented—simply by becoming medical professionals—to facing any level of risk, however high, including that of certain death. No one believes that. Indeed, we ask soldiers to *volunteer* for especially risky missions, and we treat their willingness to face almost certain death as heroic and *above the call of duty*. Similarly, we understand that there are some limits, however vaguely specified, to the risks physicians have agreed to face. Fox (1988) suggests that a historical precedent for this conclusion can be found in the special contracts societies have in the past negotiated with certain physicians to act as "plague doctors." Clearly these societies did not assume that all physicians had agreed, merely by having become physicians, to accept extraordinary risks of death.

Since risk-taking must involve consent, the best way to construe this feature of the AMA position is to modify it. In keeping with the way I earlier spelled out explicitly the argument of the revised AMA statement, the requisite modification would go something like this:

Physicians consented to face some standard level of risk when they
   agreed to enter the profession and trained for it.
The risks of nosocomial HIV infection are not so high that they
   require additional consent.

Consequently, refusing to treat HIV patients is invidious discrimination.

Even this modified position may need further qualification, depending on information about nosocomial risks. Specifically, further refinement may suggest a middle ground between the extreme positions that characterize this controversy concerning duty to treat: the blanket affirmations on the one hand and the absolute denials on the other. Let us turn now to see what we know about this important issue—the evidence of the risks of HIV transmission during treatment.

The Risks of HIV Transmission During Treatment

The Aggregate Risks of HIV Transmission Are Low

Are the facts about the real risks to health care workers, including physicians, consistent with the modified AMA position? Consider first the data available at the time the AMA formulated its policy, in the late 1980s. The aggregate data, in more than half a dozen studies, suggest generally low risks of HIV transmission to health care workers. Allen (1988:4), summarizing combined studies of almost 1,400 health care workers and 1,300 dental personnel, concludes that "the risk of HIV infection even after mucous membrane exposure or parenteral [inserted into the body other than through ingestion, e.g., through a cut or needlestick] inoculation of infected blood, fluids, or secretions is extremely low—probably less than one per 200 incidents." A summary by the Centers for Disease Control of 1,107 health care workers tested after exposure, mostly by needlesticks, showed only four to be HIV positive, for a conversion rate of 0.0041. All of these were exposed by needlesticks, one had an HIV positive sexual partner, three had no risk factors, and two of them were emergency technicians injured by co-workers during resuscitation attempts (Centers for Disease Control, 1989; Fahey et al., 1989; Marcus et al., 1988a, 1988b). This conversion rate is probably a maximum estimate, or we would be seeing a much higher proportion of health care workers who are HIV positive.

Three important observations can be made about the level and distribution of risk to health care workers. (1) *Health care workers seem to be at no greater risk than the public as a whole.* Some employment information is known for about 86 percent of the first forty thousand AIDS cases. Of those where employment informa- tion is available, 2,232 (5.6 percent) reported employment in a health care setting before or at the time of diagnosis. This is almost exactly the percentage of persons in the workforce as a whole who are in health services. (2) *Health care workers who have AIDS fall into the same high-risk groups as the population as a whole and in the same proportions.* (3) *The 2,232 health care workers with AIDS were dis- tributed among all categories of health care workers.* Among this group, 108 fall into no known risk category. And of these, seventeen died, and 50 percent are still being reviewed; 33 percent still had no known risk factor after their cases were carefully reviewed. Surgical specialties were not overrepresented; only housekeeping and mainte- nance workers were disproportionately likely to be infected in the absence of an identified risk (v. Allen, 1988:3). A study of military reservists employed in health care settings showed that the only category of workers showing higher HIV prevalence than among non–health care reservists were single white and black males em- ployed as nurses or medical technicians (Cowan et al., 1989).

The most recent figures from the CDC (Centers for Disease Control, 1993), in their continuing surveillance of exposed health care workers, confirm the same conclusions. By September 1993, there were thirty-nine cases of HIV-infected health care workers (eleven had AIDS) whose reported occupational exposure to HIV was documented by the CDC and whose infection could not be ex- plained by their membership in a high-risk group. There were eighty-one other cases in which job-related exposure was reported but could not be documented. Among the documented cases, fifteen were clinical laboratory technicians and thirteen were nurses, sug- gesting a higher concentration of (reported) exposures in these groups of workers than the earlier figures indicated. (Caution should be exercised in assuming that the reported rate of exposure reflects the actual rate of exposure, since some groups may be more willing to report exposure than others.) No surgical cases were reported and documented. The known rate of seroconversion from needlesticks is 36 out of ten thousand (or about one third of one percent). (Tokors et al., 1993).

These increased numbers of infected health care workers might seem more alarming than the figures from the late 1980s, but they are consistent with all the major conclusions drawn from earlier studies. The higher numbers simply reflect another five years of a growing epidemic, not a higher rate of transmission (Centers for Disease Control, 1993).

Breaking Down the Nosocomial Risks

In general, the risk particular physicians face will be the result of (1) the general risk of seroconverting (testing positive for HIV antigens) per incident of exposure (for example, per needlestick), (2) the frequency of exposure incidents (such as needlesticks), and (3) the proportion of their patients who are HIV positive. Hagen and colleagues (1988) estimated the frequency of needlesticks to be about one in forty cases. Using high estimates of HIV seroconversion rates and high estimates of HIV prevalence among patients, they still conclude that the "surgeon's risk of HIV infection when operating on an infected patient appears to fall between one chance in 130,000 and one chance in 4500." They argue for the plausibility of this estimate on the grounds that there would otherwise be a high rate of HIV infection among surgeons operating in high-risk areas (the same kind of reasoning I used in the previous section to argue that Allen's conversion rate is probably a maximum estimate).

Emanuel (1989) breaks down the statistics with somewhat different conclusions. Assuming a rate of forty needlesticks per year (which implies 1,600 operations a year if Hagen et al. are correct about the rate), a 1 percent risk of seroconversion per HIV-infected needlestick (which is three times the CDC's estimate of .36 percent [Tokors et al., 1993]), and a patient prevalence of 4.6 percent, Emanuel concludes that emergency department surgeons face a 2 percent annual risk of infection. If, as Dr. Lorraine Day—whom we met at the beginning of this chapter—claimed, 33 percent of her patients are HIV positive, then she faces a 12 percent per year risk of HIV infection, or 49 percent for five years, a very high level of risk indeed. For comparison, Emanuel claims that medical house staff face an annual risk of death comparable to that of Boston firefighters. Dr. Day's annual risk of death, on the other hand, he concludes is higher than the risk faced by military personnel in Vietnam during the war.

Emanuel's estimates face a serious problem: They are much higher than observed rates of HIV infection among health care workers, and the pattern of the distribution of HIV infection among health care workers does not resemble what we would expect if these estimates are accurate. (Even with HIV's long latency, we would probably have seen some of the predicted effects on health care workers by now if the nosocomial risks conformed to Emanuel's estimates.) Still, these estimates come from honestly made extrapolations, not out of an attempt to inflame opposition against a duty to treat. Indeed, Emanuel firmly believes in such a duty, basing it on "the concept of medicine as a profession and on the physician's particular professional role" (Emanuel, 1988:1686), and he concludes that only extraordinary risks—like those estimated for Dr. Day—are beyond the call of duty.

Leaving this problem aside, we see that Emanuel's estimates raise reasonable questions about the risks a minority of physicians face. And because of these questions, it is not unreasonable for some physicians to believe they face risks higher than the standard level to which all physicians presumably consented. Since consent to risks is essential, we should (1) attempt to firm up the estimates of these risks, (2) do what we can to reduce the exposure of the vulnerable physicians, both by improving measures to prevent exposures and by increasing the access of HIV patients to other physicians, and (3) provide conditions under which consent to these special risks can be obtained.

Hepatitis B (HBV) versus HIV

We still need a positive characterization of the standard level of risks to which physicians have presumably consented on the modified AMA view. The risks of hepatitis B are a useful reference point: Physicians like my friend Peter are aware of the risks, yet do not refuse to treat those who might be infected with HBV. If the risks of HIV do not exceed those of HBV, can we infer consent to the former from consent to the latter? In fact, the risk of seroconverting to HIV and then dying is lower than (but almost the same as) the risk of seroconverting to HBV and then dying. Hepatitis B is much more prevalent in the patient population, by a factor of ten, and is much more highly contagious than HIV, by a factor of about forty; but though it is a serious disease, it is less likely to kill than HIV [Centers for Disease Control, 1989;38(S-6):5–6].

Annas (1988:28) concludes that "as long as scientific estimates place the chance of becoming infected with HIV and dying at less than the probability of becoming infected with hepatitis B and dying, there is no objective data to warrant discriminating against an HIV-infected individual." This point seems to support the AMA contention that refusal to treat HIV patients is invidious discrimination. This quick comparison between the risks of hepatitis B and those of HIV ignores some relevant differences, however, differences that count against the claim that consent to risking HIV is included in consent to risking HBV. First, people judge the risk to be worse when there is near certainty of death upon infection (as in HIV)—even though there is less risk of infection. That is, a fairly general bias skews the reaction to risk. Second, there is less risk of sexual transmission of HBV to heterosexual partners. This means there is also less risk from HBV of a conflict with obligations to protect family members from harm. Third, there is less stigma attached to having HBV than to having HIV. Fourth, there is a vaccine for HBV infection that is more than 90 percent effective (Centers for Disease Control, 1989;38[S-6]:5–6); the risk of infection followed by death is reduced by a factor of almost twenty for vaccinated health care workers.

In view of these differences, some physicians may insist that they consented to the risks of hepatitis B but not of HIV. (Peter claimed this.) Still, I do not believe that the differences here are sufficient to establish that physicians typically have consented to one kind of risk but not the other. The hepatitis B vaccine is only recently available, and therefore the level of risk to which most practicing physicians presumably consented was the prevaccine level. Moreover, although the certainty of death following HIV may be the factor that impresses some physicians, I also believe most underestimate the combined probability of dying from nosocomial hepatitis B. The conclusion we are led to is this: There is in general good reason to treat consent to the risks of hepatitis B as tantamount to consent to the risks of HIV, but the differences between these risks are such that we cannot simply regard as disingenuous someone who is impressed by the differences and denies having consented to the risks of HIV. We cannot, in other words, simply dismiss all instances of reluctance to treat as examples of reneging on a prior commitment.

Consent and Variations in Risk

The *revised* AMA position as I modified it comes to this: Refusing to treat HIV patients is invidious discrimination because (1) physicians have consented to some standard level of nosocomial risks when they trained for the profession and entered it, and (2) the nosocomial risks of HIV infection are not so high that they require additional consent. The evidence about HIV risks is for the most part consistent with this position, but two qualifications already hinted at are in order.

First, the *estimated*, but *not observed*, cumulative risks to some physicians who practice in high-incidence areas exceed the standard level of risk. Despite the speculative nature of the estimates, this minority of physicians is neither unreasonable nor disingenuous to insist that additional consent to these particular risks is necessary. In cases of reasonable disagreement about these risks, we should err in the direction of seeking explicit consent rather than continue to insist that a duty already obtains. Since some of the alleged risks are elevated as a result of society's failure to meet its clear obligations to eliminate problems with insurance and other barriers to access, it would be hypocritical to insist that physicians comply with their contested obligations.

Second, some people perceive the risks of hepatitis B and HIV differently, despite the fact that the combined risk of infection followed by death is similar (sans vaccine). For such individuals, consent to the risks of HBV is not tantamount to consent to the risks of HIV. Here, too, we must err in the direction of seeking more explicit consent rather than automatically treat disagreement about risks and the consequent reluctance to treat as attempts to renege on a prior agreement.

With these qualifications, the revised AMA position occupies a reasonable middle ground between blanket affirmation and blanket denial of a duty to treat.

Justifications for Duties to Treat

Consent as a Constraint on Justifications

I believe I have shown that there must be consent to the risks involved in a duty to treat. This imposes constraints not just on the scope or content of such a duty, as we have seen, but on the kinds of justification—or foundations—we can provide for it. One might think such an observation was uncontroversial: After all, professional obligations are acquired obligations, and acquired obligations in general result only from actions or roles one undertakes consensually. Unfortunately, however, this relatively straightforward point has been made controversial. Some have claimed, for example, that the very "concept" of being a medical professional implies a duty to treat despite nosocomial risks. Others have tried to ground the duty in appeals to what history tells us were at some time the standard virtues or duties of such professionals.

Deemphasizing consent to risk is a necessary prelude to making a general "duty to treat" immune to claims such as "I may have consented to some risks on entering the profession, but not to *those* risks," or, "Maybe earlier practitioners consented to risks of infection, but I entered the profession when there were few such risks and did not consent to them." On the view I have been defending, these denials of consent have to be taken seriously. And that entails gathering evidence about the types of risks people did know about and then inferring that the risks HIV poses for most physicians do not exceed the risks to which they in fact consented on entering the profession. (Some physicians may reasonably insist they face cumulative risks beyond the requirements of duty—basing their claim on extrapolation rather than direct observation.) The defense of a duty to treat is thus cumbersome and inelegant, which has led to a desire to find justifications that might avoid this level of detail.

By examining some of these justifications briefly, I want to show either that the alternative accounts incorporate consent to risk without acknowledging it, or they fail to provide a foundation for a duty to treat. I also want to draw some lessons from these accounts that point to a plausible model of professional obligations in general. Understanding this model will help us see how best to respond to the reluctance of physicians to treat HIV patients.

Justice and Duties to Treat

Numerous claims have been made that justice, including rights to health care, cannot be the basis for a duty to treat (v. Zuger and Miles, 1987; Arras, 1988; Emanuel, 1988). The problem with grounding a duty to treat on appeals to justice is this: If individuals have a right to health care, there must be a correlative *social* obligation to guarantee that appropriate health care is provided—this social obligation does not, however, lead directly into an obligation of each physician or provider to deliver that care. (I have no objection to this point; v. Daniels, 1985:Ch.6.) Instead, society might be able to guarantee the delivery of all necessary care by letting physicians contract individually to deliver whatever care they choose. Such a system of voluntary contracts involves no general moral duty to treat that is binding on all physicians; rather, physicians have only specific contractual duties to treat the patients they choose to treat.

Proponents of this line of argument turn elsewhere, for example to claims about what it is to be a virtuous physician, to find foundations for claims about duties to treat. Yet the argument fails to show that we must seek alternative foundations for such claims. To see why, observe that the duty of physicians to treat anyone they are competent to treat, despite the nosocomial risks, divides into two independent components: First, physicians might have a duty to treat anyone they are competent to treat, provided there are no nosocomial risks. That is, there is no choice about whom to treat, except that self-protection overrides the duty. Second, physicians might have a duty to disregard (at least some) nosocomial risks in deciding whom to treat without having a general duty to treat any patient they are competent to treat. That is, they can select patients on any basis except nosocomial risk. Note then that questions of justice may have a bearing on each of these distinct duties to treat. Under some conditions access to care can be assured without establishing a binding duty to treat—of either kind—on all physicians; under other conditions, however, justice may require us to impose on physicians one or both of these duties to treat (for example, as a condition of licensing, or as a condition of eligibility for third-party reimbursements), because that is the only—or the best—way to guarantee adequate and equitable access to care. Whether justice requires us to impose either or both duties to treat depends on many facts about the design of the health care system, the willingness of physicians to accept patients of all kinds, and the kinds of needs that have to be met—not merely on the fact that physicians are professionals. Moreover, the imposition of such duties is compatible with the requirement of consent: In agreeing to pursue a career in medicine when a duty to treat was a condition of licensing, physicians would be consenting to accept certain obligations and the risks that they entail. Although such conditions clearly restrict the options open to individuals—one cannot be a physician without agreeing to the conditions—imposing them need not violate any basic liberties of individuals and thus involves no inconsistency within the requirements of justice itself (v. Daniels, 1985:Ch.6).

The argument that justice cannot provide foundations for a duty to treat fails because it assumes, without justification, that a duty to treat would have to apply to physicians under all conditions simply by virtue of their being physicians. To be sure, if we assume that either of the duties to treat that we distinguished must be independent of facts about what arrangements of institutions and obligations assure access to care, then justice—which is sensitive to these facts—is not the basis for those duties. But such an assumption begs the question against a justice-based account; it takes moral duties binding professionals to be *transcendent*, that is, independent of facts about the delivery system and thus binding in all medical systems. Justice can provide us with foundations for perfectly adequate duties to treat, even if not for such transcendent ones as may exist.

Arguments from the Concept of a Virtuous Physician

In an excellent discussion of the concept of a virtuous physician, Arras (1988) spells out two distinct "virtue ethic" accounts of the duty to treat—one conceptual and the other historical. Zuger and Miles (1987:1927) typify the conceptual approach. They trace their view to Scribonius, a first-century Roman physician: "To be in a profession implied a commitment to a certain end (*professio*), and thus an obligation to perform certain functions or duties (*officia*) necessary to attain that end. In the case of medicine, the *professio* is healing, the *officia* is treatment of sick persons presenting for care. Professional virtues are the attributes of character needed to honor the commitment to healing." Because physicians have voluntarily committed themselves to the end of healing, they are obliged to accept the duty of caring for HIV-infected patients; physicians who refuse to treat "are falling short of an excellence in practice implicit in their professional commitment" (Zuger and Miles, 1987:1927).[1]

This conceptual approach errs because it assumes that the end to which physicians have committed themselves is that of healing in general. Obviously each physician cannot treat everyone who needs or even seeks healing; that is not an achievable end. What *would* be an achievable goal is to treat the patients one chooses to take on, or the patients assigned to one in a health maintenance organization (HMO) or the patients one can squeeze into a forty-hour week. (That is roughly how the AMA Code, Principle VI, for example, construes the commitment.) Physicians have a right to choose whom to treat, provided no morally objectionable or illegal discrimination is involved; we cannot infer which patients healers must treat from the Scribonian concept of a healer that Zuger and Miles describe.

Furthermore, properly understood, the conceptual approach does not show that we need not worry about consent to risks. Quite the opposite. This approach really asserts that physicians have already consented to all nosocomial risks because they have adopted the unrestricted end of healing, an end that logically commits them to facing all nosocomial risks. But it simply does not follow that if I have a goal of healing (some) people, then I have that goal regardless of the obstacles that arise to carrying it out. I might have the goal of healing (some) people *provided that doing so does not become too dangerous.* Such a proviso does not introduce a logical or conceptual inconsistency between my goal of healing (some) people and my concerns about my safety, because from a reasonably circumscribed goal of healing, nothing follows about the levels of risk one is willing to take to achieve that goal.

In discussing the modified AMA view, I concluded that those who consented to becoming physicians—by doing so—accepted some standard level of risks and a duty to treat in the face of those risks. Physicians learn to distinguish standard from exceptional risks through medical education, clinical training, and observation of the role models who surround them in various institutions; nothing about the risks or their consent to them is inherent in the concept of a physician.

Historical Accounts of Virtue-Based Duties

For reasons similar to mine, Arras (1988) rejects the conceptual approach to deriving virtues. Instead, he suggests that we try to abstract from the historical record a pattern of virtuous-physician behavior to which physicians appear to have been committed. At least in the past century or two (with foreshadowings even before that), he concludes, professional organizations and society as a whole have expected physicians to be willing to face significant risks of contagion or infection, in times of epidemic for instance. Virtuous physicians would feel an obligation to treat even at risk to themselves.

The historical approach also faces several problems, most of which Arras acknowledges. First, the historical record is spotty. As Fox (1988) notes, in many epidemics physicians have hardly been paradigms of the virtues Arras extols, and concludes—as I noted earlier—that voluntary arrangements to serve as plague doctors (usually for hazard pay or other special compensation), have been traditional solutions to the problem of excessive risk during epidemics. Second, from the fact that virtuous physicians behaved one particular way under conditions existing long ago, one cannot conclude that virtue is manifest in the same way now. Many things about medical practice have changed in the interim: our understanding of disease, the product physicians deliver, the institutional framework through which it is delivered. Since everything else is so altered, we must remain skeptical that the virtues are unchanged—unless we are given powerful reason to believe otherwise.

Acknowledging that the virtues are not immutable (and that they depend on context), Arras suggests that ongoing negotiation between the profession and society is responsible for the emergence of a historically determined model of the virtuous physician. This means that virtues are "fragile" (Arras's term). We—society and the profession—renegotiate what virtues we want physicians to exhibit as conditions change. Therefore, obligations that derive from past virtues are binding now only if we still subscribe to those virtues. If contemporary physicians (or their professional organizations) insist they have not consented to the risks past physicians accepted, then renegotiation is clearly already under way.

Once we accept the fragility of virtue, we have to see that the historical approach to grounding a duty to treat must ultimately rest on consent and is not, after all, transcendent. Despite being rooted historically, the ideal of a good physician responds to changing conditions in medicine and in the health care system. In any case, with or without change and negotiation, a historical version of the virtue ethic does no more than set the stage for a consensual undertaking. History makes it possible to be explicit about the virtues that people entering the profession have incorporated through their education, their training, and their emulation of the role models of good physicians. But this is a consensual undertaking, and thus the picture of how the virtues of the good physician are articulated and become internalized is consistent with my central point: Consent to risk acts as a constraint on any account of the foundations for a duty to treat. Dissecting the virtue-ethic account, we find consent at its core.

This should not really surprise us, even though virtue theory is sometimes cast as an alternative to a "contractual" model of foundations. Rather than an alternative to consent, virtue theory specifies the content of that consent. For example, virtue theory might tell us that physicians consented to facing nosocomial risks of HIV because they entered a profession dominated by a traditional model of virtue that included such risk-taking. But although that account gives us historical *evidence* about the content of such consent at a particular point in time, it helps us the least when we most need it, i.e., when there is an ongoing dispute both within the profession and within society about precisely what those virtues involve.

We learn an important lesson from the virtue theorist's motive in deemphasizing consent. It is not, after all, simply up to individuals entering a profession to tailor-make contracts that suit their wishes. The shape of the professional obligations to which an individual consents is determined over time through negotiation with society. The negotiation process is complex because at the heart of it is a complex problem: What departures from the requirements of common morality should society allow—or require—professionals to make? Such exceptions are desirable from society's point of view (v. Freedman, 1978). For example, lawyers must keep clients' confidence and plead their defense even in the face of a belief that the clients are guilty. Similarly, physicians must respect their patients' confidences and act as their advocates even when such behavior by others would not be morally acceptable. Allowing professionals to live by a special morality leads to better treatments.

This whole structure of morally required and permissible professional behaviors is not up for renegotiation by each individual, however. On entering the profession, individuals adopt the whole package—which has the wisdom (and biases) of a tradition behind it. Those individuals cannot omit the duty to treat, for example, and accept the rest. I believe it is this fact that motivates the virtue theorist to attack contractarian views. Focusing on the risk-taking involved in the duty to treat provides a forceful reminder that consent cannot be dropped out of the account.[2]

Some Points of Agreement About Professional Obligations

Several features of a more general view of physician obligations emerge from this discussion of competing foundations for a duty to treat. These points of convergence give guidance for the response to physicians' reluctance to treat HIV patients.

First, as virtue theorists like Arras (1988) remind us, individuals cannot custom-tailor the obligations they undertake on entering a profession; I have insisted that if the "package" of obligations includes a duty to treat, individuals must consent to some standard level of risks that limits the duty. These points are compatible.

Second, justice both constrains the negotiations between society and the profession and limits what physicians are permitted and required to do. For example, the liberty to select patients—which the AMA insistently defends—must be exercised in ways that are not discriminatory. Moreover, justice may require imposing some special obligations on physicians. If access to care cannot be assured without imposing restrictions on physician autonomy to choose patients, then that autonomy may be restricted—as, for instance, when a condition of licensing or eligibility for third-party reimbursements might be that physicians must treat patients regardless of their type of insurance or despite some level of nosocomial risks.

Note that consent is involved here, too: Physicians accept these constraints when they apply for their licenses or seek third-party payments, *knowing that these conditions obtain*. The virtues a "good" physician exhibits can thus be shaped by what society believes it has social obligations to guarantee.

Third, society may want virtues in its physicians that go beyond what justice requires. Society may want physicians not only to be advocates for their patients and to put their patients' interests before their own in certain ways—believing that physicians guided by an ethic of agency will exhibit greater respect for their patients and deliver better care. We may want physicians to make "pure" clinical judgments, untainted by calculation of the physician's interests or views about the social worth of the patient; we may want physicians to put their patient's interests before their own by treating regardless of some level of nosocomial risks. So even if justice did not require us to impose such a duty, we might have good social reasons for wanting physicians to accept it. These socially imposed obligations, like requirements of justice, are sensitive to facts about the design of health care systems and are thus not fully transcendent, either.

These three features combine to yield the following picture of professional obligations: The socially negotiated ideal of the good physician is constrained by, but not limited to, what justice requires; it thus stands as a relatively fixed conception from the point of view of any individual. The individual entering a profession must consent to adopting this conception, and cannot custom-tailor consent by picking and choosing among the obligations. Although becoming a doctor means accepting *this* set of obligations, the ideal is not immutable and is renegotiated as conditions in and outside medicine change.

Expansive as this model of professional obligations is, it unfortunately still leaves room for the kind of controversy that surrounds the duty to treat HIV patients. There can be—and is—disagreement both about the level of standard risks covered by a duty to treat and about whether the nosocomial risks of HIV exceed that level. Where evidence is complex, reasonable people may differ—but the ground is also fertile for unreasonable biases and fears to produce dogmatic stands.

This account of professional obligations fits quite well with the anti-discrimination requirements of the Americans with Disabilities Act of 1990. The ADA prohibits discrimination against HIV-infected individuals in many settings, including health care settings. The ADA reinforces the American Medical Association's injunction against "invidious discrimination." (The AMA code in effect converts what is now a legal obligation not to discriminate into a professional obligation.) But the empirical issue remains: Are the risks imposed by infected patients "significant" risks to others? If HIV-infected patients impose "significant" risks on providers, then measures to protect against those risks, perhaps including some refusals to treat, would not violate the ADA injunctions against discrimination. My argument about professional commitments to a standard level of risk suggests that HIV-infected patients offer no significant extra risks beyond those physicians are ordinarily committed to facing. If I am right, then the ADA and the position I have developed here about professional obligations complement each other. If the risks imposed by HIV-infected patients *are* significantly higher than we now believe them to be, however, then both professional and legal obligations will need modification—and in similar ways.

How Should We Respond to Reluctance to Treat?

This model suggests four types of response to the reluctance of physicians to treat HIV patients: reaffirming a duty to treat, respecting its limits, renegotiating professional obligations, and assuring equitable access to care. Let's look at each in turn.

Reaffirming a Duty to Treat

We have obligations to take certain risks only if we have consented to adopt those obligations and face those risks. Contemporary physicians—regardless of whether they entered the profession during Pax antibiotica or earlier, pre- or post-HIV—should have understood from their education, training, and emulation of role models that treating patients carried some moderate risks of nosocomial infection (for example, risks of contracting hepatitis B). All physicians know a possibility of encountering antibiotic-resistant strains of infection exists and that new or previously undiagnosed diseases might emerge. They know that it is standard practice for physicians to treat patients within their competence despite this moderate level of risk; indeed, in their training, these physicians observed cases in which risks exceeding the standard level were present. They further observed the special protections offered immunocompromised or pregnant health care workers, suggesting that individuals are not obliged to take risks that exceed some moderate standard. I therefore infer that contemporary physicians have accepted a duty not to refuse to treat HIV patients, unless the cumulative risks of treating exceed the standard level of risk that limits the duty to treat. As we saw earlier, extrapolative estimates—not observations—suggest that nosocomial risks of HIV infection exceed that standard level only for a small number of practitioners in certain high-incidence areas.

Reaffirming in this way the duty to treat draws attention to the need for several kinds of education—both about the actual nosocomial risks of HIV transmission and about the reasons for claiming that physicians have accepted a duty to treat in the face of some modest level of risks—and for clear and honest discussion of the actual nosocomial risks of HIV transmission. Education and discussion are essential because it appears that some physicians are heavily influenced by anecdotal evidence. Fear is sometimes compounded by bias against those in high-risk groups and by a political belief that the government agencies responsible for monitoring data on these risks are politically constrained to underestimate the risks. The result is an educational process slow and uneven in its effects; many physicians will feel the risks they actually face exceed their duty to treat.

The educational effort must also be clear about the reasons summarized above for asserting that physicians have this duty. It only confuses the issue to claim, as some have, that physicians are bound to this duty now simply because past physicians were. Similarly, it does not help to say that physicians have this duty because "virtuous" physicians have always affirmed it. Nor will it help to claim that the "concept of a healer" implies it. The effort must rather be to show physicians that *they have already adopted the duty*—though it is a duty limited to some reasonable level of risks.

A reaffirmation of the duty to treat also calls for moral pressure from professional colleagues and organizations, though this must be exerted with sensitivity. Moral pressure can influence people positively, but not if the pressure appears in the form of self-righteous exhortation by those who face few risks or none. The duty to treat is sensitive to actual levels of risk, and exaggerated affirmations of a duty to treat regardless of risk—as in the AMA's 1987 statement—will likely backfire. A difficult issue facing professional organizations is what recourse they offer those HIV patients who feel physicians have excluded them from their practices, or to physicians who feel certain colleagues are unjustifiably reluctant to treat—and what help to offer those who honestly believe the risk *does* exceed the standard level of risks. Another difficult and pressing issue is raised by the importance of role models in medical education. House staff often complain that they bear the burden of treating HIV patients and that some physicians are notoriously difficult to track down when referrals for HIV patients are involved. (Remember Peter's remark: "He can't get out of it, and I can.") If we tolerate such a double standard, eventually there will be a legitimate basis for new practitioners to say that they never accepted a duty to treat in these circumstances because it was never really part of the package most physicians live by. Clear policy in teaching centers can help. Unfortunately, many teaching centers refrain from adopting explicit policies affirming a duty to treat, and even those that do have such policies do not all enforce them in an evenhanded way.

Respecting the Limits of a Duty to Treat

The duty to treat despite some standard level of nosocomial risks is a limited duty, as I have pointed out several times. If risks exceed the standard level—however roughly understood that level is—then we have a case "beyond the call of duty." The difficulty is that we have only speculative, extrapolated estimates of the cumulative noso-comial risks facing the minority of practitioners in high-incidence areas who perform procedures involving significant exposures. The softness of these estimates leaves room for disagreement. The con-sent model calls for erring on the side of caution and giving ample opportunity for individuals to provide more specific forms of consent to these risks. For example, hospitals in high-incidence areas should have explicit policies affirming a duty to treat. Agreement to work under these conditions would amount to the special consent needed, though of course the policy must be supported in an evenhanded way for all personnel (not merely for those with the least power).[3] Society then also has an obligation to reduce the concentration of these risks on a small number of practitioners by increasing access to care (I return to this point shortly).

Respecting the limits to a duty to treat means that we must appeal to the special commitment and courage of those who are willing to face higher risks or to act under conditions where consider-able uncertainty obtains. One such example: We do not really know what the risks are of certain procedures, such as unprotected mouth-to-mouth resuscitation of someone at high risk for HIV in emer-gency situations, especially where exposure to blood is involved as well. Nurses and other health care workers have often attempted resuscitation in these situations, believing that certain death for their patient outweighed *uncertain* risks to themselves. The duty to treat can not be presumed to cover such situations (v. Macklin, 1990, for a discussion of this emergency situation), though—oddly—we do not look on such acts as acts of heroism, as we might in other rescue situations. If we better understood the degree of the uncertainty, we would be more likely to acknowledge this heroism.

Renegotiating Professional Obligations

The persistent denials of a duty to treat by some physicians and professional organizations are most charitably viewed as an attempt to renegotiate the duty to treat recognized by others. Society has created the conditions under which such renegotiation does not seem extraordinary. For example, offering physicians direct economic incentives to deny some treatments to their patients, as is done in some capitation schemes [a scheme in which a physician or group is paid a fixed fee to cover the costs of all services used in a given period of time], undermines physicians' belief that they must act as advocates for their patients' interests. Professional organizations tolerate many conflicts of interest between the economic interests of physicians and the medical interests of their patients, eroding the ethic of agency, the requirement that physicians act in the best interests of their patients without consideration of personal gain. In this climate, it makes perfect sense to many physicians to deny a duty to treat in the face of nosocomial risks.

Society should oppose renegotiating the duty to treat, but we cannot effectively single this duty out as sacrosanct while we create incentives that undermine the dispositions and commitments of physicians to act as agents for their patients. Virtue is indeed fragile, as Arras has said. To preserve the duty to treat we must act to preserve a more encompassing patient-centered ethic, and we can do that only if we preserve—or establish—institutional arrangements that sustain such commitments. A health care system that will assure access to all and allocate health care resources without trying to convert physicians into gatekeepers motivated by their own economic interests is achievable. But unless we demonstrate a commitment to such goals, we will not be able to resist those who would renegotiate the duty to treat.

Assuring Equitable Access to Care

Justice requires that adequate access to treatment be available for HIV patients. As many have noted, one way to reduce the concentration of nosocomial risks on those physicians and health care workers practicing in high-incidence areas is to improve access to care (if we do that, we then spread those patients over a broader range of physicians); another is to eliminate problems with insurance and other barriers to access. If it requires a universal, compulsory health insurance scheme to eliminate barriers to insurance, then HIV simply points us toward a measure already indicated by other problems of access and coverage in the health care system (see Chapter 8). But insurance—or the lack thereof—is not the only barrier that must be overcome. We lack adequate facilities and personnel in both inner-city and rural areas. Addressing these problems of access, which will require new programs and incentives, will do far more to improve access than exhorting physicians to be more willing to treat. Unless society fulfills its share of the responsibility for making sure there is equitable access to care, focusing primarily on the reluctance of (some) physicians to treat will be both ineffective and hypocritical.

Furthermore, once society demonstrates a commitment to treating HIV patients, addressing the reluctance of physicians to treat will become easier as well as more appropriate. Educational and moral appeals will be more credible. And once we eliminate financial and geographical barriers to access, we can take stronger measures against physician reluctance—if it persists—by, for example, linking commitments to treat to working conditions in hospitals, health maintenance organizations, and other reimbursement schemes. If necessary, we could require physicians to accept HIV patients as a condition of eligibility for licensing or reimbursement—and we could do so without violating any basic liberties of providers. But it may be that none of these steps will be necessary, if other measures to improve access are taken first. We can best reaffirm that physicians have a duty to treat despite risk of infection if we show our societal commitment to assuring access to care in every feasible way.

3

HIV-Infected Surgeons and Dentists: Public Threat or Public Sacrifice?

"I find little difference between the HIV-infected homosexual or intravenous drug abuser who continues to have unrestrained sexual activity and the surgeon who is infected and continues to practice surgery."
—Dorsett D. Smith, MD,
Physicians for Moral Responsibility
(Smith, 1990)

"Based on current evidence of risk, a comparative risk analysis, and the availability of the less restrictive alternative of improving infection control generally, prudence dictates that HIV-infected health workers continue professional practice [including invasive procedures], as long as they rigorously adhere to basic infection control practices and are functionally able to continue to work." (Barnes et al., 1990:324)

"There is no black and white here. The patient is right to have his emotions. But I'm a human being, too. I have the right to work. They don't have the right to know if I'm not affecting their health."
—Dr. Neal Rzepkowski,
physician with HIV
fired from Brooks Memorial Hospital
(Wolff, 1991a:A1)

"In a perfect world . . . where people would listen to facts and act rationally, I would not have had to [fire Dr. Neal Rzepkowski]. But that is not the way reality is. This scares the heck out of people, and in a small community like this, the emergency room would be closed because of the outcry. It would not take a lot of people to wreak havoc."
—Richard Ketcham, President,
Brooks Memorial Hospital
(Wolff, 1991b:B2)

39

The Firing of Dr. Rzepkowski

Dr. Neal Rzepkowski learned he was infected with HIV in 1985 while working at St. Clare's Hospital in Schenectady, New York. He informed his hospital supervisors. " 'They did not curtail me,' he said. 'Nor should they have, because I was protected by human rights and by law' " (Wolff, 1991a:A10). He also let selected patients know—those he thought were "informed enough about AIDS to handle it." For example, he told a veterinarian whose three children he had delivered, thinking she would understand. The veterinarian said, "He was, in fact, a gifted doctor. . . . I have never regretted for a moment receiving his medical care" (Wolff, 1991a:A10). Continuing his policy of openness ("I have never hid from anyone about this" [Wolff, 1991b:B2]), Dr. Rzepkowski also reported his condition to hospital authorities at Brooks Memorial Hospital, in Dunkirk, New York, where he had begun working in the emergency room in the spring of 1990.

In July 1991, shortly after the Centers for Disease Control issued new guidelines for health care workers infected with either HIV or HBV, Dr. Rzepkowski was forced to resign his position at Brooks Memorial. Richard Ketcham, the hospital president, insisted that there had been no risk to patients, including his friends and relatives who had been treated by Dr. Rzepkowski, but he believed CDC guidelines allowed no other decision. These guidelines require HIV-infected health care workers to refrain from "exposure prone" procedures, leaving it to "medical/surgical/dental organizations and institutions at which the procedures are performed" to identify which procedures are involved (Centers for Disease Control, 1991b:5). In an example of how concerns about liability are likely to compel hospitals to assume a conservative stance, the Brooks Memorial Hospital board decided to count even the removal of stitches as an exposure-prone procedure. Because Dr. Rzepkowski was often the only physician available in the emergency room, it became impossible for him to continue.

The hospital also sent a letter to the 4,100 patients treated in the emergency room in the year and a half Dr. Rzepkowski had worked there, informing them that they might have been treated by an HIV-infected health care worker; the letter claimed there was "no risk" of infection. In response, one man called the hospital, shouting, "You took away my right to choose! You took away my rights!" Another said, "Yeah, he treated my wife and I'm angry. Someone ought to tell him he's not God" (Wolff, 1991b:B1, B2).

Dr. Rzepkowski defends the fact that he informed only some of his patients of his condition, claiming that "They don't have the right to know if I'm not affecting their health" (Wolff, 1991a:A1). The American Medical Association, however, takes a different view. At its June 1991 meeting, invoking the "Do no harm" principle, the AMA affirmed that doctors are under an obligation to find out whether they are infected, and that—if they are—they must either cease performing invasive procedures [no specific definition is provided but this may include any procedure that inserts equipment or materials into a patient's body in any manner] or disclose their condition to their patients, allowing the patient to make the decision whether to proceed with treatment (Wilkerson, 1991). CDC guidelines in 1991 also required that an infected health care worker generally refrain from "exposure prone" procedures. These procedures were to be specified by professional organizations or provider institutions and were intended to be a special subset of "invasive procedures." Both AMA and CDC guidelines allowed a special review panel the power to grant infected physicians permission to perform certain invasive procedures—provided they inform patients of their condition.

Late in the fall of 1991, proposals were made to modify these policies by giving local authorities more power to regulate and monitor the practice of infected professionals. In October of that year, Congress passed a bill allowing state legislatures to adopt either the June CDC guidelines or substitute rules (Hilts, 1991). New York and Massachusetts indicated they would not follow CDC guidelines (Bass, 1991; Sack, 1991). Nearly all professional organizations (Altman, 1991b,c,d; Reuters, 1991), ultimately including the AMA (Leary, 1991), refused to provide lists of exposure-prone procedures. Faced with these refusals, in late November the CDC released "draft revisions" of the guidelines (Altman, 1991b; Centers for Disease Control, 1991c), calling for local committees to review infected health care workers who perform certain invasive procedures. These committees were to restrict the performance of certain procedures on a case-by-case basis, after judging the competency of the physician to comply with infection control measures and to perform the procedures in question without additional risk; alternatively, the committees could require physicians to inform patients of their status. Within weeks, the AMA similarly modified its guidelines (Leary, 1991).

The CDC revisions were never adopted, however, and the 1991 regulations are still officially in effect. It is worth noting that the central issues raised so clearly by the June 1991 CDC and AMA guidelines would not have disappeared with the proposed CDC and AMA revisions, although the proposals made these issues less visible. In fact, by leaving so much to the discretion of local committees, the draft revisions would have opened the door to highly variable and inequitable treatment. I concentrate in what follows on the issues underlying the CDC regulations and Dr. Rzepkowski's case.

Workers versus Patients: Risks and Rights

Do the CDC or AMA policies violate Dr. Rzepkowski's rights as a handicapped worker? Do patients' rights to be protected against the (low) risks of HIV transmission, or rights to know about those risks, constitute reasonable limits on the rights of an infected professional?

The conflict between the rights of the infected and those of the uninfected is the sharpest yet encountered in the HIV epidemic. Early on—when parents fought to keep HIV-infected students out of their children's schools (resorting to violence in at least one case)—the drama was high, but the complexity of the issue was low. Even though many could identify with the fears of the parents, once it became clear that the risks of casual transmission from student to student were immeasurably small, "right" seemed clearly on one side; public sympathy readily shifted toward the infected schoolchildren. Similarly, in all employment contexts—except health care settings involving invasive procedures—the rights of HIV-infected workers have been broadly recognized as a matter of ethics and law, to the point of their inclusion in the recent Americans with Disabilities Act of 1990 (Parmet, 1990), which I mentioned in Chapter 2. In fact, the scientific assurance that HIV is not casually transmitted, but requires sexual contact or *exposure to blood*, set the stage for the conflict in Dr. Rzepkowski's case: Blood-to-blood contact was precisely the issue.

Health care workers themselves may have helped to build a strong public fear of blood-to-blood contact in health care settings. Physicians and dentists in large numbers, showing exaggerated fears of the risks, have refused—sometimes loudly and openly—to treat patients they suspect may be HIV infected. Although many professional associations have insisted that there is a "duty to treat," other associations (as also noted in Chapter 2)—largely as a concession to the fears of their own members—have not ruled that treating HIV patients is a professional obligation. Many individual professionals have insisted they never undertook any such obligations and have no duty to treat in the face of risks of infection (Daniels, 1991b). Even when a dentist is fined for turning away a patient with AIDS, as in two recent cases in which the New York City Commission on Human Rights became involved, it reminds the public that at least some health care workers believe they have something to fear (Fill, 1991).

Whether or not these fears are themselves contagious, they are widely exhibited by professionals and a 1987 Gallup poll reported that 86 percent of those sampled thought patients should be told if their physicians had HIV (cited in Gostin, 1989:32). A more recent survey showed that 59 percent thought surgeons with AIDS should be excluded from practice, 52 percent thought dental hygienists and dentists should be so excluded, 50 percent would exclude nurses, and 45 percent would exclude physicians with AIDS (Gerbert et al., 1989). These fears were registered at a time when there was no concrete example of transmission from professional to patient, an event that would almost certainly heighten the fears and raise the percentages further.

Just such a focal example or "signal accident," to use a term from the risk-perception literature (Slovic, 1987:283), was provided by an initial CDC report that a female patient of an infected Florida dentist—Dr. David Acer—had in turn become infected. (I alluded to this case in Chapter 1.) The effect of this now well-known example was intensified because the patient herself launched an emotional campaign to dramatize her plight and to call for stricter regulation of infected health care workers. Eventually, five (and more recently, a sixth) of Dr. Acer's patients were found to have a strain of HIV similar to his, and public fears—as well as media attention—grew. The media vigorously reported the panic reactions that followed the "discovery" of additional dentists, surgeons, or other physicians practicing with HIV infection (Kantrowitz, 1991). Dentists were besieged by patients seeking reassurance that they routinely followed appropriate sterilization protocols and that they were not infected with HIV (Muro, 1991; Navarro, 1991). Studies have so far revealed no likely incidents of transmission to patients in any case except Dr. Acer's, and even in his case experts are by no means persuaded the patients were infected by accidental exposure to Dr. Acer's blood (Altman, 1991a).

The June 1991 guidelines were crafted by the CDC in the context of this growing public fear and loud calls—even from the AMA—for more restrictive measures on health care workers. Did the climate of fear unduly influence the CDC recommendations? Were the restrictions on infected workers performing invasive procedures in part a concession to those fears? Were the rights of infected workers sacrificed in a calculated attempt to quiet public fear or to ward off calls for even more restrictive measures? Or did the guidelines represent the best judgment of experts about the level of risk involved?

When framed by questions such as these, this seems to be a largely empirical, rather than moral, problem. One might think that matters could be settled simply by first finding out how high the probability of transmission is from doctor to patient and then determining the specifiable level of risk at which the rights of patients to protection or information outweigh the rights of handicapped health care workers to work. If the level of risk did *not* reach the point at which the patients' rights limit those of handicapped workers, we would have a clear case of political sacrifice of health care workers. But this way of settling matters presupposes that we have a clear ranking of the respective rights for various levels of actual risk—which, in fact, we do not.

Furthermore, the picture just painted oversimplifies what is really at issue in at least three important ways. First, because there is considerable *uncertainty* about the level of risk that exists, we may have to make a choice about where to place the burdens of a policy—on patients or on physicians. Gostin points to this as a key point in the policy debate about the CDC guidelines:

> At the heart of the differences of opinion over the management of HIV-infected professionals is who ought to bear the burden of scientific uncertainty (professionals or patients) and should public health authorities err on the side of patient safety? There is no "correct" choice, but as a matter of public policy, I prefer to emphasize patient confidence and patient safety (Gostin, 1991b:142).

This issue of uncertainty is one to which I have already drawn attention, at the end of Chapter 2; I will have more to say about its role below.

Second, *perceptions* of the level of risk differ greatly, quite apart from uncertainty about actual probabilities of HIV transmission. To many medical professionals and members of the public, even a low probability of HIV transmission is perceived as a serious risk. To many other experts, the low probabilities of transmission suggest that the risk is small, and that there is no need for restrictive measures on infected professionals. The disagreement here is thus not merely one between experts and the public, as it often is in risk-management policy, but among experts from different domains whose professional biases lead them to perceive the risks differently. An expert in public health measures, for instance, may think the risk of HIV transmission is too small to be addressed in a cost-effective manner by removing infected professionals from practice. Experts in malpractice litigation or in risk management at a hospital, on the other hand, will more likely seize on the possible repercussions of the fact that no steps were taken to eliminate a known risk. Professional biases such as these reflect the differing *interests* different parties have in assessing the risks. Whose perceptions of risk are to count? Must we respect the experts' judgments? And if so, which experts? To what extent do we dare allow policy to reflect public fear when—by expert assessment—the fear is exaggerated, and responding to it would be imprudent or unfair public policy?

Third, there may be *moral disagreement* about where limits on rights should be drawn as a result of the risks of transmission. The simple picture that one principle takes priority over the other at a specifiable threshold of risks does not hold here. This should not surprise us. Rights, after all, are general and abstract notions. They draw their content from the purpose we have in asserting them in particular contexts, for example, sparing us from particular harms or providing us with particular benefits. To protect us, rights must provide specific responses to the actual threats we face in the situations in which we assert them. So putting muscle on the schematic bones of a right involves *pragmatics*—a body of assumptions about what features of the situations in which we appeal to them are salient and relevant. These assumptions derive from the purpose behind asserting this right.

The degree of objectivity (or subjectivity) of our perspective on risks will depend on pragmatic considerations, as I have indicated. For example, patient rights to know and control the risks they face have developed as a defense against the paternalistic imposition of risks by physicians; there is thus a point in taking patients' perceptions of those risks more seriously than the experts' medical judgments. In contrast, the insistence on protecting the rights of handicapped workers is intended to protect them against the exaggerated or fabricated perceptions of fellow workers and employers; the tendency is to insist that the significance of the risks they impose on others be objectively determined.

There may be no easy way to specify our agreement about how to rank conflicting rights of these sorts, in part because they are governed by different pragmatic considerations—one set emphasizing patients' subjective perceptions of risks, the other, experts' objectively determined probabilities. Moreover, these differences may well be reinforced by the professional biases that influence perceptions of risk, as noted in the preceding paragraph. Thus any *simple* picture of a threshold of risks is bound to be seriously misleading.

My goal here is to shed light on the following policy questions: Should we allow infected health care workers to perform any procedures they are competent to carry out (relying on barrier (e.g., gloves) and other infection control measures to reduce the chance of transmission), as the American Civil Liberties Union (ACLU) and other groups argued in hearings before the CDC when it was drawing up its guidelines? Should we oblige infected professionals to avoid seriously invasive or exposure-prone procedures (where the risk of transmission is theoretically greatest), as specified in the CDC guidelines? Should we require infected professionals to inform patients of their status (thus making room for patients to decide what risks they want to take), as the AMA suggested? Should we engage in mandatory testing of health care workers to ensure that there is compliance with whatever restrictions we eventually decide should be imposed? Should we criminalize the failure to comply with such restrictions? To answer this series of questions, however, we must first undertake to discover whether there are good reasons for favoring patients' rights over infected health care workers' rights—or vice versa. And that means addressing some of the difficulties to which I have just alluded.

The Probability of Transmitting HIV from Professionals to Patients

Despite the public panic about the risks of catching AIDS from their dentists or doctors, current evidence is that the probability of contracting HIV infection in this way is exceedingly small. But even those who acknowledge that the probability is small perceive and respond to the risk differently.

Our information about probability of disease transmission in health care settings is of two types. One source of information is the frequency of examples—usually clusters of cases—of actual transmission from health care workers to patients. The CDC, for example, cites reports of twenty clusters of documented transmission of HBV from infected health care workers to more than three hundred patients since serologic testing for HBV became available in the 1970s

(Centers for Disease Control, 1991b:2). In contrast, there is only *one* cluster where there is likely transmission of HIV from a health care worker to patients—the six patients of the Florida dentist Dr. Acer, already mentioned. Moreover, retrospective studies of the patients of several dentists, physicians, and surgeons who have HIV—involving the testing of nearly one third of all their patients—revealed *no* other clusters of infected patients (Centers for Disease Control, 1991b:3; Lyall, 1991). We must be careful, however, not to confuse these data—based on happenstance discovery and reporting—with hard actuarial data about frequency of death from a given source. Because these examples came to light retrospectively and in an uncontrolled way, not through any systematic screening process, we cannot reliably estimate the probability of transmission from them—though they may reasonably be thought to suggest whether the problem before us is large or small.

The example of Dr. Acer's patients raises more questions than it has so far answered. One patient, with no other known risk factors, first experienced a fever characteristic of becoming HIV-positive one month after undergoing a molar extraction by Dr. Acer; this is consistent with an exposure during the procedure. Moreover, as pointed out above, she and five other patients had a very similar genetic strain of HIV to Dr. Acer's. These two facts, though strongly suggestive, do not *establish* that Dr. Acer transmitted his virus to each of these patients through accidental exposure to his blood. For one thing, although there was evidence that Dr. Acer did not adequately sterilize equipment between patients, there was no clear evidence that he punctured his skin in any of these cases. Investigators thus consider it an open question how many, if any, of the five patients in question were infected through accidental exposure to Dr. Acer's blood. (Other hypotheses, including the bizarre one that Dr. Acer might have deliberately injected these patients with his blood, have been actively but inconclusively explored (Altman, 1991a; Boyd, 1991; Barr, 1994). If the route of infection was from contaminated instruments—that is, from patient to patient—or was deliberate, then we point the finger of blame at the wrong target in singling out infected health care workers for restrictions on their practice. Much more to the point—and much more effective—would be a resolute effort to improve infection control techniques.

More generally, the puzzles surrounding this particular cluster show how inappropriate it is to let opinion generated by one highly publicized example determine public policy. In this case, as we have seen, the "signal accident" is not even a clear-cut example of what it has been reported to be, namely, an infected worker accidentally giving his or her virus to a patient. But even if it is eventually proved that this case involved accidental transmission from Dr. Acer to his patients, we should not let it determine policy; by itself, it tells us very little about the probability of transmission in other cases and the degree of risk in the long run.

The second source of information about the probability of transmission derives from more careful study of the mechanisms underlying transmission in these and related examples, and the construction of a statistical model based on them. For example, the most likely mechanism for transmission would involve an infected health care worker suffering a minor puncture wound (like a needlestick, or a bone chip or scalpel puncture), and bleeding directly into a patient. How likely is a patient to be infected by such an accident? To answer this question we need a model that includes estimates of how frequently skin punctures take place and how frequently they lead to transmission of the virus (as discussed generally in Chapter 2). Review of such events as glove punctures yields only approximations to the overall frequency of puncture wounds; nor can we rely on mere reports of punctures, since some may go undetected or unreported (Hagen et al., 1988). Moreover, surveillance of even just those patients known to have percutaneous exposures to infected blood through needlesticks depends on making assumptions about which cases of seroconversion involve other risk factors. Modeling the transmission of infection from health care worker to patient on estimates of transmission in the opposite direction requires yet further assumptions; for example, about the likelihood of a worker bleeding through a glove after a puncture compared to the direct delivery of infected blood from patient to worker by needlestick.

As a result of all these assumptions and uncertainties in the statistical model, the probability of transmission can be estimated only within a considerable range, sometimes greater than an order of magnitude. Thus, the CDC estimates the risk of HIV transmission to the patient in a seriously invasive procedure to be somewhere in the range between one in forty thousand and one in four hundred thousand (Centers for Disease Control, 1991a). The probability of transmission from a dentist to a patient is even lower: between one in 260,000 and one in 2.6 million (Kinsley, 1991:4). (By contrast, as we saw in Chapter 2, a widely quoted estimate of the risk of transmission *to* health care workers *from* an infected patient was between 1/4,500 and 1/130,000 [Hagen et al., 1988:1358].)

All these estimates are based on the assumption that the health care worker (or patient) is HIV positive. If we want to know the probability of a patient becoming HIV positive from an invasive procedure when we do *not* know the HIV status of the health care workers, we must further multiply these already low probabilities by the incidence of HIV in the health care worker population, which is the same generally low incidence that exists in the population of the United States as a whole. When we do this, we see that the probability of becoming infected with HIV through an invasive procedure would be less than one in eight million to one in forty million if one half of one percent (or one in two hundred) of all health care workers are infected.

These estimates are extremely sensitive to the assumptions underlying the statistical model used by the CDC, which may rely too heavily on the following mechanism of transmission: A needle sticks an infected health care worker and then sticks a patient. Yet this of course is by no means the only possible mechanism for transmission. In the case of direct bleeding from a cut suffered by an infected worker, for example, the risks to the patient may be higher still. Yet we have no good way to quantify these risks—or to judge their relative seriousness (Dickey, 1991).

These problems aside, the CDC estimated—using its own calculation of the probability of HIV transmission from health care worker to patient—that between thirteen and 128 patients may have been infected during invasive surgical procedures in a ten-year span (Rosenthal, 1991a:C5). Many critics believe even this fairly low estimate is too high and in fact *no such patient has yet been identified.* In contrast, forty health care workers who were infected by patients have been identified, which is compatible with the general view of experts that the risks to health care workers are higher than the risks to patients. Again using the CDC estimate, some have focused not on the probability of HIV transmission from an infected worker to a single patient, but on the cumulative risk imposed on all the patients that a health care worker treats. Thus Gostin supports the CDC's guidelines because the risk of one in forty thousand becomes a risk of one in forty that some patient will be infected if an infected surgeon performs one thousand operations over a period of years. The CDC estimated that an infected surgeon who continues to practice for seven years has a one in twelve chance of transmitting HIV infection to some patient (Kinsley, 1991:42). (Of course, the risk to each individual patient remains between 1/40,000 and 1/400,000.)

Comparing these probabilities with those involved with HBV transmission is instructive. The presence of hepatitis B e antigen

(HBeAg) is associated with higher levels of circulating virus, and we find higher infectivity from needlesticks where the source is HBeAg positive. The CDC reported about a 30 percent risk of HBV transmission following percutaneous exposure to HBeAg-positive blood (Centers for Disease Control, 1991b:3) and estimated that twelve thousand health care workers become infected with HBV each year through exposure to patients' blood, resulting in 250 annual deaths and about one thousand active HBV carriers (Centers for Disease Control, 1989). The risk of transmitting HIV through a single percutaneous exposure to infected blood is about one hundred times *less than* that of transmitting HBV. There is a risk of 0.3 percent for HIV compared to 30 percent for HBeAg-positive blood (Centers for Disease Control, 1991b:3; Gerberding et al., 1987; Henderson et al., 1990). To be sure, HIV is far more likely to be fatal, once contracted, than HBV. Still, the *overall risks of becoming infected and then dying* from HIV and HBV infection as a result of exposure to blood in health care settings are fairly similar (a point I noted in Chapter 2). The CDC estimated the risk of death due to HBV infection after an invasive procedure by an HBeAG-positive surgeon was from .7 to 13.2 per million and estimated the risk of death after an invasive procedure by an HIV-positive surgeon was from 2.4 to 24 per million (that is, 1/40,000 to 1/400,000). Given the lack of precision in the component estimates, this is a very similar level of risk (v. Feldblum, 1991).

Despite the similarity in overall risk of death in this setting, many people (including health care workers) are more fearful of HIV than of HBV and view the risk to themselves as higher. The fact that HIV is more likely to be fatal if contracted seems to be the salient feature of the risk and scares people more than the fact that they are just as likely to die, statistically speaking, from transmission of HBV as from HIV in health care settings. (This point was also noted in Chapter 2.) Perhaps this *perception* of risk helps explain why it was only in the wake of the attention paid to the single cluster of possible HIV transmissions that the CDC has made more restrictive recommendations in its 1991 guidelines regarding health care workers infected with *either* HIV or HBV. The evidence about HBV transmission has been available for some time, but it had never led to such preemptive restrictions. Of course, the CDC guidelines would have been even more questionable from a moral point of view if restrictions had been passed at this stage for health care workers infected with HIV but not for those infected with HBV.

Follow-up studies of health care workers exposed to HIV in ways other than through percutaneous inoculation reveal no measurable risk in these cases at all. This fact should compel us to limit our *reasonable* concerns about health care workers to contexts in which it is likely for percutaneous exposures to take place. Thus the CDC's 1991 guidelines urge the more careful definition of exposure-prone procedures and explicitly deny that any restrictive measures are appropriate for infected "HCWs [health care workers] with HIV or HBV who perform invasive procedures not defined as 'exposure-prone,' provided the infected HCWs practice recommended surgical or dental techniques and comply with universal precautions and current recommendations for sterilization/disinfection" (Centers for Disease Control, 1991b:5).

The CDC guidelines are intended to guard against the kind of unjustifiable exclusions of health care workers from employment we have seen in many cases. In one such instance, patients stopped seeing a pediatrician in private practice after a local newspaper revealed he was HIV positive, even though the CDC argued that he posed no risks to patients (Applebome, 1987). Similarly, after a New Jersey otolaryngologist was diagnosed—at the hospital where he had admitting privileges—as having AIDS, those privileges were suspended. The hospital restored them with the proviso that the physician in question present all his patients with an informed-consent form describing his infection and the "potential risk of transmission." That effectively ended his ability to continue in professional practice (Sullivan, 1989). We have yet to see whether such a proviso, or the way the 1991 guidelines leave physicians like Dr. Rzepkowski vulnerable to discharge, is justifiable.

Probabilities of Death: Some Comparisons

How should we react to the CDC estimate of our chances of infection from an HIV-infected surgeon? For simplicity of reference, I shall round off that estimate of surgical risk to 1/100,000 chance of such infection—which is similar to a recent estimate of one chance in 83,000 per hour of surgery (Lowenfels and Wormser, 1991). This figure is also roughly mid-range between the 1/40,000 and the 1/400,000 probabilities that the CDC gives. Correspondingly, the chance of being infected by a surgeon whose HIV status we do not know would drop to considerably less than 1/20,000,000. Is this a big risk? The answer to that depends in part on how it compares to other chances of death we take in everyday and medical contexts. Even though we know that people do not judge and respond to risks in ways strictly proportional to the underlying probabilities of death associated with the risks, it helps put this probability in perspective if we place it among others we routinely face.

Each of the following activities involves a risk—I ignore the differences in reliability of actuarial and theoretical estimates—of about 1/1,000,000 of death from the cause noted in parentheses: living two days in New York City or Boston (air pollution); traveling six minutes in a canoe (accident); traveling ten miles by bicycle (accident); traveling one thousand miles by air or three hundred miles by car (accident); living with a smoker for two months (any one of various diseases from secondhand smoke); spending two summer months in Denver (cancer from cosmic radiation); drinking thirty twelve-ounce cans of diet soda (cancer from saccharin) (Wilson, 1979). These probabilities of death are thus at least twenty times *greater* than the probability that we will contract HIV and die when we go for an invasive procedure and do *not* know the HIV status of our surgeon. Similarly, we have more than ten times the chance of being killed by lightning, four times the chance of being killed by a bee, and about twice the chance of being hit by a falling aircraft as we do of being infected with HIV by surgeons in general. If we know our surgeon is HIV positive, then our probability of contracting HIV (1/100,000) is similar to the probability of death (from the causes noted above) in the following everyday activities: taking a one-hour canoe ride while on vacation; our child bicycling two miles each way to school for one month; drinking one diet soda a day for ten months; living with a smoker for a year and a half; spending a sabbatical year in Denver.

We can also compare the probability that we will become infected with HIV during an invasive procedure with other chances we take in medical contexts. Our chance of dying from anesthesia while on the operating table is approximately 1/10,000—roughly ten times greater than our chance of being infected by a surgeon known to have HIV infection, and two thousand times greater than our being infected in the process of undergoing invasive procedures in general. The risk of death from allergic reaction to penicillin is about 1/100,000; a mother who approves a penicillin shot for her toddler with a throat infection incurs—implicitly accepts—that level of risk (Landesman, 1991). I very much doubt mothers are often specifically informed of the probabilities at work in such instances; at best, most pediatricians are likely to say only something like, "There's a minute chance of an allergic reaction"—even as they ready the child for the injection.

Because the CDC's estimate tells us what extra chance of death we face from being operated on by an HIV-infected surgeon, it may be particularly instructive to consider other chances we take when we choose surgeons. Suppose we must choose a surgeon to perform a coronary artery bypass graft (CABG surgery). One recent study shows that the best surgeon surveyed had a 1.9 percent mortality rate for his procedures; the worst had a 9.2 percent mortality rate (O'Connor et al., 1991). That means that patients face an *extra* risk of death in selecting the worst surgeon of more than 7/100, or 7,300 *times the extra chance of death the patient would face if his or her surgeon were HIV infected.* Similarly, patients deciding in which medical center to have a bypass operation might face an extra 3 percent risk—or three thousand times the extra risk faced by going to a surgeon who has HIV. If it were better known that such data are available, patients might well demand "consumer report" information about the success rates of individual practitioners and medical centers. But outcomes research in medicine is still in its infancy, and of course if everyone were to demand this kind of information, it might well become harder to get it: The incentive to practitioners to obstruct such information gathering and to disguise their failures would increase dramatically. We might even be worse off, because of the increased difficulty in learning what contributes to high failure rates (Berwick, 1991).

Rationality and Perceptions of HIV Transmission Risks

A recent *Newsweek* survey, confirming the Gallup poll results noted earlier, showed that 90 percent of Americans want health care workers to reveal their HIV status (Gross, 1991:A20). A majority of doctors at a recent AMA meeting said they would not seek treatment from an infected doctor (Gross, 1991:A20). The United States Senate voted eighty-one to eighteen, supporting an amendment introduced by Jesse Helms, to jail doctors who fail to inform patients that they are HIV positive. (The amendment was never enacted into law.) Yet Americans in general—including doctors and even senators—normally face without concern much higher probabilities of death involved in everyday life and medical contexts. The AMA does not, after all, require surgeons to report their individual fatality rates to prospective patients.

Is this apparently inconsistent response to the underlying probabilities irrational or otherwise morally indefensible? Posing the question this way echoes a long-standing debate in the field of risk perception and public policy. Some years ago it was noted that expert judgments of risk tend to correlate much better with probabilities of death than lay judgments do (Slovic, Fischhoff, and Lichtenstein, 1979). Moreover, public budgets seemed skewed by these "distorted" public perceptions of risk; judged by expert standards, we spend too much money regulating some risks and too little regulating others. One response to this gap between expert and lay perceptions of risk was to invest in efforts at "risk communication," with the aim of learning how better to educate the public about "real" risks in order to obtain support for the efficient promotion of public health and safety.

Unfortunately, public perceptions seem resistant to such educational efforts. Systematic studies of risk perception have revealed a rich array of factors that affect nonexperts' judgments of risk. Thus voluntariness, familiarity, dread, and the ability to control are important factors; so too are judgments about the benefits that accompany the risks and how those benefits are distributed. Many of these factors have some heuristic value, enabling people to track information relevant to these risks and to adjust their behavior in ways that have some plausibility, given the lack of more precise information available to nonexperts (Slovic, Fischhoff, and Lichtenstein, 1982). It would be wrong, then, simply to assume that we have an instance of irrational or otherwise unjustifiable response to risk wherever there is a perception of risk accompanied by a response to it that is disproportionate to the underlying probabilities.

This point is much clearer if we examine it from an individual perspective. How people perceive and respond to the risks associated with various activities is not just a function of the underlying probabilities or even of the individual's awareness of them. Jane, who likes to feel fit, relishes a canoe or bicycle ride, while being repulsed at the prospect of "polluting" her body with a diet drink and risking cancer (which she especially fears); yet she is aware of the underlying probabilities of all these activities noted earlier. James, more sedentary by nature, accepts the risks of the soft drink but thinks canoeing too dangerous; he remembers a canoe accident in his hometown in which a child died (which left him believing this to be a particularly dangerous activity). Mario, who is terrified at the prospect of dying in a plane crash, chooses to drive—where he can exercise some control over outcomes, even though he is aware that flying imposes lower probabilities of death. Some people imagine that some kinds of death are preferable to others (people may have special fears of cancer and

AIDS, for instance), and we are apt to particularly dread some other outcomes (for example, those involving catastrophes).

Just as nonexpert perceptions of risk reflect individual preferences and values, so, too, judgments about risk made by experts from different professional domains will reflect their *interests* and training. A public health official noting the very low probability of HIV transmission from professionals to patients, and the very high cost for little health benefit of restricting an infected health care worker, will probably view the risk as very low—one better addressed by instituting broad infection control measures than by singling out a particular infected professional. A malpractice litigator will seize on the fact that a medical center knew it had an infected surgeon on its staff and "did nothing to reduce the risk" to a patient who has—as a result—contracted HIV infection. Hospital counsel, well aware of the likely reaction of malpractice litigators, will insist that the risks are too great to ignore. Such different reactions—professionally determined—to the same probability of transmission are hardly to be discounted as irrational. Professionals react to risks in ways largely dictated by the interests, goals, and standards of their professions.

How individuals—experts or lay—react to risks thus reflects the many other preferences and values they hold. In weighing benefits against risks, people rely on their individual conceptions of what is good in life. To insist that people should respond primarily to the underlying probabilities implies, in effect, that we believe people do not have a clear conception of what is good for them. Yet it does not seem irrational for individuals not to focus solely on their chances of death, but rather to say, "I will take steps, investing my resources in reducing my dread of certain outcomes. We all have to die, and even if in general I like an environment with less chance of death, I also must live comfortably in whatever environment I am in. I'd rather face somewhat greater chances of death while feeling more secure than face lower chances of death while living in fear." This point can be generalized. The public, responding to expert complaints about distorted public budgets for risk management, can say: "We prefer *feeling* more secure, despite somewhat greater chances of death, to *being* actually safer but full of unreduced fears. Public investment should aim at more than simply reducing chances of death." To insist that either an individual or the public in general is wrong to argue this way is to engage in a rather strong form of paternalism.

The point can be made especially vivid if we think about choices made in medical settings. The mother who knows her toddler faces a

1/100,000 risk of death from an allergic reaction to penicillin might conclude that the benefits outweigh the risks; there may be no alternative with a better benefit-to-risk ratio. But if her child needed surgery and she knew that the surgeon was HIV infected, she could avoid the risk of HIV transmission with no cost beyond that of switching surgeons. Although switching may reflect the phobia she has about HIV—a fear exaggerated by prejudice or the social stigma attached to HIV disease (Landesman, 1991:657)—it may also reflect a perfectly rational risk/benefit calculation.

Similarly, the same mother contemplating surgery might also try to find a family member to donate the blood that would be needed in the surgery, again seeking to avoid the risk of about 1/100,000 of HIV infection (this time through the public blood supply). Once again, her behavior could be seen as a reflection of her exaggerated fear of HIV transmission, but it may also reflect a reasonable risk/benefit calculation. The mother can achieve the benefit of transfusion without any cost except switching to a more trusted donor. To put this another way: The cost of living with the dread that HIV may be contracted is much higher than the cost of switching surgeons or finding a family member to act as a blood donor. There seems to be nothing irrational about viewing one risk (death from allergic reaction) as routine (and unavoidable, if there is no feasible alternative) and another (contracting HIV) as a special risk to be avoided (in part because it is avoidable and there are alternatives).

While discussing a patient's right to be informed of a health care worker's HIV status, Gostin points out that this is a case in which the patient (or mother) not only wants to know something, but will act on that knowledge—which may mean altering the originally intended action (Gostin, 1989:33–34). From the individual's perspective, the knowledge seems both relevant and important. Furthermore, a given patient's risk-averse behavior—even if it is motivated by exaggerated fear or phobia—is not individually unreasonable. Patients can dodge a low probability of a bad outcome—which they "phobically" perceive to be an unacceptable risk—at low cost to themselves. The cost of living with the dread that accompanies not switching surgeons or donors may be higher than the cost of switching, even if the reduction of probability of death is quite small and of an order of magnitude we elsewhere tend to ignore.

If this is true, it is unlikely that we can justify a straightforwardly paternalistic refusal to give any weight to the patient's desire to know the HIV status of a health care worker. We are not, after all, protecting the patient against acting in a way that all can see is irrational—even if we believe from the start that the person seems more afraid of HIV transmission than the probabilities justify.

These observations suggest that the problem actually has the following structure: Underlying the policy choices we face is a controversy about whether to give priority to patients' rights or to the rights of handicapped workers, given the risks of HIV transmission. One way to resolve the dispute would have been to denounce the strong public fears—so exaggerated as to count as irrational—of HIV transmission. But this approach appears to be unjustifiably paternalistic. An alternative strategy would be to short-circuit the dispute about rights, claiming that HIV-infected professionals have obligations—accepted when they entered their profession—either to refrain from imposing risks on their patients or to inform them of the risks. If this is to be a successful way to get around the debate about rights, however, it must be because the obligations do not themselves derive from the rights of patients and because professionals waive any conflicting rights they might have as handicapped workers. I shall turn next to an exploration of these ideas.

Professional Obligations: "Do No Harm"

Remember that when Dr. Rzepkowski discovered he was HIV infected, he informed his superiors, he continued to perform invasive procedures (some of them exposure-prone), and he informed *some* of his patients of his status (though only those he judged capable of understanding the situation). Did he have a professional, moral obligation to refrain from those procedures? Did he have a professional obligation to inform *all* the patients on whom he performed such procedures? Did the fact that he told the patients he thought would not overreact suggest that he felt an obligation to inform patients but that he was willing to carry out that obligation only in a self-serving way? Or was telling *any* patients merely optional or discretionary from his point of view? (If so, then telling some but not others violated no obligation.)

If, as some professional organizations insist, Dr. Rzepkowski had both the obligation to refrain from exposure-prone procedures and the obligation to inform patients of his HIV status, that might seem to reduce the debate about conflicts between patients' rights and handicapped workers' rights to a nullity. This would then be just another instance—it might be argued—where infected professionals waive appeal to handicapped workers' rights when they enter the profession and undertake the special moral obligations inherent in it. On the other hand, some may object that professional obligations cannot conflict with the general moral or legal rights that all other workers have or require professionals to waive those rights. We need to examine these alternative claims about professional obligations carefully, especially since the organizations to which professionals belong do not agree what they are.

The claim that a physician has an obligation to refrain from imposing the risks involved in HIV transmission to patients is quite distinct from the claim that there is an obligation to obtain consent from patients specifically informed of that risk. The *obligation to refrain* at least appears to be the kind of obligation a physician might have independent of any prior rights of patients. For example, if the physician has a duty to "do no harm," and if imposing a risk of HIV transmission constitutes doing a harm, then we need not first determine whether a patient has a right not to be harmed before deciding that the physician has a duty to refrain. In contrast, the *obligation to inform* is less plausibly construed as an obligation that a physician has independent of any prior rights of patients to know about the physician's status or the risk of transmission in certain procedures. If a physician's professional obligations include respecting the rights of patients, and patients have a right to know about the risk of HIV imposed by their surgeon, then the physician's obligation to inform is *derived* from the prior right of patients. I believe claims about physicians' obligations generally are based on such a view: Physicians have an obligation to inform *because* a patient has a right to know and to make decisions about what risks to take. I shall defer discussion of an obligation to inform to a later point, when I turn to look at the patient's right to know (from which I am claiming the obligation to inform is derived). For now, in this section, I shall focus entirely on the claim that Dr. Rzepkowski had a professional, ethical obligation to refrain from certain invasive procedures.

Consider the AMA position that there is such an obligation. The AMA's Judicial Council took the following position in 1988: "The Council believes that if *a risk* [emphasis added] of transmission of an infectious disease from a physician to a patient exists, disclosure of that risk to a patient is not enough; patients are entitled to expect that their physicians will not increase their exposure to the risk of contracting an infectious disease, even minimally. . . . If a risk does exist, the physician should not engage in the activity" (American Medical Association, 1988:1360). Reaffirming and clarifying this statement in the aftermath of the Acer case, the AMA stated:

> Physicians who are HIV positive have an ethical obligation not to
> engage in any professional activity which has an *identifiable risk*
> [emphasis added] of transmission of the infection to the patient. . . .
> In cases of uncertainty about the risks to patient health, the medi-
> cal profession, as a matter of medical ethics, should err on the side
> of protecting patients (American Medical Association, 1991).

The AMA specifically imposes two obligations on physicians: (1)
Those who are at risk of acquiring HIV infection and who perform
invasive procedures should determine their HIV status; (2) until uncertainty about risks is resolved, HIV-infected physicians should refrain from performing invasive procedures that pose an identifiable
risk or should disclose their HIV status—performing the procedure
only if there is informed consent from the patient. How important to
this position is the fact that we still have some "uncertainty" about
the level of risk? It could be very important: If uncertainty can be
removed about the level of risk, and it turns out to be very low, then
there may in fact no longer be a duty to refrain. Commenting on the
AMA position, however, Dr. Nancy Dickey—an AMA trustee—
noted that "the risk of transmission from an HIV infected physician
during certain invasive procedures is very low but real. So some restraint on invasive procedures is necessary as a matter of the oldest
precept of medical ethics—that *the physician shall do no harm*"
(Dickey, 1991:2; emphasis in original). This seems to suggest that the
AMA already views the level of risk under discussion by the CDC and
other experts as one that carries with it an implied duty to refrain.

Regardless of the level of uncertainty, however, it seems to follow that the AMA has a clear view of what *procedures* involve
"identifiable" risk, since HIV-infected physicians are urged to refrain from performing *them*. Nevertheless, in the wake of the CDC's
call for instructions from professional associations about which procedures are exposure-prone, Dr. Dickey, defending the fact that a
majority of professional groups have declined to identify exposure-
prone procedures in their specialties, argued that "since there has
never been a documented doctor-to-patient transmission, groups are
concerned about being able to label any given procedure as being an
at-risk procedure" (Coleman, 1991:3). But if no procedure can be
labeled "risky" in the absence of a documented case of doctor-to-
patient transmission, then it is difficult to see why the AMA rules
that surgeons performing certain invasive procedures pose an "identifiable risk" and would be "doing harm" if they performed those
procedures without obtaining informed consent from patients aware
of their HIV status.

The AMA position that physicians must impose "no identifiable risk" on patients seems much too strong. Physicians and other health care workers often carry infectious conditions that might have an impact—in some cases a very serious one—on patient health. Even if that danger of infection is remote, it represents an "identifiable risk"; thus, if we take the AMA line literally, we would have to conclude that no surgeon—or surgical nurse—should ever operate. Broadening the "no identifiable risk" requirement to include other mechanisms for harming patients, including all the factors that might affect physician performance—such as stress, fatigue, medication side effects, substance abuse, family problems—we quickly see that the requirement is much too strong (these points have been made by numerous commentators; v. Barnes et al., 1990:314–15). Indeed, it would oblige every surgeon who generally performed worse than the best surgeon to refrain from surgery, since performing surgery with less-than-optimal skill entails imposing an identifiable risk on patients (in the case of coronary artery bypass surgery, as we saw, it is a risk up to 7,300 times the risk of HIV transmission). Indeed, it just is the case that performing surgery at all imposes an identifiable risk on patients.

A weaker claim might be that a physician has a duty to refrain from imposing any identifiable *avoidable* risk. If HIV-infected surgeons know their status, for instance, they can avoid imposing the risk by not operating. But surgeons may not always know when they have other infectious conditions, or they may be unaware of the effects of, say, marital stress; so those are unavoidable risks. Furthermore, there will always be a *range* of "competent" surgical performances, and it would be prohibitively costly to remove all surgeons from practice who were competent but not optimal (strictly speaking, that would mean removing all but the best surgeon).

Even this weaker claim could still be too strong, since—if we are willing to devote enough resources to the effort—we can probably at least reduce most avoidable risks significantly. Certainly that is true for the identifiable, avoidable risks associated with other infections, other performance-affecting conditions, and "below-optimal" but still competent performance. On the other hand, if we interpret "avoidable" to mean "avoidable given an appropriate weighing of the benefits against the costs," then the claim that a physician has a duty to refrain from imposing those risks is too weak. The cost of restricting all HIV-infected health care workers from performing exposure-prone procedures probably outweighs the benefits. (I shall return to this point below.) In any case, it is highly probable that there are many other "avoidable" risks that can be reduced far more cost-effectively than can the risk of HIV transmission by infected health care workers. If so, it seems arbitrary to single out this particular avoidable risk from among all the others—many of them much greater—that are routinely ignored.

Nor can we simply modify the AMA position so that it says "Impose no avoidable risk to which the patient does not consent." Such a stricture would presuppose that the patient is entitled to consent to all risks, even the risks of HIV transmission in this case, and that the duty to refrain is itself *derived* from the right of the patient to consent. But we are considering an *independent* duty to refrain, and thus this is a way to save the AMA position only if we are willing to change the ground rules.

Yet another way to try to save the AMA position would be to make it depend heavily on there being *uncertainty* about the degree of risk. Then the position might be this: "Given the considerable uncertainty about the risk of HIV transmission, the physician has a duty to refrain from imposing it." A statement of this sort implies that the duty to refrain should be lifted if the level of risk turns out to be—as in the current CDC estimate—a very small risk already deemed insufficient to warrant a duty to refrain when the "no avoidable risk" standard is too strong. There is a problem, however, with simply hiding behind uncertainty and claiming that the CDC estimate may be too low: To do so feeds public hysteria about the risk. Of course, the statistical model underlying the estimate can be challenged at crucial points, and the risk may be somewhat higher than its estimate (though we would expect more observed cases of transmission if that were true). But the small likelihood that the risk is *much* higher should not count for as much as this argument from uncertainty requires. It is odd, for example, to let the *mere possibility* that the risk of HIV transmission is higher than the CDC estimate count for more than the *known fact* that the extra risk involved in going to a surgeon who performs poorly is significantly higher than the extra risk of HIV transmission is likely to be under even worst-case scenarios.

Strictly speaking, I have not actually shown that surgeons have no ethical or professional duty to refrain from exposure-prone procedures, but I *have* shown that the AMA has not demonstrated that there is such a duty. The AMA has not given us adequate grounds for deriving a duty that singles out risk of HIV transmission in this way. Moreover, if we are to have such a duty in the case of HIV transmission—on anything like the grounds the AMA cites—then it commits us to much more withdrawal from medical procedures than the AMA or anyone else believes appropriate. Of course, it is logically possible that HIV-infected surgeons have a duty to refrain, as do all other surgeons in many cases where their performance is now viewed as routine. But since no one is claiming—and many would reject—such an outcome, the argument for a duty to refrain in the case of HIV transmission remains unpersuasive.

By now it should be clear that we cannot short-circuit the controversy about the conflicting rights of patients and infected health care workers; I therefore turn next to a discussion of that apparent conflict.

Do Patients' Rights Override Handicapped Workers' Rights?

The firing of Dr. Rzepkowski seemed to raise a rather straightforward question: Are the risks of his infecting his patients sufficiently great that we must rank the rights of patients to know those risks (or to be protected against them) higher than his—the doctor's—rights as a handicapped worker? Thus posed, the question suggests there is some threshold level of risk beyond which one set of rights takes priority over the other, and that all we have to do is solve the problem of discovering whether the risks in question have reached that threshold. I want to develop here my reasons for thinking that the controversy has deeper roots than a mere empirical dispute about the level of risk.

We should suspect the problem is a greater one when we note the complexity of the relationship between those rights and the choice of particular policy options. For example, as we have already seen, the CDC's June 1991 guidelines involve restrictions on the procedures HIV-infected professionals are to be allowed to perform. Such a policy can be justified in two distinct ways.

One justification would be the claim that the risks HIV-infected professionals impose in these procedures are "significant" and that these handicapped workers are therefore in fact not "otherwise qualified" to perform all the essential tasks in their job; their rights as handicapped workers are *limited* to contexts in which they impose no significant risks on others. (The quasi-technical, legal use of the term "significant" needs some explanation, which I will come to shortly.) On this view, if the risks were not significant, the rights of the handicapped workers would take precedence over any patient's right to know and to consent to the risks involved. In effect, on this account, significant risks form the undisputed boundary between these rights. The simple picture of a threshold of risk would seem to be adequate, and the search for empirical answers would be on—if this were the whole story. But it is not.

A different justification for the CDC policy ascribes full priority to patients' rights. It presupposes that the rights of patients to know and to consent to the risks they face take precedence over handicapped workers' rights, even if the risks imposed by HIV-infected workers are not "significant," as the term is understood in this context. Since, however, actually informing patients of the HIV status of professionals carries with it extra costs, including the broad violation of the rights of those professionals to medical confidentiality, we can accomplish the same benefit to patients at a somewhat lower social cost by simply restricting the practice of the infected professionals.

A more paternalistic variation on this justification presupposes that patients cannot reliably assess the risks of infection or poor performance imposed by professionals, because professionals cannot or will not provide reliable information about the risks they impose (as opposed to the risks of the procedures themselves) (Feldblum, 1991:134–35). We must therefore restrict the practices of those individuals who pose a risk of transmitting certain infections. Both of these full-priority justifications of the CDC policy turn, not on *empirical* and *legal* questions about whether the risks to patients are significant, but rather on *moral* and *legal* judgments that patients' rights take precedence over the rights of handicapped workers.

Because there are these *two* possible lines of justification for the CDC's June 1991 policy, merely showing that the risks of HIV transmission to patients are not "significant" would not suffice to show that the CDC policy has no adequate justification. It might still be the case that we are morally required to give priority to patients' rights. This renders the boundary concept of "significant risk" a distinction without force in this dispute. That is, even if "significant risk" defines the scope of handicapped workers' rights when they are in conflict with the preferences of other workers or their employers, it does not define their scope when they are in conflict with the stronger, more specific, and better-defined rights of patients. In effect, patients have a right to know and to consent to—or to be protected against—even those risks that fail to count as significant in other employment contexts. Or so it might be claimed.

A persuasive argument has in any case been made that the probabilities of HIV transmission do *not* constitute a "significant risk," when we judge the risk from the perspective of employment discrimination law, including the ADA of 1990 (v. Barnes et al., 1990:315–16; v. also Feldblum, 1991:135–36). First, a "significant" risk has to be more than a merely "speculative" risk. In the absence of any real explanation of how Dr. Acer's patients became infected, and supported only by a statistical model, the CDC estimate of transmission risks does appear speculative; the probabilities involved make the risk a "remote" one, certainly a "minute one," because it represents at most a minute elevation of risks of death generally present in medical contexts and usually tolerated with little attention being paid. For example, we tolerated for a long time the risks of HBV transmission without restriction, though current CDC regulations now do impose restrictions. We continue to tolerate much larger risks of death that derive from variations in the competence of professionals or medical centers. All these points count heavily toward a conclusion that the risk of HIV transmission for each patient is *not significant* in the legal sense.

Some who think the risk to individuals is admittedly small nevertheless think the risk to the *pool* of patients treated by a physician is significant; that is, they think the cumulative risk should be viewed as significant even if the risk to a single individual is unimpressive (Gostin, 1991a:306; 1991b:141). This change of focus may be misleading; we are apt to be unduly impressed by the larger probabilities that of course emerge in this larger context. For example, although the cumulative risk seems high (for example, the 1/40 to 1/100 chance that an infected surgeon will infect some patient over the course of a thousand exposure-prone procedures), to judge whether this risk is really significant would require us to compare the cumulative risks involved here with those from other sources. Cumulative risks are simply multiples of the risks in single cases, however, and we should not let higher probabilities *by themselves* trouble us. The point is that each of us takes not a 1/40 or 1/100 chance, but only a 1/40,000 or 1/100,000 chance.

Significance is thus judged in an objective way when we think about the rights of handicapped workers. We compare the underlying probabilities of harm to other risks people take in those settings. This emphasis on objective characterization of the risk is no accident; it is a fundamental feature of what I earlier referred to as the "pragmatics" of the appeal to the rights of handicapped workers. The point of asserting that handicapped workers are otherwise qualified to perform their jobs unless they impose (objectively) significant risks on others is to defend those workers against the standard forms of bias they encounter. Such workers have in the past been discriminated against simply because those who worked with them (or their customers or employees) believed that they imposed risks, and employers have often rationalized their reluctance to accommodate handicapped workers by imagining risks such workers might impose on themselves or others. To defend handicapped workers, then, we must not let the *subjective* perceptions of risks held by others count at all. The pragmatics of the appeal to handicapped workers' rights requires discounting subjective fears and insisting on high, *objective* standards of demonstrable risk; it shifts the burden of proof to those who would show these workers impose a significant risk and are thus not qualified for their jobs.

This means that if the CDC estimates are wrong, and the probabilities of transmission are much higher, then all could agree that the risks were significant. The higher risks would mark a clear *limit* to the rights of infected workers, and the CDC policy would be justified. Given the actual CDC estimates, however, and judging from within the pragmatics surrounding the appeal to the rights of handicapped workers, we should ignore the exaggerated fears of patients. Giving in to them (by giving weight to the subjective fears of colleagues and employers, etc.) would be tantamount to abridging the rights of handicapped workers to equal opportunity. There *are* no significant risks here—whatever all those patients we call "the public" perceive to be the case.

The argument about significant risk as we have looked at it so far takes place from within the framework (including the pragmatics) imposed by the rights of handicapped workers. The attitudes of patients, on this view, are assimilated to all those potentially hostile "others"—fellow workers, clients, employers—who would unfairly restrict handicapped workers' employment rights. This is not, however, the only framework that bears on this controversy.

Moral principles governing the rights of patients, including the right to exercise informed consent about medical procedures, have a certain history, and this history controls their strength and scope in the standard context of their application. They are intended to protect patients against the traditional imbalance of power that exists in the doctor-patient relationship. The principles are sharply drawn to prevent the paternalistic imposition of risks common not many years ago in the United States (and still prevalent in many other societies). It does not matter that the more "objective" judgment of medical experts—physicians—is that a risk is small or that it is outweighed by the benefits of a procedure. Instead, we must let the subjective risk-benefit assessment of the patient be decisive if we are to assure control—for the patient—over risk-taking. In a sense, the principle assuring that informed consent is obtained, or rather, the manner in which it is standardly applied—what I have called the pragmatics—exaggerates the threat to the patients in order to protect them.

What kinds of risks does a patient have a right to be informed about when giving informed consent is at issue? The risks are sometimes described as those that a "reasonable person" would want to know about—because they can "reasonably" be expected to have some bearing on what such a person might decide to do. We have already observed how people polled overwhelmingly want to know the HIV status of the health care professionals who treat them. It is difficult to assert that what most people want to know is not what a reasonable person would want to know; the "reasonable person" standard should not be defined in such a way that most people are shown to be unreasonable. Moreover, although the majority's perception of the risks seems exaggerated when we look simply at the underlying probabilities of transmission, the fear is real—and it can be reduced at low cost by patients' switching from infected professionals. Clearly, then, information is rationally related to the choices being faced and is "material" to the decision being made; that is, it will affect the decision about what to do.

The pragmatics here are aimed at eliminating, at least as the general case, instances of physicians failing to inform patients of risks because they (the physicians) think the risks are worth taking. The overriding goal is rather for the patient to remain the judge of what risks are worth taking. Thus the pragmatics must stack the deck in such a way that the patient's *subjective* perception of the risk is the determining factor in how the hand gets played. In general, where risk-taking is involved, we have long been accustomed to accepting the individual's right to consent to risks: This is the usual mechanism for distributing the benefits and burdens of risk-taking. Only when people appealed to imagined risks to justify refusals to give handicapped workers fair equality of opportunity did we need to impose more objective requirements on the assessment of risk.

One countervailing consideration to this argument is that courts have ruled in the context of tort litigation that "remote" and "minute" risks need not be revealed to patients. Because there are so many minute or remote risks, no professional can take the time to reveal them all. In any case, it is impossible to tell ahead of time which of these a "reasonable person" would want to know about.

But the "minuteness" of the risk of HIV transmission, judging solely by probabilities, is not decisive here, because we already know that patients specifically want to know about it and view it as material to their decisions. This is *not* simply another minute risk, but rather one that a malpractice lawyer would pick out as salient.

Another way to restrict the scope of a patient's right to information has a bearing on the patient's perceptions of risk. Suppose a patient has racist views, for instance, about the inferiority of doctors belonging to a certain minority group. The fact that the patient perceives the risks of being treated by, say, an Asian or Jewish doctor as greater than the risks of being treated by some other doctor would suffice to convince us that the patient has a right to information about the religion or race of his physician. We would hardly condone (or formalize opportunities for) switching behavior based on perceived risks with such racist roots—though the behavior almost certainly takes place and there is little we can do to prevent it in a system that generally provides open choice of practitioners). Similarly, it might be claimed, the exaggerated perception of the risks of HIV transmission may have their basis in other discriminatory attitudes, such as homophobia. The stigma attached to HIV infection may itself derive from homophobia, and it may be this relationship that leads to heightened perceptions of risk. If this is true, then allowing the rights of HIV-infected health care workers to be compromised by the discriminatory attitudes of patients seems very much like allowing other handicapped workers' rights to be limited by other discriminatory attitudes harbored by co-workers or employers.

Although there is some merit to the claim that the stigma attached to HIV infection is rooted in homophobia, and we should not adopt policies that countenance the effects of homophobia, it is also true that many people fear HIV infection simply because of its inevitable effect—death. Moreover, they think there is a *risk* of transmission because they are aware there is a *mechanism* for transmission, and respected experts are concerned that statistical models of the probability of transmission suggest that some people will be infected in this way each year. Despite the partially apt analogy to the fabricated claims about risk that may traditionally have hurt handicapped workers, the risk of transmission perceived by patients cannot be dismissed entirely on this basis.

The conflict now takes this form: A risk that is not significant—judged from within the pragmatics of the rights of handicapped workers—is viewed as serious and material by patients. Such a conflict cannot be settled simply by saying, "The probability is only

1/100,000," however, because just what the objective probabilities are is precisely what is *not* at issue from within the pragmatics of patients' rights. That concern arises only from the perspective of the rights of handicapped workers. In other words, unless we have an *independent* argument about which perspective on risks—which rights, that is—must be given priority, we cannot settle the question merely by stating, "The risks are [or are not] significant" any more than stating the probabilities settles anything. We encounter this unusual source of indeterminacy because the rights of handicapped workers and patients rarely come into conflict, and the pragmatics surrounding each in general do not have to take the force of the other set of rights into account.[1]

Can we find an independent argument that establishes which perspective on risks, or rights, should be given priority? I am not aware of any such general, independent argument. Handicapped workers' rights derive from a general principle of distributive justice guaranteeing *fair equality of opportunity* and have substantial legal recognition, including the recent ADA legislation. Similarly, there is solid moral and legal support for the right to control over one's body, including the risks that are imposed on it in the context of medical care. However, even if there is no general argument showing that one right takes priority over the other, there is a specific argument that granting full priority to patients' rights as a way of responding to the risks of HIV transmission can make *each* of us worse off—at least if certain empirical assumptions are true. If the argument I explore in the next section is persuasive, it gives us good and adequate reason to restrict the exercise of patients' rights *in this instance.*

How We Can All Be Worse Off if We Each Try to Do Better: The Switching Dilemma

Although the probability of HIV transmission is very low, we have seen that most individuals view it as a significant risk—and one they want to avoid. Since the cost of switching health care providers is small, each of us can do better if we try to avoid the risk by seeking information about a provider's HIV status and switching if necessary. I want to show, however, that if we all act in that manner, we will then each be worse off. The only way for all of us to be better off is if we cooperate in refraining from seeking information about HIV status and acting on it. Let's look at this apparent paradox, to see why this is so.

A situation with this structure is known in game theory as a many-person prisoners' dilemma. The fact that the Switching Dilemma, as I shall call it, manifests this structure has important implications for arguments about testing health care workers or imposing practice restrictions on them. Dilemmas of this sort are really very familiar; they arise in many contexts. Consider a standard example: We are all fishermen. If all the other fishermen respect a limit on their catch, I can do better by exceeding the limit. If the others violate the limit, I would clearly do worse than they if I persist in sticking to the limit. But if we all try to catch the most fish we can, then we all do worse than we would if we respected a limit, because the fish population will collapse.

Similarly: Suppose we could all derive a significant benefit from the clean air that would result if we each invested in anti-smog devices for our cars. If everyone except me buys the device, I will be better off, since I get clean air without having to pay for it. If others refrain from buying the device, I would be a fool to buy one; I would have spent money to no avail, because the air still would not be clean (my anti-smog device alone will not suffice to clean it up). Whatever action others take, then, I do better if I do not buy the device. Yet—once again—if we all reason this way and act accordingly, we are all worse off than if we cooperate.

These examples are commonly thought of as "public-good" problems; our Switching Dilemma is likewise a kind of public-good problem, because the same kind of scenario gets played out when it comes to avoiding the risks of HIV transmission. Suppose all of us refrain from demanding information about the HIV status of surgeons who will operate on us, accepting the cost of living with the fear that they may infect us. We will then all be better off for several reasons: Resources will be available for infection control because they will not be diverted to testing, regulating, and enforcing compliance from surgeons or other health care workers. As a result, our chances of actually catching HIV will be lower (better infection control barriers are the most effective protection against transmission in health care settings). Services provided by HIV-infected surgeons (and other infected health care workers) will still be available to us— and to all those patients with HIV. Uninfected health care workers will be more willing to treat HIV-infected patients if the risks they face in doing so are not aggravated by policies that would penalize them if they were to become infected.

Of course, if everyone else refrains from demanding information about the HIV status of health care workers, but I can get and act on the information, then I will do better. I will have the benefits noted above, *and* I will avoid the "cost" inherent in my fear of contagion. I would also be a fool to refrain from seeking the information if everyone else demands it and acts on it, because—in that case—not only would I not have the benefits that derive from everyone refraining, but I would also still have to live with my fear. So whatever others do, I am better off trying to find out my surgeon's HIV status and switching if appropriate. But if all of us reason and aim to improve our situations in this rational way, we will all be worse off. That is the Switching Dilemma.

Now, to be sure, my description of the situation rests on some robust empirical assumptions. I assume that we get better protection against HIV transmission by emphasizing infection controls than we do by isolating and switching from, or restricting the practice of, HIV-infected surgeons and other health care workers. (This assumption underlies our existing practice regarding the protection of health care workers from the *higher* risk of transmission from patients.) I also assume there is a significant benefit to be gained from having a health care system in which there is less fear of treating HIV patients. (If physicians fear not only HIV transmission but the loss of their own livelihood if they become infected, they will be even more reluctant to treat HIV patients.) I further assume that the services provided by HIV-infected health care workers are of considerable value. (Some of these workers concentrate their efforts on treating other HIV patients, providing services many uninfected health care workers are reluctant to offer.)

Additionally, I assume there are significant costs to enforcing a system of information gathering intended to identify infected health care workers. Even if the government does not make testing mandatory, liability insurers are likely to require evidence from hospitals or individuals that they are not HIV infected. If we manage to avoid the costs of mandatory testing, we still have the costs of assuring compliance by health care workers (especially those who know they are infected). Considerable unwillingness has been shown on the part of such infected workers to comply with the CDC guidelines (Gross, 1991; Rosenthal, 1991a). A survey carried out in the wake of the CDC announcement of the 1991 guidelines found that HIV-infected health care workers are reluctant to tell their employers or patients about their condition, to restrict their practice to nonrisky procedures, and to have themselves tested or to seek treatment for fear that their status will put them at risk of losing their jobs (Rosenthal, 1991b:C5). If such noncompliance is widespread and people become aware of it, fears of contagion may persist despite the measures put into place to detect infected providers. Moreover, the noncompliance may come from professional groups as well. Dr. Roy Schwarz, an AMA official— explaining why dozens of medical groups are refusing to cooperate with CDC calls for guidelines about which procedures in each specialty are exposure-prone—said, "The prevailing attitude was that compiling a list implies there is a significant risk, and thus would mislead the public and capitulate to public fears" (Altman, 1991:A1, A19). Dr. Nancy Dickey explained: "Since there has never been a documented doctor-to-patient transmission, groups are concerned about being able to label any given procedure as being an at-risk procedure" (Coleman, 1991).

A further assumption is that a system that imposes restrictions on HIV-infected physicians or that indirectly—through liability insurance—requires testing of physicians and other workers will produce a demand for the mandatory testing of patients as well. Physicians are at greater risk of infection from patients than patients are from physicians, and they therefore perceive it as unfair that they should be asked to undergo testing and restrictions if patients are not. We may also see particular organizations of health care providers claiming that they can assure better patient safety through administering CDC-type guidelines than other providers, using the fear of transmission and their greater assurances of safety as a marketing device. For example, Kaiser Permanente has had a policy of keeping HIV-infected surgeons from performing invasive procedures—but it also has a policy of retaining the services of these physicians, which markedly reduces their incentive *not* to report their condition. Kaiser can then claim that their close monitoring of physician behavior makes their services safer than those provided by community hospitals. While this may be a successful marketing strategy, it tends to build rather than calm public fears of infection.

One final assumption in the Switching Dilemma is that the fear of contagion from professionals will persist. In fact, however, if people refrain from seeking information about the status of providers and efforts are instead focused on infection control, and if the benefit of this use of resources becomes better known, then over time the dread of HIV transmission will diminish. Moreover, the costs—such as they are—are borne by everyone. This means that it is possible to describe a new situation, a Long-Term Switching Dilemma, which includes the benefits of gradually diminishing dread over time. Once again, individuals who do not cooperate with others—seeking instead to cut their own short-term, temporary dread—will do better individually; but if all behave this way, all will lose the benefits of cooperation described earlier as well as the benefits of long-term, permanent dread reduction that derive from cooperation.

The Switching Dilemma has implications both for the CDC guidelines as well as for AMA policies. The AMA position that physicians have an obligation to know their status and report it to their patients if they are HIV positive sets the stage for switching. Although it might seem that the CDC guidelines escape the Switching Dilemma (because they do not call for producing a body of information that individuals other than the infected health care workers themselves can act on—they do not, for example, call for mandatory testing), in fact the CDC's June 1991 guidelines are challenged by the Switching Dilemma. By removing HIV-positive health care workers from certain invasive procedures, the CDC guidelines (paternalistically?) take the switching out of the hands of individual patients; the result is that everyone can switch without the embarrassment of having had to acquire information about infected providers. In effect, by giving in to the demand for knowledge about providers' HIV status and by enabling patients to switch, the guidelines virtually assure that all *will* switch—at least in the restricted cases where exposure-prone procedures are involved. Thus although the June 1991 guidelines may limit the *scope* of switching behavior, containing the more widespread damage that unrestricted switching would introduce, they also produce the damaging effect that comes from everyone switching in cases where exposure-prone procedures will take place. The Switching Dilemma has implications for the CDC guidelines as well as for policies—like the AMA's—that leave switching to individuals.

What follows from the fact that acting on our fears of contagion can lead to the Switching Dilemma? The dilemma tells us that we will all be worse off if we rely on and continue to respect individual autonomy unequivocally in situations of this sort. We can avoid the problem if we enforce some form of cooperation: The cost to each person will be that they will have to live with their own dread (although that may diminish in the long run, once full cooperation takes hold), but they will in fact have less to fear because they will have a better health care system; indeed, it will be one in which there is less chance of HIV transmission, because infection control measures will be more scrupulously adhered to. The enforced cooperation would take the form of protecting the rights of infected workers to continue practicing the procedures they are competent to perform.

The justification for ignoring individual preferences to know and to switch is not, however, the strong paternalism that seemed objectionable earlier. We are not saying that people do not know what is good for them and have to be protected against irrational acts. Rather, we are saying that people may make themselves worse off even when they act rationally, as a result of the effects produced when everyone behaves in the same rational way. The problem is that rational behavior by individuals can undermine a common or public good. In other words, we each do not end up with as safe or productive a health care system if we allow people to engage in switching behavior *even when that behavior is, individually, rational.* Specifically, if we grant full priority to patients' rights and allow people to engage in switching behavior, we are each worse off because our system is not as safe or productive as it would be if we refrained from full exercise of our patients' rights. Because all can agree to the importance of the public good, we are justified in limiting the range of choices open to us as individuals; only by so doing can we achieve the collective benefit.

This argument for restricting the exercise of patients' rights does not constitute or depend on a general argument that the rights of health care workers must take precedence over the rights of patients. The argument is tied to very specific assumptions about the effects of everyone exercising their rights as patients; change some of the mechanisms underlying these assumptions, and the argument does not work. Thus we have arrived at a justification for some policy options, not because we have settled once and for all how the underlying rights should be ranked, but because seeing that we must avoid the Switching Dilemma allows us to sidestep the apparently intractable problem of ranking conflicting rights. The opposition to the CDC guidelines that follows from this argument does not depend on saying, as some have argued (Barnes et al., 1990; Feldblum, 1991), that we have no basis for limiting the rights of handicapped workers because the risks fail to meet the threshold of "significance."

Implications for Public Policy

I have argued that we are each worse off if we adopt policies that either allow unrestricted exercise of patients' rights to know and to engage in switching behavior or have substantially equivalent effects. Since the AMA and CDC guidelines call for withdrawal of infected professionals from exposure-prone procedures (unless, under special conditions, they obtain informed consent from patients to perform those procedures), these guidelines must be included among policy options that make us collectively worse off—at least if the assumptions underlying the Switching Dilemma are correct as I have sketched them. And of course, more restrictive policies—such as calls for mandatory testing of all professionals or criminalization of failures to inform patients of a positive HIV status—serve only to push us deeper into being collectively worse off. Thus the argument offered here, although it does not settle in a general and principled way the conflict between patients' rights and the rights of handicapped workers, very definitely has policy implications. (Recall, however, that I have emphasized how, if the risks of transmission are substantially greater than current estimates suggest, the payoffs of our policy options change dramatically, and the Switching Dilemma disappears. Similarly, if the increased risks of transmission count as clearly significant, we will have to limit the rights of infected workers accordingly.

Given the Switching Dilemma, what policy options are appropriate? I briefly note the following:

(1) *Improve compliance with existing infection control measures.* "Universal" protections are not universally used. This may be especially true in private-practice settings, such as individual doctor and dentist offices. The public was clearly alarmed at the discovery of apparently grossly sloppy procedures in Dr. Acer's office. We should use this alarm to promote vigilance about protective measures (not to enflame the public about possible doctor-to-patient HIV transmission).

(2) *Invest in research and development to improve infection control measures.* Concern about threats to surgeons has led to some informative studies of needlestick and glove-puncture accidents; more such research must be done, and procedures and equipment must be modified in light of what is learned.

(3) *Encourage voluntary testing and treatment by practitioners who suspect they are at risk.* We have seen how restrictive policies may produce attempts to avoid testing and treatment. If practitioners are able to determine their HIV status without fear of reprisals, they may decide on their own to refrain from some procedures, or they may modify their practice in others, and they may be more likely to consult with others (confidentially) to discuss how to minimize risks.

(4) *Resist efforts to impose restrictive measures in order to manage liability.* Fighting for a standard of care that emphasizes infection control rather than singling out and removing infected personnel is both difficult and important. The argument has to be that an emphasis on infection control and other measures to reduce risks to patients represents a more effective form of quality control than does imposing restrictive measures on infected professionals.

(5) *Continue to monitor HIV (and HBV) transmission in health care settings.* Since the policies recommended here turn on the risks of transmission being as low as current estimates suggest, it is essential that we not view the matter as settled. We need more and better research, including prospective studies of infected practitioners, to learn more about the real risks.

(6) *Increase efforts to reduce the public perception that risks are great.* Public fear of infected workers and students has diminished as a result of strong support for the rights of those workers and students and of extensive public education. Similar efforts should work in the case of fears of transmission from health care professionals. A highly visible campaign aimed at infection control and other measures to reduce risks to patients would do much to generate confidence that risks are being taken seriously in appropriate ways.

We should not be under any illusions about the difficulties and challenges in following the policies recommended here. We may well yet find some clear cases of HIV transmission from health care worker to patient—clearer than those involving Dr. Acer's dental patients. If the assumptions behind my argument are correct, however, we should have *fewer* such cases if we put our emphasis on infection control than if we tried to eliminate "threatening" infected professionals from health care settings (for an excellent discussion of the benefits of a policy focused on infection control, v. Barnes et al., 1990:324). But it will be difficult to show that we have fewer cases: Any case that does appear is likely to seem to be another signal accident like the Acer case. It will require careful public education, including of those in the media, to put any putative cases of HIV transmission from health care worker to patient in proper perspective. Nevertheless, the alternative is worse. Even if we put stringent restrictions on infected professionals, the lack of compliance such policies may produce—plus the lack of emphasis on infection control that results when we divert resources into treating infected workers as the source of the risk—could easily produce *even more* cases of HIV transmission. That is, the CDC or AMA guidelines may actually give us more, not fewer, cases that can become signal accidents, in the process greatly inflating public fears. The Switching Dilemma tells us, as some public health proponents have pointed out as well, that more-restrictive policies may thus intensify rather than diminish public dread. If this happens, we will feel pushed to ever more drastic measures that are in turn even more likely to be collectively self-defeating.

Whether or not Dr. Rzepkowski's rights were violated, there is no question that we make ourselves collectively worse off if we adopt policies that restrict his and other health care workers' rights under present conditions. That gives us good reason *not* to adopt the restrictive measures that led to Rzepkowski's firing.

4

AIDS and Insurability: Ethical Issues in Underwriting

The Common Practice of Exclusion

Underwriting and Access to Medical Insurance

We live in a society in which more than 37 million people do not have insurance coverage for any health care services. These are primarily working people (and their dependents) who lack the kind of coverage typically available through employee group plans and yet who are ineligible for public insurance coverage. Their numbers grew considerably throughout the 1980s. In the face of rising health care costs, governments have restricted eligibility for public insurance, and some employers have reduced benefits—especially for dependents. The resulting "insurance gap" is a large part of why so many people have begun to urge major reform of our mixed public-private insurance system—and to ask what we gain and what we lose from a system that relies so heavily on private insurance.

A particularly dramatic and visible feature of the growing insurance gap in recent years has been the way that those who have AIDS (or who test positive for HIV, virtually assuring they will get AIDS) have found themselves increasingly either unable to get insurance or losing the insurance coverage they had once it becomes known that they have AIDS. The fact that so much of even the private insurance in this country is integrally tied to employment plays a major role here, since those with AIDS generally find they have to give up their jobs precisely at the point where their need for health care services (and thus insurance coverage) becomes greatest.

As a first step toward forming an argument about what our social obligations are, with respect to assuring that those with AIDS (and other especially nasty, complex, and expensive-to-treat diseases) retain their insurability, we will look at how standard underwriting practices currently work. Once we understand what is meant by "actuarial fairness," we can begin to assess whether the gains from a system that relies heavily on private insurance outweigh the losses; we will, in other words, be in a position to evaluate whether actuarial fairness is—as insurers are wont to claim—the equivalent of fairness in general. We will be in a position to ask: What are the obligations of insurers in a mixed system to facilitate access to coverage? Do standard underwriting practices interfere with social obligations to guarantee access to health care? Is there a sound moral justification for them? And, finally: What does justice require in the way of access to medical insurance—and does the present mixed public-private system provide that in a just manner? The answer to these questions will prepare us to see why reform of insurance underwriting has become a point of agreement among alternative proposals for national health care reform (see Chapter 8).

Standard Underwriting Practices and AIDS

Once debate forced into the open questions about access to medical insurance, public attention began to focus on the underwriting practices of medical insurers. For example, the *New York Times* reported that many private insurers have decided not to underwrite insurance for certain small groups and individuals and that their underwriting decisions go beyond mere efforts to protect themselves against those at risk for AIDS (Freudenheim, 1990). AIDS is, of course, but one of a multitude of diagnoses that are medically uninsurable; the phenomenon of people being (or suddenly becoming) "uninsurable" has been with us for a long time.

Nevertheless, the HIV epidemic has brought this troubling problem of uninsurability (and attendant general concerns about underwriting practices for medical insurance)—as it has so many others—to the forefront of public consciousness. In part this is because the cost of medical care for those with AIDS is frequently so prohibitively high that, suddenly, a very visible group of vulnerable people has been forced onto public budgets because they have lost insurance coverage or because they cannot get access to it once they have AIDS or have been exposed to HIV. In Washington, D.C., in Massachusetts, and in some other states, there have been vocal public debates about underwriting practices and their impact on those with or at risk for AIDS; legislation restricting these practices was ultimately struck down by the courts. Underwriting for AIDS thus serves to illustrate a much larger issue.

According to an Office of Technology Assessment survey (1988), nearly all insurers deny coverage to individuals who have AIDS. The only exceptions are certain "open-enrollment" Blue Cross/Blue Shield plans, some of which—largely as a consequence—have very high AIDS patient loads. These plans are given special reimbursement rates by state regulators (for example, in New York). Even these plans have exclusion clauses, often for eleven months, for preexisting conditions. Some commercial insurers are treating exposure to HIV, as measured by antibody tests, as a preexisting condition or as an indicator of high risk for developing AIDS and denying coverage on that basis.[1] Some commercial insurers and HMOs insure only individuals at low risk for AIDS; they apparently feel no obligation to insure high-risk individuals. Different insurers use a whole range of methods for determining risk classification, such as personal history questionnaires, attending physician statements, and laboratory tests, including HIV antibody tests. There is clear evidence that some insurers have attempted to determine sexual orientation through quite indirect indicators (occupation, marital status) as a way of assessing risk (v. Office of Technology Assessment, 1988:2).

Underwriting for AIDS, as we will see, involves the *standard underwriting practices* of denying coverage or of offering more expensive and substandard coverage to those who have a disease or are at higher risk of contracting it in the future (as determined by various medical examinations, tests, or records, or other "predictors" of risk). Because it heightens awareness of these practices and their social consequences, the HIV epidemic forces us to consider ethical issues that have been little discussed.

Justifying Standard Underwriting Practices

One justification for these standard underwriting practices is that they are really dictated solely by the economic interests of private insurers. In that case, the considerations relevant to justification are clear. We must simply weigh the benefits that are gained from having a mixed public-private insurance scheme against the costs, including the social costs of an increased insurance gap.

Although the structure of this justification is clear, little about the conclusions it yields is. What the benefits and costs of a mixed system are remains controversial, as does the issue of how to compare these benefits and costs to feasible alternative systems (and how to figure out what is politically feasible). A justification for standard underwriting practices that rested on these kinds of comparisons would therefore be constantly open to challenge. What is worse, disagreement about the relevant facts would quickly turn attention from the standard practices to the justification for a mixed public-private insurance system as a whole.

Strategically, this line of defense of standard practices is risky for insurers, who want to protect their economic interests. They must show why their interests are worth protecting in the face of complaints about injustice. A much more promising strategy, from an insurer's point of view, would be to develop a knockdown argument that showed we are *morally required* to use standard underwriting practices. The main objection to such practices is that they are unjust because they leave many people without insurance. But if it could be shown that it was unjust or unfair *not* to use these practices—that is, that they are requirements of justice—two things would be accomplished. First, defenders of standard underwriting practices could lay claim to high moral ground, meeting an argument from fairness with one of equally potent moral force. Second, the logic of the justification would prevent us from digging deeper and spreading controversy to the mixed insurance system as a whole. And, indeed, some insurers have developed just such an argument. They claim it is *actuarially unfair* (and therefore generally unfair) to those who are at low medical risk if insurers do not exclude those who are at high risk, such as those at risk for HIV, from insurance pools. Thus the term, "actuarial fairness," widely used in the literature, expresses the *moral* judgment that fair underwriting practices must reflect the division of people according to the *actuarially accurate* determination of their risks.

This Argument from Actuarial Fairness, as I shall refer to it, is an important one that deserves a careful analysis and reply. In the next section, I show that insurers are wrong to treat actuarial fairness as if it were an obvious requirement of justice or social fairness; doing so involves presuppositions that are both controversial and implausible. Moreover, we often depart from actuarially fair practices for reasons of social justice (or for other social purposes), which suggests that we do *not* treat actuarially fair practices as fundamental moral requirements. Indeed, as I go on to argue, in a just health care system—whether public or mixed—actuarial fairness disappears as an issue of any fundamental interest to consumers of insurance; playing only a "bookkeeping" role and thus confirming the claim that it has little to do with justice or social fairness after all. Because the Argument from Actuarial Fairness fails, insurers will be forced to defend standard underwriting practices by defending the merits of a mixed insurance system as a whole. No such system will be just unless it explicitly divides the responsibility for guaranteeing access between the public and insurers, as we have failed to do. Finally, at the end of this chapter, I will turn my attention to some ethical issues concerning the methods of risk classification used in standard underwriting practices.

Is It Unfair to Underwrite High-Risk Individuals?

Market Forces and the Descriptive Content of Actuarial Fairness

Let us begin by thinking solely about the risk-management aspect of medical insurance, ignoring for the moment any special moral importance we might attribute to assuring access to health care services. From this perspective, health insurance (like other insurance) is no more than a way for rational, economic agents to manage their risks of serious losses under conditions of uncertainty. The market for such insurance exists because most prudent people are willing to face modest losses (premiums) on a regular basis, rather than face catastrophic losses at unpredictable times. The modest losses are perceived as the cost of security.

The absence of information about when losses will occur is what gives people a common interest in pooling risks. In the general case, we can imagine that there is a symmetry among all parties with regard to the lack of information. Under these conditions, prudent consumers of security will have a common interest in sharing their risks.

An important change takes place when we acquire information that allows us to distinguish the different risks and thus sort people into stratified risk pools. For example, in the case of homeowner's fire insurance, we can differentiate risk pools because we acquire actuarially relevant information about the construction, age, density, and location of houses, and information about available fire-fighting facilities and relevant fire safety codes. In the case of medical insurance, the differentiation can be the result of information about individual medical histories, genetic disposition to disease or genetic disorders (v. Antonarakis, 1989), or lifestyle choices.

Two forces emerge when risk is stratified in this way. First, those purchasing insurance may now see themselves as having distinct rather than common interests. Those who are at lower risk will see an advantage in premiums priced to reflect those risks; they will want to pool their risks only with those at comparably low risk, because it will then be less expensive to "buy security"—which is what they are attempting to achieve by buying insurance in the first place. Why, they ask, should we want to—or, worse, *have* to—subsidize security for those at higher risk? If the only constraint at work in such an insurance market is that it be structured so that consumers have a chance to pursue their own economic advantage, then it seems reasonable for those at lower risk to pursue a divided pool with premiums that reflect risks. (We should not, however, confuse the rational behavior of people operating *within* a given institutional arrangement that provides incentives for such behavior with the moral judgments those same people might make about the appropriateness of that institutional framework. Surveys suggest that a majority of Americans would prefer a system of universal, compulsory health insurance, which puts everyone in the same risk pool [v. Blendon and Donelan, 1990].) And, indeed, those at high risk will seek the security bargain offered by insurance that pools high- and low-risk individuals together. (Insurers refer to this practice as "adverse selection.")

The second force drives the insurer. At a certain level of abstraction, it does not matter to the insurer what the structure of the risk pool is. Opportunity to profit from the provision of security exists in both "community-rated" pools and risk-rated pools. Under certain market conditions, however—for example, where participation in the insurance scheme is not compulsory and where information is available to participants about their individual risks—adverse selection and other problems will arise for insurers. Those who suspect that their risks are high will seek out insurance, and those who think their risks are low may avoid insurance or seek cheaper insurance elsewhere. Competition will then drive insurers to keep premiums low by excluding high-risk individuals. The standard underwriting practices we are examining are thus a consequence of providing health insurance *in a specific marketing context* with certain underlying assumptions about the social function of the insurance (v. Hammond and Shapiro, 1986). Most fundamentally, the assumption is that health insurance is a market for individual security in which consumers must be allowed to pursue their individual interests, as determined by information about their risks. This assumption is far from morally neutral, as we shall see.

The concept of actuarial fairness could be assigned a purely *descriptive* as opposed to *normative* content in the kind of insurance market we have just been considering. On such a stipulation, saying that a premium is "actuarially fair" would mean no more than that it reflects the actuarial risks the purchaser actually faces or is known to face, or, in other words, that it is actuarially accurate. Similarly, saying that the refusal to insure those at high risk is actuarially fair would mean only that such underwriting practices yield insurance markets in which premiums reflect risks. As a result, the cost of insuring some people is simply too high for standard insurance, and such people may not find insurance available at any price. In an ideal insurance market, it could then be argued, market forces would drive premiums in the direction of actuarial fairness for the economic reasons just described.

This purely descriptive notion of actuarial fairness does not carry with it the *moral* claim that such a system of exclusions from coverage and risk-based premiums is a fair one, that is, that justice requires us to have it. The notion of actuarial fairness that we find in the insurance literature (understandably) goes beyond this purely descriptive content, however, and carries the implication that actuarially *accurate* underwriting practices are also *fair* or *just* ones. It is this moral notion that is crucial to the Argument from Actuarial Fairness—to which I shall now turn.

The Argument from Actuarial Fairness

Clifford and Iuculano (1987) defend standard underwriting practices, such as permitting HIV testing and denying coverage to those at high risk, with a version of the moral argument I have called the Argument from Actuarial Fairness. Claiming that insurance "is founded on the principle that policyholders with the same expected risk of loss should be treated equally," they conclude that bans on HIV testing "would seriously distort the fair and equitable functioning of the insurance pricing system" (Clifford and Iuculano, 1987:1807). Similarly, they go on to say: "The primary goal of underwriting is the accurate prediction of future mortality and morbidity costs. An insurance company has the *responsibility* to treat all its policyholders fairly by establishing premiums at a level consistent with the risk represented by each individual policyholder" (Clifford and Iuculano, 1987:1809, emphasis added). The authors bolster this appeal to actuarial fairness by citing requirements of the Unfair Trade Practices Act, which mandates "fair discrimination" so that individuals are charged premiums in accordance with their risk, but prohibits "unfair discrimination" between individuals who face comparable risks. The authors claim that HIV testing is a fair and valid underwriting tool.

In effect, Clifford and Iuculano argue that it is *unfair* if insurers *fail* to deny coverage to those at high risk. Specifically, it will be unfair to those at low risk if they are made to pay the higher premiums necessary to cover the costs of those at high risk. Their remark about the "responsibility" of insurers suggests that it is an *obligation* to refuse to underwrite those at high risk for AIDS—but the claim that standard underwriting practices are *obligatory* is a *strong* claim indeed. The *weak* claim, that it is (sometimes) *permissible* to use such practices, is more plausible—but it does not offer insurers the strategic advantages noted in the previous section. Instead, it provides a defense of standard underwriting practices only if it can also be shown that our mixed system is compatible with our moral obligations to provide access to health care. If standard practices undercut our ability to meet these obligations in a mixed system, then they obstruct justice and are therefore impermissible. The strategic advantage—from the insurers' point of view—of the strong claim is that it allows them to avoid having to make such a defense of the mixed system as a whole, and that it meets an accusation of unfairness—not simply with a denial, but with a countercharge.

Put in its simplest terms, my objection to this argument is, as I intimated above, that it confuses *actuarial fairness* with *moral fairness* or *just distribution*. These are two altogether different notions: Actuarial fairness is neither a necessary nor a sufficient condition for moral fairness or justice in an insurance scheme—most especially not in a health insurance scheme. To forge the link between fairness and actuarial fairness as Clifford and Iuculano do is to presuppose that individuals are entitled to benefit from any and all of their individual differences, including their different degrees of risk for disease and disability. Such a presupposition is highly controversial and, I shall argue, false. (The weak claim noted earlier—that it is [sometimes] permissible to use standard underwriting practices for medical insurance—has a correspondingly weak presupposition, namely, that following standard underwriting practices is not unfair if information about individual differences in medical risk provides a basis for competitive advantage. But this weak presupposition is also false.)

A Controversial Assumption About Individual Differences

To get from the merely descriptive notion of actuarial fairness, which has no justificatory force, to the moral claim about fairness found in the insurers' argument, we need to add some moral assumptions. Specifically, we have to add what I will call the *strong assumption*, the claim that individuals should be free to pursue the economic advantage that derives from any of their individual traits, including their proneness to disease and disability. This strong assumption might be used in an argument that echoes some recent work on distributive justice: (1) Individual differences of any kind constitute some of an individual's personal assets; (2) people should be free to— indeed, are entitled to—gain advantages from their personal assets; (3) social arrangements will be just only if they respect such liberties and entitlements; (4) specifically, individuals are entitled to have markets—including medical insurance markets—structured in such a way that they can pursue any advantages that might derive from their personal assets.

This skeletal argument might be elaborated, and the strong assumption it contains be defended (or attacked), in a number of different ways within different theories of justice. For example, Nozick's (1974) libertarianism begins with certain assumptions about property rights and the degree to which certain liberties, such as the liberty to exchange one's marketable abilities or traits for personal advantage, must be respected even in the face of what many take to be overriding social goals. Consequently, schemes that are actuarially unfair in effect confiscate property without consent.

Other political philosophers claim that just arrangements are the result of a bargain made by rational people who want to divide the benefits of mutual cooperation (v. Gauthier, 1986). On this view, bargainers who have initial advantages in assets would accept only those social arrangements that retain their relative advantages; they would argue that *just* arrangements preserve the advantages of those at low risk of disease through insurance markets that use standard underwriting practices.

An attractive feature of bargaining theories of this sort (for some people) is that they justify principles of justice through the most straightforward appeal to the interests of each moral agent. Others, however, will note that—unfortunately—the significant inequalities such theories justify can be traced back to initial inequalities for which there is little moral justification, surely reason enough for rejecting the bargaining approach. If bargaining can yield agreement only if unjustified initial advantages are preserved, then bargaining does not—*cannot*—tell us what justice requires.

An alternative to the "bargaining" theory of justice avoids incorporating initial inequalities in this way by constructing a "hypothetical" contract in which all participants are treated fairly and impartially. On Rawls's (1971) theory, for example, "free" and "equal" moral agents are kept from knowing anything about their individual traits; they must select principles of justice that would work to everyone's advantage, including those who are worst off. Exactly which individual differences should be allowed to yield individual advantage thus becomes a matter for deliberation *within* the theory of justice, not a starting point for it.

Such an approach breaks the grip that initial inequalities have in a real bargain, but it does so at a cost. We now need an argument why this model for selecting principles is fair to all people and why we should count its outcome as justified (Rawls, 1980, 1993). Thus we can see that the debate about the relevance of individual differences to the just distribution of social goods goes very deep and lies at the heart of the conflict between alternative approaches to constructing and justifying theories of justice (v. Barry, 1989, for a brilliant discussion of the alternative theories of justice). These complex, foundational disputes cannot be resolved here, but their prominence should give pause to any who hoped for a simple, straightforward way to tell what counts as "just." Showing that the strong assumption about individual differences is deeply controversial at the level of the theory of justice is obviously not, in itself, a refutation of the Argument from Actuarial Fairness, but it does give us good reason not to accept the assumption without a convincing argument. I shall endeavor to underscore why such a "convincing argument" is so difficult to make.

As it stands, the strong assumption is much *too* strong. Some individual differences are ones we clearly think should *not* be allowed to yield advantage or disadvantage; recent legislation in the United States has established a legal framework to reinforce these views about justice. For example, we believe that race or gender should not become a basis for advantage or disadvantage in the distribution of rights, liberties, opportunities, or economic gain. Under some conditions, being of a certain race or gender might—indeed, does—have market advantages. But though in practice we fall far short of what justice demands, we nevertheless believe that justice requires us to sever consideration of race, gender, and handicaps from deliberations about hiring, firing, and reimbursement for services performed. (What makes a policy of Affirmative Action so controversial is that there race and gender *are* allowed to play an explicit role so that certain social goals can be achieved.) Thus we reject the view—in its most general form—that all individual differences can morally serve as the basis for advantage or disadvantage.

Although we agree that race and gender are unacceptable bases for advantage or disadvantage, we have less agreement about how to treat some other individual differences. We allow talents and skills, for example, to play a role in the generation of inequalities, and yet we tax (to some degree) those with the most highly rewarded talents and skills in ways that—in principle—help those who lack them (though not to the maximal extent, as Rawls, 1971, would have it). How much inequality we allow is controversial in practice, just as it is in theory. Some people think that individuals are entitled to derive whatever advantages the market allows from their talents and skills, and they view income redistribution as an unjustifiable tax on talents and skills (v. Nozick, 1974). Others argue that talents and skills such as intelligence or manual dexterity are the results of a "natural lottery," not desert, and that it is a matter of luck who enjoys the family and social structures that encourage the traits of character such as diligence that are essential to the refining of basic talents. On this view, redistributive schemes are a morally obligatory form of social insurance that protects us against turning out to be among those who are worst off with regard to marketable talents and skills (v. Cohen, 1989; Dworkin, 1982; and Rawls 1971, 1993).

Even among those philosophers who want to treat talents and skills as individual assets, however, only the strictest libertarians treat health status differences as merely "unfortunate" variations and believe that there is no social obligation to correct for the relative advantages and disadvantages caused by disease or disability (Engelhardt, 1986). The design of health care systems throughout most of the world rests on a rejection of the view that individuals should have the opportunity to gain economic advantage from differences in the level or degree of their health risks. Despite variations in how these societies distribute the premium and tax burdens of financing universal health care insurance, our mixed system is nearly unique in allowing the degree of risk to play such a role. Moreover, as I noted earlier, surveys show that most Americans would prefer a universal system that abolished that practice. Far from being a self-evident or intuitively obvious moral principle, the strong assumption is in fact widely rejected.

Two Observations About Actuarial Fairness and Insurance Practices

The Argument from Actuarial Fairness rests on an assumption that is controversial in theory and fails to match the moral beliefs, not only of most Americans, but of the rest of the world as well. We do not settle moral arguments by a vote, however, and I will in the next section offer a solid reason for rejecting the view that health insurance must be structured so that individuals can derive benefits from their differences in medical risks. But first I want to draw lessons from two further observations about the role of actuarial fairness in our insurance practices.

The first observation is that in both medical and nonmedical contexts insurers are highly selective about which information they will use to determine risks. This selectivity adds an element of *moral arbitrariness* to the notion of actuarial fairness. We can accept this arbitrariness only if we believe that insurance markets give us a fair procedure for recognizing all and only those differences among individuals it is appropriate to recognize. That is, the need to justify reliance on a market model returns to haunt us again, even though the strategic appeal of the Argument from Actuarial Fairness was that it seemed to avoid this messy issue. To see why this is so, consider three different interpretations of what actuarial fairness might require regarding the acquisition and use of information about risks.

In the first place, actuarial fairness might require that we *discover* or *seek out* all relevant information about the risks people face. If what really matters for purposes of justice is that individuals have different risks that can be brought into play as individual assets, then it might be thought the fair arrangement is one in which we make a reasonable effort to find out precisely what these differences are. This might mean, for example, that insurers are obliged to develop new medical technologies, including genetic tests, that allow more accurate predictions of risks for subgroups to be made. On this interpretation of the requirements of actuarial fairness, insurers might be obliged to commit resources to mapping the human genome and to developing tests relevant to underwriting practices.

A second interpretation is that actuarial fairness might require only that insurers *use* all relevant, available information about those risks. This view allows a slight loosening of the connection between individual differences and the distribution of advantages, for people are entitled to derive benefit only from those differences in risks about which information happens to be available. For example, if technologies such as the ELISA test for HIV happen to be available because they were developed to screen blood, then insurers are obliged to extend their use into insurance contexts because the tests mean that information about HIV risks is obtainable. Similarly, if mapping the human genome leads us to develop diagnostic screening tests for various medical conditions, then insurers would be obliged, on this view of actuarial fairness, to use them for underwriting purposes. (We need to be alert to this possible use—actually an abuse, if I am right—of the results of mapping the human genome.)

Actuarial fairness might, in the third interpretation, simply allow insurers to use information about risks whenever it is in their economic interest to do so. This approach loosens even more dramatically the connection between individual differences and the advantages that result from them within insurance schemes. In effect, it says we are entitled to benefit from our differences only if the market makes it profitable for insurers to allow us to so benefit.

No one (including Clifford and Iuculano, 1987) who feels the moral pull of the Argument from Actuarial Fairness actually pushes the first interpretation, making research obligatory. I do not believe that standard insurance practice endorses the second interpretation, requiring that all available ways of determining and categorizing risks be used, either. Insurance practice seems rather to follow the third path: When the strong assumption about individual differences is made operational in insurance markets, this interpretation simply says that people are entitled to gain advantage from those differences that insurance markets happen to reward. This no longer sounds like a fundamental or basic principle of distributive justice; rather, it appears to be something purely adventitious.

If we could be persuaded that insurance markets provide a *fair procedure* for recognizing which individual differences should be rewarded, then the arbitrariness would be less troublesome. We would simply be saying the market is a kind of lottery that determines in an arbitrary—but nonetheless fair—way which individual differences will yield advantages to their holders. Without a justification for relying on markets to provide us with such a procedure, however, the arbitrariness is morally troubling, since its consequences for individuals—including the ways in which it magnifies inequalities—are serious. To be sure, cost factors can be pervasive in markets without making them unfair. My point is not that the market is unfair because such happenstance factors as information and costs play a role in what distinctions it makes. Rather, my point is that we need to be shown the market is at least as good as any alternative procedure at making distinctions among individual differences of the sort society thinks should be rewarded.

My second general observation about the role of actuarial fairness in our insurance practices is that society does not in fact trust the insurance market to make all and only those distinctions it is fair to make among individuals. This is made evident by the way we regulate both medical and nonmedical insurance markets, making explicit social judgments about *how* insurance companies may draw distinctions among individuals for underwriting purposes. We act as if we do *not* think insurance markets are procedurally fair. In effect, we allow many considerations—both of justice and of other goals of social policy—to *override* appeals to actuarial fairness. This suggests that we do not consider actuarial fairness as a basic requirement of distributive justice in insurance contexts after all. Some examples will help make this clear.

Even in insurance markets where no general social obligation is felt to make security against loss available to all, e.g., in fire or theft insurance, it is generally recognized that certain underwriting practices are unacceptable forms of discrimination. Thus "redlining" whole geographical areas was thought to contribute to the economic decline of neighborhoods and to "racial tipping" and "white flight," and that particular underwriting practice was condemned in the late 1970s as unacceptable. No one questioned, however, the utility of redlining as a (rough) device allowing insurers to predict their risks of loss. The point is that *considerations of justice* overruled the *advantage to insurers* of what hitherto had been standard underwriting practices. Similarly, unisex rating is a rejection of an "actuarially fair" and efficient method of underwriting and pricing groups at differential risk. In this case, we override standard underwriting practices because we give more importance to a principle of distributive justice assuring the equal treatment of a group that is traditionally discriminated against (typically it is women, though in some instances men have also been victims of gender discrimination) than we do to "efficiency" in underwriting practices. Some states require high-risk drivers to be insured, setting up special insurance pools or rate regulations, subsidizing high-risk drivers to make sure no one has to encounter uninsured drivers. Here our social interest in guaranteeing a public good (the reduced risk of encountering an uninsured driver) is allowed to overrule otherwise sound (and actuarially fair) underwriting practices that would have denied these drivers insurance.

Turning to medical insurance, we also find examples in which other social goals lead us to override considerations of actuarial fairness. As noted earlier, some states tried to ban the HIV testing of individuals for health insurance, not because of a concern about the accuracy of the screening device, but because of concerns about privacy and the importance of access to treatment. More generally, about one third of the states have established insurance pools that guarantee no one is deemed uninsurable because of prior medical condition or high-risk classification. Where such pools are funded by insurance premiums paid by low-risk individuals, we simply have an enforced "subsidy" from those at low risk to those at high risk, overriding concerns about actuarial fairness. Finally, if we think about our combined private and public insurance schemes, and the corresponding premiums and taxes, our health care system is largely "actuarially unfair" to working adults, who must pay a combined tax-plus-premium that covers the health care needs of children and the elderly. (The combined scheme looks actuarially fair only if we think about premiums and benefits paid out over the whole lifespan, assuming the scheme is stable and that benefit ratios remain roughly comparable for different birth cohorts [v. Daniels, 1988].)

These examples confirm that we override standard underwriting practices for various reasons, and that we do not wholly trust insurance markets to draw the distinctions between those occasions when actuarial fairness is acceptable—morally fair—and when it is not. Put more bluntly, the way we handle the drawing of distinctions strongly suggests *we do not believe actuarial fairness is a basic requirement of justice.* I turn next to a discussion of further reasons to support that belief.

What Happens to Actuarial Fairness in a Just System?

Justice and Differences in Health Risks

My argument so far has been negative, challenging a crucial assumption underlying the Argument from Actuarial Fairness by showing that it is controversial at the level of theory and that it is inconsistent with important features of our practice. By relying on a more positive account of what justice requires in the distribution of health care—my fair-equality-of-opportunity account, which I reviewed in Chapter 1 (v. Daniels, 1985, 1988, for a full development of this view)—I hope to sharpen the contrast between what justice requires and what standard underwriting practices involve when individuals face actuarially distinct risks. Specifically, on this view justice requires that there be no financial barriers to access to health care and that the system allocate its limited resources so that they work effectively to protect normal functioning, and thus fair equality of opportunity, for all—not just the privileged (or wealthy) few. We can then address the question: What happens to actuarial fairness in a just health care system?

The view of health care as critical to fair equality of opportunity requires rejecting the Argument from Actuarial Fairness. A health care system is just *only if* it protects fair equality of opportunity. A system, like ours, that uses standard underwriting practices based on actuarial fairness fails to protect equal opportunity, because access to care depends on ability to pay. A just health care system must thus reject the insurers' argument that actuarial fairness assures that the insurance system is just. It will be clear from what follows that standard underwriting practices are not a necessary condition for justice, either.

Actuarial Fairness in Just Insurance Schemes

One common way to try to meet social obligations regarding access to health care is to institute a universal and compulsory health insurance scheme (see Chapter 8). We need to look at what happens to standard underwriting practices in such schemes. Typically, under insurance schemes established as part of social policy, prior medical conditions and risk classification cannot serve as the basis for either underwriting or pricing insurance coverage. Rather, because society acts on its obligation to meet all reasonable health care needs, within limits on resources, there will be subsidies from the well to the ill and from low-risk to high-risk individuals, as well as from the rich to the poor. The social insurance scheme thus *requires* what a private market for health insurance would condemn as actuarially unfair.[2] From the perspective of private insurers in our mixed system, denying coverage to those at high risk seems completely unproblematic ("You can't buy fire insurance once the engines are on the way," they will tell us). But this perspective is persuasive only if the most important function of health insurance is risk management. Since health insurance has a very different social function, however—protecting equality of opportunity by guaranteeing access to an appropriate array of medical services—then there is a clear *mismatch* between standard underwriting practices and the social function of health insurance. A just, purely public health insurance system thus leaves no room for the notion of actuarial fairness.

Ironically, a just, but mixed, public and private health insurance system makes actuarial fairness a largely illusory—perhaps even deceptive—notion. Suppose that high-risk individuals are excluded from private insurance schemes in a mixed insurance system, for the kinds of reasons we have noted earlier. Because the system is just, these people will nevertheless not be left uninsured (as many are in the United States today) but will be covered by public insurance or by legally mandated high-risk insurance pools subsidized by premiums from private insurance. Lower-risk individuals left in the private insurance schemes might think that actuarial fairness has protected them from higher premiums. But here is where their savings are largely illusory. The premiums of those in the private insurance schemes will either cross-subsidize to some extent the high-risk individuals who are insured in the special high-risk pools, or their taxes will cover the costs of insuring high-risk individuals through public schemes. Their actual insurance premiums are thus their private ones *plus the share of their taxes* that goes to public insurance.

Because such a system is intended to protect fair equality of opportunity, I am supposing that the high-risk individuals are not being asked to bear the full burden, or even the major burden, of the higher health care costs they are likely to incur. Because protecting fair equality of opportunity is a societal obligation, it would seem reasonable for those obligations to be financed through the most progressive transfer system in the society, presumably an income-based tax. In contrast, taxing those at high risk through higher insurance premiums would be giving weight to individual differences that the principle of fair equality of opportunity renders morally irrelevant. Retaining standard underwriting practices in a mixed (but just) system would primarily serve a bookkeeping role, helping us to distinguish the costs of insurance to be borne by premiums as opposed to taxes.

Some will want to argue that I have overstated the point about illusion. Perhaps so. In a mixed system, assuming that publicly financed insurance is more progressively financed than private insurance, there will be some special distributive effects of putting high-risk individuals into public schemes rather than leaving them in private ones—but how *big* these effects are will depend on the rela-

tive size of the two sectors and how progressively financed the public schemes really are. The main point of the principle remains,
however: In a just system, low-risk individuals share the burden of
financing the health risks of high-risk individuals. In sharp contrast
to the way the Argument from Actuarial Fairness would have it, true
fairness *requires* that these risks be shared.

Actuarial Fairness and Individual Responsibility for Risks

I want to comment briefly on the issues raised by self-imposed risks,
which might be thought to raise problems for my account of justice
and health care. In the fair-equality-of-opportunity account to which
I have appealed, the crucial underlying intuition is that individual
differences in risks of disease and disability are the results of a natural lottery. The fact that people do not in any important sense *deserve* the advantages such a lottery offers gives us ample reason to
avoid magnifying these inequalities into socially approved ones if
there is a reasonable alternative. But what if people bring their risks
of disease and disability on themselves? We may then believe that
social obligations to protect equality of opportunity do not apply,
that people are responsible for the shortfall of opportunity they bring
on themselves. Some people clearly believe they should not have to
subsidize the risky behaviors of others, even if they should share the
costs incurred by unavoidable risks of disease. Strikingly, the attitudes of many persons toward different categories of victims of the
HIV epidemic turn on whether those individuals appear to be "inno-
cent" victims, or victims who are culpable because their own behaviors have harmed them—i.e., they are persons who "brought it on
themselves." (This judgmental attitude persists even though the me-
dian interval between HIV infection and AIDS is so long that many
current victims, even more than a decade after AIDS was discovered,
could not have known of any connection between their behavior and
its risks.)

    Several very serious problems with the notions of responsibility
and culpability are at work here. We seem untroubled by many lifestyle choices that carry with them significant risks of disease and
disability. We rarely ask that those who like risky sports be specially
penalized in order to reduce the likelihood that they will raise our
health care costs. We fall well short of imposing major penalties on
those whose smoking, alcohol consumption, and eating habits increase their health risks—though we increasingly look with favor on
regulations aimed at limiting the harm to others from those behav-

iors, and we generally look favorably on some insurance incentives (as in life insurance policies) that reward risk-lowering behaviors.

The more we examine the factors that contribute to some groups being more prone to risky behaviors than others, the more cautious we have to be about overemphasizing individual culpability for choosing the risky behavior. Class, education, and cultural factors— many effectively beyond an individual's control—are very powerful predictors of behavior. We also do not have a good grasp of the factors that play a role in converting lifestyle choices, like smoking, into real risks of disease: Recent studies suggest important genetic factors may play a major causal role in determining which smokers get cancer (Foreman, 1990). In the case of HIV, we must be very suspicious of the vehemence with which people raise the issue of self-imposed risks. This may largely be a smoke screen masking homophobia, racism, and social antipathy to drug abusers, rather than a deeply held and consistent conviction about the importance of the distinction between natural and self-imposed risks. For many reasons, then, I believe a just health care system must steer clear of penalties and sanctions for self-imposed risks, though it may be important to consider some incentives; certainly it is important to invest resources in learning more about how to modify people's behavior, including behaviors (like sex and addiction) that are deeply resistant to intervention.

Dividing Responsibilities in a Mixed System

Some people believe that insurers in our mixed system are under an obligation to share the burden of guaranteeing access to health care. The view is that sharing that burden is part of the "overhead" of doing business in a mixed system, an implicit quid pro quo for being allowed to profit from what otherwise might be a social insurance scheme. The use of standard underwriting practices to exclude (for example) those who have been exposed to HIV is thus criticized as an abrogation of responsibility. Is this criticism fair?

The obligation to assure access to health care services is primarily a *social* obligation, not a private or corporate one. This obligation is directly discharged by the state in a compulsory universal health insurance system. In a mixed system, however, there must be a division of responsibility between private insurers and the public. The exact terms of that division must be *explicit* and must lead to assignable legal duties to assure access to care (v. Buchanan, 1989). Precisely which categories of people will be eligible for public insurance and will therefore fall outside the responsibility of private insurers must be clear. Those who are at high risk, for example, would become the responsibility of the public if we set up tax-subsidized insurance pools that cover them (independent of means-tested insurance for those with ordinary risks who cannot afford insurance). Alternatively, they could be made the responsibility of private insurers, if states mandated insurers to subsidize such an insurance pool through revenues from premiums paid by those with ordinary risks. Another option is to share the burden: High-risk insurance pools could be jointly subsidized by taxes and premiums provided by private insurers. For instance, Medicaid might spread the burdens of guaranteeing access by participating in such insurance pools. The point is this: Justice requires that society establish some adequate scheme, and the act of establishing it must include making explicit who has what responsibilities; the failure to divide responsibility explicitly is bound ultimately to lead to injustice. (Insurance gaps will appear, because both public and private sectors will pass the buck—or, rather, try to hold on to it.)

An analogous point can be made about the obligations of physicians and hospitals regarding access to medical care. Our social obligation to provide access to care does not directly translate into obligations for hospitals or physicians to treat every patient who seeks their care. We can of course divide responsibility, through legislation or regulation, placing certain obligations on those who would be licensed to deliver services. But then these obligations should be thought of as contractual: Physicians or hospitals agree to the imposed obligations as conditions on their practice, and thus the conditions need not be seen as violations of any basic liberties of providers (v. Daniels, 1985:Ch.6). What we cannot do, however, is infer that every provider has an obligation to assure access to care simply because there is a social obligation to do so (on these points, see Chapter 2). Exactly which obligations we want different providers— or insurers—to undertake must be the result of an explicit division of responsibility in a mixed system.

It should also be obvious that *real obligations* to underwrite such normally uninsurable individuals should be distinguished from *tactical decisions* to underwrite some of them in order to reduce social pressures for the redesign of the insurance scheme. Even an informal sense of "mission," or a community-spirited effort to offer open enrollment as long as the competitive market still allows robust cross-subsidies, falls short of being a real obligation to underwrite those with disease conditions or at high risk for them. If there are genuine obligations, they must be part of the explicit design of the system. Thus the community-oriented mission of some Blue Cross/Blue Shield plans, which offer open enrollment and engage in "community rating" for individual health insurance, is part of a quid pro quo. Special tax status and special discounts on hospital rates (such as are available in, for example, New York) constitute a contractual arrangement to depart from standard underwriting practices. As competition and cost-containment measures intensify, however, any such arrangements will have to be made more explicit because of the decreased opportunity to offset losses through cross-subsidies.

The current crisis in underwriting for those with HIV exposure also requires society to undertake a more explicit division of responsibility regarding access to care. Those who are not being underwritten through private insurance are falling as burdens on narrowly financed public budgets (such as those at local or state public hospitals.) The result is that the burden of guaranteeing access to those in medical need is improperly distributed even in the public sphere—and that access to care for many is restricted.

The problem of underwriting high-risk individuals and those with prior conditions highlights a failure, not of the private sector but of the public one. It is hardly fair to fault insurers for responding to the incentives that exist in the current system. If we are dissatisfied with the output of that system—and we should be—we have a public responsibility to modify it. Further, it is unfair to fault insurers for defining their obligations to underwrite health insurance quite narrowly, within the limits of "fair" underwriting practices conceptually tied to the ways private insurance is used to manage many kinds of risks. That is exactly what we should expect when we allow a private insurance system—and within that context, private insurers have not (for the most part) violated their business ethic.

Insurers can be faulted, however, to the extent that they have lobbied to obstruct the emergence of an insurance system that would solve the problems of access faced by those at high risk. They cannot simply wash their hands of the access problems that result from standard underwriting practices, when they have exercised political and economic power to reduce the sphere of public insurance schemes. Nonetheless, culpability is not the same as obligation (even if we do have an intuitive sense that insurers "owe" something to those made worse off by insurers' opposition to alternatives to our mixed insurance system). The real moral failure is a public or social one.

When I first introduced the Argument from Actuarial Fairness, I noted its strategic advantage for insurers—allowing attention to be deflected from a careful examination of the *justice* of our mixed system and consideration of alternatives to it. I did not completely rule out a limited, bookkeeping role for appeals to actuarial fairness or other standard underwriting practices in a just mixed system. The constraint on that role is strong, however: Standard underwriting practices must not undermine the just distribution of health care services. They must never lead to gaps in insurance coverage or to significant burdens on those at high risk. Otherwise, fair equality of opportunity will not be protected by the health care system—which is what I have argued justice, by definition, requires. What this means is that we must, after all, examine the purported advantages of a mixed public and private insurance scheme, such as its efficiency (but v. Evans, 1989; Fuchs and Hahn, 1990). We must see whether those advantages outweigh the risks that standard actuarial practices pose to the just distribution of health care—precisely the sort of examination insurers hope to avoid. By now it should be clear that actuarial fairness can play only a subsidiary role in a just, mixed system, and that we cannot use the notion to avoid answering more basic questions about justice in our health care system.

Techniques of Risk Classification

Gathering the information necessary to classify risks for underwriting purposes poses ethical issues. My discussion in this section—though narrowly focused in a sense—will serve to highlight general ethical issues, for once again it turns out that concentrating on the particular issues raised by AIDS (here: risk classification for those with AIDS) can give us a point of entry into a broader arena. The central point I will develop here is consistent with conclusions of the earlier sections: Ultimately, considerations of justice and of other social goals and costs override the interest insurers have in making risk classifications that are actuarially fair. More specifically, considerations of justice rule out attempts to use sexual orientation as a criterion for risk classification, and concerns about discrimination and other social costs weigh against using HIV testing as a method of risk classification. Let us turn to look more closely at why this is so.

Considerable evidence exists that some insurers have used sexual orientation as a method of risk classification (Office of Technology Assessment, 1988; Schatz, 1987). Schatz (1987:1787) notes that one insurance company distributed an "AIDS Profile" that urged agents to separate out applications by single males in occupations (such as design, hairdressing, and dealing in antiques) that require little physical exertion. Other insurers, Schatz also notes, have used information about living arrangements, or zip codes, to classify risks.

The use in underwriting of stereotyped predictors of sexual orientation, or the use of sexual orientation itself, is morally unacceptable—and would be *even if they proved to be actuarially accurate.* The use of such predictors leads to the imposition of further serious harms on a group already subject to vigorous discrimination. For instance, as a result of such insurance policies employment opportunities may be affected, and access to credit or home mortgages may be limited (Schatz, 1987:1788). Fears about such discrimination may work as a disincentive to open communication by gays with physicians, itself an important step toward combatting the spread of AIDS. Finally, denying a benefit to a large group of individuals because *some* of its members are at higher risk of disease clearly resembles a form of discrimination that has been found totally unacceptable in the case of race or religious background. For example, some states have prohibited the use of (even) accurate medical tests for the presence of sickle-cell anemia or Tay-Sachs disease in underwriting, in part because coverage denials would fall disproportionately on groups that have historically been discriminated against in various other ways. Indeed, in the case of race, insurers have been explicitly barred from using "economic necessity" arguments to show risk classifications that impose special burdens on one race are nevertheless justifiable (Schatz, 1987:1791). Where access to important goods and opportunities generally provided by insurance is blocked by racial, sexual-orientation, gender-based, or other forms of stereotyping, the courts have backed growing public sentiment that equality of opportunity *must* be preserved, even if it costs insurers (or other premium payers) something to protect that equality.

Significantly, organizations representing insurers of several different types—the Blue Cross/Blue Shield Association, the Health Insurance Association of America, and the American Council of Life Insurance—have all agreed that the use of sexual orientation in underwriting is unacceptable; the "model bulletin" developed by the National Association of Insurance Commissioners discourages the effort to use sexual orientation for underwriting purposes—though none of the recommendations of these organizations is binding on particular insurers. Furthermore, as Schatz (1987:1792) notes, although the National Association of Insurance Commissioners strongly rejected the underwriting use of sexual orientation or proxies for it, it could not arrive at an agreement about the use of HIV testing. Nevertheless, the unified organizational stand suggests there is wide recognition that considerations of justice constrain the use of sexual orientation for underwriting purposes.

The public debate surrounding HIV testing for health insurance purposes has focused less on its predictive value than on the social costs of permitting its use for underwriting purposes. The argument about social costs weighs the costs to insurers when HIV testing is not permitted against the costs to others—the externalities, as the economists would have it—when testing is permitted. For example, given the high false-positive rate of HIV testing in low-incidence populations, the ratio of burdens imposed on others to savings to insurers is likely to be high. Protecting insurers through testing thus potentially involves a very significant cost to many others. In any case, many critics of HIV testing (e.g., Peter Hiam, the former Massachusetts insurance commissioner who resigned in protest against then-Governor Michael Dukakis's plan to allow some testing for HIV by life insurance companies) have argued that the economic threat to insurers when they are not allowed to test has been exaggerated. Not only are costs not so high as original estimates suggested, but there are many steps insurance companies could take to control costs before a step as socially problematic as HIV testing would be justifiable.

Testing for HIV would protect medical insurers against only a very small proportion of their AIDS liability. Many individuals in at least one of the groups among which the infected can be expected to be found (gay men) are employed and covered by group plans, for which no testing is envisioned. Others presumed to be at high risk (such as drug abusers) are not likely to seek out insurance at all. In addition, there are other ways for insurers to limit liability for the costs of AIDS than by resorting to testing for HIV. For example, case-management techniques have shown considerable success in limiting costs and improving the delivery of services to AIDS patients. Finally, the burden of costs can be reduced by spreading the risk among insurers, either by establishing voluntary risk-sharing pools or by cross-subsidizing in ways that cut against standard actuarial practices—provided some agreements can be reached among insurers in areas where the risk for AIDS is especially prevalent. In sum, if it can be shown that the burden to insurers is not so great as originally suggested, and the actual burden can be managed and spread in a way that minimizes burdens on particular insurers, then the argument *for* testing is seriously undercut.

The argument *against* testing is in any case quite powerful. As many commentators have pointed out (v., for example, Schatz, 1987:1795), there are many less objectionable ways of gathering information about AIDS risks than requiring AIDS testing or asking questions about prior test results. The most powerful argument against allowing insurers to test is the concern that it will lead to other forms of discrimination (v. Schatz, 1987:1800); that is, it will impose very high costs on others. Some insurers do not have a good record of protecting confidentiality, despite their claims to the contrary, and in the absence of specific state laws that impose serious sanctions on the abuse of medical information, many opponents of testing believe that insurers cannot be trusted with such sensitive information as HIV test results. Those at risk for AIDS greatly fear endemic breaches of confidentiality. If insurers add to the demand for compulsory testing, then there will be a serious disincentive to voluntary testing by individuals who ought to know their status. Even worse, insistence by insurers that physicians provide information about prior test results will dramatically impair the effect of educational and preventive programs surrounding AIDS. We are likely to see interference with efforts to encourage people to be tested voluntarily (e.g., prior to pregnancy, or for research purposes). When we add the risks of discrimination and the negative effects on efforts to prevent the spread of AIDS, there is a compelling argument against allowing insurers to test. And, indeed, it is noteworthy that the Blue Cross/Blue Shield Association has adopted a policy that seeks to avoid testing in favor of other risk classification techniques.

I will conclude with one comment about the policy proposed by various insurers, that we should "treat AIDS like any other disease." If this policy is intended to counter the hysteria and discrimination that has accompanied the early phase of the AIDS epidemic, then it is to be applauded. It is clear, however, that this policy has been advocated by some insurers as an argument in favor of permitting HIV testing and the usual underwriting practices that accompany the identification of high risk individuals or those to whom only substandard coverage is offered. Treating AIDS "like any other disease"—for those who argue this way—could lead to a kind of justification for testing, since medical tests for some other conditions are standard practice.

The argument we have just reviewed, however, shows that treating AIDS like any other disease would also mean that we should subject underwriting practices and claims about actuarial fairness in the case of AIDS to careful examination. If AIDS *is* exceptional, because of the climate of discrimination that surrounds those at high risk for it and because of the need to enlist the cooperation of those at high risk if its spread is to be stopped, then we have adequate social reasons for not permitting testing or other forms of risk classification. That is, after all, what we already do in other cases: Actuarial fairness is a principle we readily compromise when other principles give us social reasons for doing so. Thus a policy of treating AIDS like any other disease may in fact require us to avoid morally problematic and socially costly methods of risk classification; it may also be a policy that, after close analysis, would lead us directly to require some form of underwriting for those at high risk for this disease.

The Unfairness of Insurance Exclusions

The HIV epidemic has focused criticism on standard underwriting practices that exclude from insurance coverage those with AIDS or those who are at high risk for it. Insurers have denied the charge that these practices are unfair, claiming instead that whatever is actuarially fair is fair or just. But this form of self-defense will only work if we assume that individuals are entitled to gain advantages and deserve losses merely as a result of their adventitious health status. That assumption is highly controversial at the level of theory, and—more importantly—it is inconsistent with many of our moral beliefs and practices (including insurance practices). We should therefore reject the insurers' argument. Justice in health care requires that we protect equality of opportunity, and that in turn implies that we must share the burden of protecting people against health risks. The insurance scheme in a just health care system, whether mixed or purely public, has to be *systematically actuarially unfair,* because its overall social function must be to guarantee universal access to appropriate care. This does not mean that, in our system as it currently stands, insurers are ignoring an obligation they have to provide access to coverage. The obligation to assure access is, rather, primarily a social one, and the failures of access in our system today are the result of *public* failures to meet those obligations. In a just but mixed system, there would be an explicit division of responsibility among public and private insurance schemes. In our mixed and unjust system, legislators and insurers alike each cynically pretend that the uninsured are the responsibility of the other. The attempt to treat actuarial fairness as a moral notion thus disguises what is really at issue, namely, the risk to insurers of adverse selection and the economic advantages of standard underwriting practices. Standard underwriting practices will be fair only if they are part of a just system—not simply as a function of being actuarially fair.

The failure of the Argument from Actuarial Fairness means that we must face an issue private insurers had hoped to avoid if we are to defend standard underwriting practices at all. In view of the clear risk that a mixed system will fail to assure access to care, the burden falls on defenders of a mixed system. They must show us that its social benefits outweigh its social costs, and that it is possible to have a mixed system that is truly just.

5

Parallel Track Use of Unproven Drugs

Introduction: Social Obligation or Fair Refusal?

Is it fair treatment of patients with life-threatening illnesses to deny them access to unproven drugs? Once again, AIDS serves as a lens to help us focus our thinking about a larger issue, in this case concerning a conflict between patients' rights and social obligations. AIDS activists—watching patients die without benefit of the promising drugs that are being subjected to lengthy testing and review—have militantly, yet with great technical understanding and expertise, attacked the extremely cautious policies of the Food and Drug Administration (FDA). My intention is not to undertake a thorough review of FDA policies with respect to new drugs, but to use the reforms those policies have precipitated to examine our obligations to dying patients.

There are really two questions we must distinguish here. The first has to do with whether society has an *obligation to provide* unproven therapies to those patients with life-threatening illnesses who would like to try them, regardless of their ability to pay. The second question raises the difficult issue of whether it is *fair to refuse* to allow HIV patients or others with life-threatening illnesses access to unproven therapies, assuming they could obtain them if we did not prohibit their use.

In general, we draw a reasonable limit on our obligations to provide treatments to patients when we require that treatments meet some standard of efficacy. The fair-equality-of-opportunity account I have been working with commits us to providing needed treatments that we have adequate reason to think will work. Of course, we retain some flexibility in deciding what counts as "adequate" and what counts as "work," since it is reasonable to let our criteria for efficacy depend in part on the condition and treatment in question. But the main point remains: We do *not* have a social obligation to invest resources in treatments when we have little reason to think they will have positive effects on normal functioning or opportunity. This seems true even if the "treatment" in question is the only action that "might" work, based on some initial evidence about its antiviral activity and safety. We are not, in other words, obliged to invest significant resources in major gambles or long shots.

Thus the boundary between proven and unproven drugs (and other treatments) is not only a prominent and standard rationing device in our health care system, but one I believe is also defensible. It is nonetheless under serious attack in our health care system, and not just by AIDS activists. Some breast cancer patients and their advocates have argued—and sued and lobbied—for insurance coverage for autologous bone marrow transplants (ABMT), even though there have been no controlled clinical trials showing improved efficacy for this very expensive last-ditch treatment. By threatening litigation—especially in the aftermath of a recent California case in which a patient's estate was awarded $89 million because an HMO had delayed providing a transplant (Eckholm, 1993)—patients have forced many insurers to provide the treatment (Pollock 1993; Ferguson, Dubinsky, and Kirsch, 1993). In Massachusetts, legislators gave in to the pressure from breast cancer advocates and passed legislation mandating all insurers to provide coverage for ABMT (Chapter 458 of Acts of 1993, An Act Providing Coverage for Bone Marrow Transplants for Certain Patients with Breast Cancer).

The distinction between proven and unproven therapies is, I have argued, a reasonable basis for restricting insurance coverage; but how is it possible to resist the threat of litigation or even legislation? In fact, we cannot resist these pressures unless we develop a publicly accountable process for making decisions about limiting coverage that is perceived to be fair and legitimate. The public distrusts insurers, even the government as an insurer—and the distrust is earned, since decisions about limiting treatment are made covertly and without public scrutiny. The public further suspects the decisions are made to protect profits or the bottom lines of budgets, not to protect patients' interests. Only by developing a public process that is respected as fair can we undercut this suspicion and create a climate in which reasonable limits on access to unproven therapies (and other reasonable limits) can be sustained. I return to this issue in Chapters 6 and 8. Here I shall concentrate on the second question of fairness distinguished earlier.

Is it fair to deny patients access—to refuse to allow HIV patients (or others with life-threatening illnesses) access—to unproven therapies that they could obtain if only we did not prohibit their use? This second difficult question lies at the heart of the campaign by AIDS activists to reform the drug-testing procedures and restrictions imposed by the FDA as well as the legislation that gives the FDA control over the legal use of drugs. In order to understand why the issue of fairness is such a critical feature of the landscape we are crossing now, we need to examine the response by the FDA to the AIDS activists' campaign.

During the late 1980s, AIDS activists, waged an effective campaign against the very slow drug-testing procedures used by the FDA. The drug-testing and approval process typically takes from seven to ten years—often literally more than a lifetime for an AIDS patient. As a result, drugs "in the pipeline" that looked promising remained unavailable to the many AIDS patients desperate to try them. In response, ACT-UP, Project Inform, and other AIDS activists challenged what they took to be a paternalistic restriction on access to these unproven treatments. They argued that the FDA was "protecting" them against their own voluntary, informed, and *reasonable* choices—presumably on the well-meaning (paternalism is always well intentioned) grounds that desperately ill people are vulnerable to quackery and have a diminished capacity to make reasonable choices.

As a result of the campaign, the FDA undertook efforts to do two things: accelerate the testing program, and make drugs still undergoing tests available to some AIDS patients (Hilts, 1989; Mariner, 1990). One procedure already in place for allowing limited use of drugs undergoing tests—known as "compassionate use"—was considered, but this requires a case-by-case approval for each patient and was clearly not a solution to the large demand for unproven AIDS drugs. Another procedure—called "Treatment IND" (investigational new drug)—was introduced in 1987. That involved approving a class of patients who would receive, on a therapeutic basis, a drug still undergoing what are known as Phase II or Phase III clinical trials. This procedure permits investigational new drugs to be used to "treat" patients where no alternative therapy exists and where the patients face a "serious or immediately life-threatening disease" (DHHS, FDA, 1988). The drug DDI, for example, was released to patients on such an expanded-access basis.

In April 1992, after much lobbying by Anthony Fauci (director of the National Institute for Allergic and Infectious Diseases) and by AIDS activists, a more accessible procedure was approved by the FDA (Public Health Service, 1992). Called "parallel track," this procedure means that a drug undergoing Phase II testing can be made available on a "parallel" therapeutic track to those who live where they cannot get into clinical trials or who cannot meet the medical requirements of the Phase II clinical trial protocol. Because some people who wanted definite access to the drug, rather than to an alternative or placebo that might be given in a controlled clinical trial, might portray themselves as ineligible for the clinical trial, a crucial proviso was imposed: The availability of the parallel track is contingent on the adequate enrollment of subjects in the clinical trial. The FDA and the drug company running the clinical trial can monitor enrollment in the clinical trial and stop access to the parallel track if it seems the availability of the parallel track undercuts the enrollment requirements of the clinical trial. In the autumn of 1992, Bristol-Myers Squibb established a parallel track for the drug d4T, which was beginning its Phase II and Phase III clinical trials (FDA, 1992). (As of 1993, d4T was the only drug officially released on a parallel track.)

It should be noted that the FDA has no authority to demand that drug companies seeking approval for Phase II testing make the drug in question available on a parallel track. The FDA cannot, for example, make approval of a clinical trial contingent on the company being willing to subsidize release of the drug on a parallel track. The company can seek to recover the cost of the drug on a parallel track from patients or insurers, but only if it makes information about the cost of developing and testing the drug available. In practice, the drug company is more likely to forgo recovering the cost in order to avoid opening its books. The availability of a parallel track is not, then, a positive right; neither society nor drug companies admit to owing patients "unproven" drugs provided on a parallel track. The parallel track is not, then, inconsistent with my claim that society has no obligation to provide unproven treatments to patients.

It is the crucial proviso that the parallel track be contingent on the adequacy of enrollment in the clinical trial that brings into sharp relief the question about fair treatment I raised at the outset, specifically: Is it fair to refuse access to unproven drugs on a parallel track if their availability undercuts enrollment in clinical trials? In order to answer that question, we need to back up, in effect, and consider first the anti-paternalist arguments advanced by the AIDS activists.

Protection for Desperate Patients

The history of unregulated drug marketing is full of examples of patients—"desperately ill" is the telling expression—who are vulnerable to unscrupulous and greedy promoters of treatments that do not work. Clearly, one role of a regulatory agency is to prevent exploitation of patients by such people. An even stronger claim is also often heard: Desperately ill patients, as a function of their illnesses, are neither competent nor in a strict sense "free" to make choices about the treatments they want to take. The threat imposed by illness, so this argument runs, is a form of coercion; patients under the threat of a fatal disease will jump at anything, and they will not give careful consideration to the risks they may be running.

Those who seek strong restrictive authority for the FDA may subscribe to a view that encompasses arguments of both sorts—the anti-exploitative and the paternalistic. In reply, AIDS activists insist that people with AIDS, just like other people facing life-threatening illnesses, should be assumed competent and free to make their own informed choices about treatment unless there is specific evidence of diminished mental competence (Delaney, 1989). From this view it would follow that while it is appropriate for the FDA to have a regulatory role aimed at reducing exploitation, it should not have one that encroaches on the autonomy of patients making even admittedly desperate choices.

Consider the matter from the perspective of a person with AIDS for whom AZT has not proved effective, and who is deliberating the wisdom of taking an unproven drug such as d4T. The temptation to take d4T (or any unproven drug at a comparable point in the testing procedures) comes from two bits of preliminary evidence of the sort that we typically have at the end of Phase I trials: It shows some antiviral activity, and it is not so unsafe as to have failed early safety tests. (Of course, the drug in question may also have been the subject of hype by the media or along the grapevine, which some desperate patients take as a third kind of "evidence"; this often further increases the temptation to take the drug.)

The following outcomes or payoffs will be seen to be possible if the drug is taken: (1) There is no effect on mortality—but there may be positive or negative effects on quality of life; (2) Death is postponed—with various possible effects on quality of life; (3) Death is hastened—with various possible effects on quality of life. Included under "death is hastened" is the possibility that taking this drug may preclude taking a more effective drug later. Considerable uncertainty surrounds the estimates of the probability of these outcomes. We cannot even assign reasonably firm probabilities, but we may be able to assign numerical rankings of probability—that is, we may "guesstimate" that some outcomes are more likely than others.

Under these conditions, it is by no means intuitively obvious what principle or strategy of rational choice someone should use in making a decision about taking the drug. One strategy is "maximining," that is, minimizing the chance of the worst outcome (in this case, hastening death). Maximining might incline us against gambling on the unproven drug. But it is clear this is not a strategy adopted by many people with life-threatening illnesses. A better match with real life is provided by the disaster-avoidance principle discussed by Kavka (1986:144). This principle tells us it is reasonable to increase our risk of hastening death if doing so reduces overall our chance of dying as soon as untreated AIDS would ordinarily kill us. Without knowing the real probabilities, however, we are unable to calculate expected payoffs—and thus we are unable, strictly speaking, to apply the principle.

People with a life-threatening illness might nevertheless conclude there is more to gain than to lose by taking the drug. They might, for example, believe they should try to take control of the situation and not wait for the lack of treatment to lead to its expected and probable outcome. They might believe it is better to die somewhat earlier trying "to fight back" than it is to die (anyway) having done nothing. Such an attitude is especially likely to come into play if there is some reasonable basis for thinking the drug may have relevant effects and is not obviously toxic—which is generally the case for drugs that have survived a successful Phase I trial. Under such conditions, these desperately ill patients are not simply grasping at straws, the argument runs, because the evidence they are acting on—though not strong—is the result of scientific efforts, not the promise of snake-oil merchants.

This point about the value of even early scientific results is important to my later argument. Having such evidence available depends on the existence of a generally reliable regulatory apparatus that requires the scientific testing of drugs for efficacy and safety. When these conditions do prevail, we cannot say is that it is *irrational* for desperate patients to take the unproven drug; it would be irrational only if some better course of action were available. Advocates of expedited access argue with repeated emphasis that if "Big Brother"—the FDA—cannot offer them anything better than what they want, then Big Brother has no grounds for protecting them against what they want (Delaney, 1989).

So far I have talked about only some of the costs to patients when they are allowed to take unproven drugs. There are other costs, too, which some have argued might make it irrational for patients to want unproven drugs; I disagree. The costs to patients of expedited access may be costs not only that they are willing to bear, but that it is in fact not irrational for them to want to bear. Costs to patients include the following: (1) increased risks of adverse drug effects (which I have already discussed); (2) dashed hopes; (3) energy; and (4) money (either for the drugs or the intensified laboratory work monitoring their effects). These are costs or burdens that many patients with AIDS are clearly willing to assume, and we can presume such patients have already figured them into the calculation that taking the drug is in their interest.

There are also costs that accrue to clinical researchers and physicians when expedited access is allowed. Because the perception is so strong that self-interest is at stake when someone is seeking to take unproven drugs, the strain that results when such a patient is denied the drugs is enormous. Numerous AIDS advocates have argued that the willingness of desperate patients to lie, to deceive, and to seek illegal routes of access where possible is a cost the system will have to bear if it does not give expedited access.

Physicians, too, may be placed under great pressure—for instance, to procure treatments for patients even when doing so considerably increases the chances of harming those patients. What the baseline "standard of care" is under these conditions could become even more difficult to determine than is usually the case. Even so, many physicians would probably be willing to accept these costs rather than be in the position of *not* being able to provide an unproven drug to a patient when providing it seems to be in that patient's best interest. On the other hand, there could also be considerable strain for a physician who has not revealed possibilities—for whatever reason—when patients are informed (by other sources) of those possibilities and then make demands of that physician. Indeed, physicians may be made liable for malpractice if they fail to inform patients of various unproven drugs available in treatment investigational new drugs or on parallel track.

One burden of expedited access is the weight it puts on the mechanism of informed consent; the burden here falls on both physician and patient. When we cannot specify risks or benefits except in a qualitative way, patients will clearly have less information than they ordinarily do in decision-making contexts; what they are consenting to is hardly a clearly defined package of benefits and risks. Still, there is nothing in this fact that renders informed consent impossible—at least not for reasonably well-educated and connected patients (I shall return to this qualification later). Another concern is the claim that no one who is in dire straits, with few options, can give "voluntary" consent. But if I am right in thinking that we cannot call "irrational" the informed decision to take an unproven drug, under the conditions we are considering, then I am troubled by the view that we should prohibit affected patients from making the decision. What we must guard against is a climate in which people are preyed upon by those pushing treatments for whose efficacy and safety there is no reasonable basis. Our best protection against that kind of climate is a viable system of drug regulation and testing.

If we cannot conclude that it is irrational to take unproven drugs under the conditions we are presupposing, then paternalistic arguments against expedited access will fail for patients who find themselves in these desperate straits. We end up with no evidence that such patients, in conjunction with their physicians, are incompetent to make rational choices. This conclusion seems ironic, if not anomalous: It is precisely patients in this class who are usually thought to be most in need of protection, because of their peculiar vulnerability. If we think that the best argument for drug regulation in general and denying expedited access in particular is that we must protect people to keep them from acting against their own interests, then the whole justificatory edifice seems in jeopardy.

Nonpaternalistic Arguments Against Access to Unproven Drugs

One AIDS activist, Delaney (1989), has suggested that a system that endorses the importance of individual liberties should not restrain people from seeking unproven drugs just because their getting those drugs may lead to under-enrollment in clinical trials. In our society, he suggests, we do not sacrifice individuals in this way for the good of society.

Delaney's objection bears a kernel of truth: It is always problematic when we coerce people into sacrificing for the benefit of others. If our justification for eliminating or restricting expedited access is that the common good—aggregate welfare—requires it, then we may be in conflict with important concerns of distributive justice. Why is it appropriate for these people to sacrifice, for the well-being of others, what they and their doctors reasonably view as their only chance at extended survival? Justifying drug regulation in this utilitarian fashion greatly strains the commitment to principle of those on whom the sacrifice falls. We should be able to do better.

Another line of justification is a contractarian version of an argument from fairness based on reciprocity. On this view, it is reasonable to expect people in these conditions to forgo what is in their self-interest because they have benefited from the sacrifices of those preceding them who have participated in clinical trials; among those (prior) sacrifices were the restrictions on access to unproven drugs that are essential if clinical trials are to be feasible. Current patients with AIDS or HIV have benefited, as recipients of information and technology that would not have been possible had such sacrifices not been made by others. It would be reasonable for people to contract to participate in such cooperative schemes over time, denying themselves access to unproven drugs, before they knew who they were (as in Rawls's device to insure impartiality, the "veil of ignorance" that prevents us from knowing about our individual traits). So it is fair that those who would prefer to take the unproven drug now abide by the restrictions such a contract would impose, especially since their preference can be counted as rational only under the conditions that contract makes possible—that is, only when some scientific evidence about efficacy and safety is available. This justification may make the burden on patients with no alternative seem more fair, but it still leaves the strain on commitment. After all, pursuing one's own interest in this case—trying to get access to the unproven drug even if it undermines clinical trials—is still the *rational* thing to do, even if it is not the *fair* thing to do.

One final line of argument not only does not involve these serious strains on commitment but also provides a more persuasive defense of the proviso that raised the issue of fairness in the first place. Like the Switching Dilemma I discussed earlier, this is an argument about the common good—specifically, what game theorists call the many-person prisoners' dilemma (see Chapter 3). If the argument succeeds, it shows that allowing clinical trials to be undermined by permitting unconstrained access to unproven drugs would make all of the patients worse off than they would be if access were permitted under the proviso that protects clinical trials.

The argument depends, however, on an empirical premise—an assumption—namely, that in general the information that emerges from clinical trials benefits, either directly or indirectly, those who have participated in them. That is, either participants benefit directly from the information produced by the clinical trial they are seeking to abandon or avoid in favor of (unconstrained) parallel track access, or they benefit indirectly as a result of the continued functioning of similar clinical trials on other unproven drugs. This assumption will not hold up for patients so close to death that they are unlikely to survive the clinical trial unless the test drug works promptly and dramatically, but the assumption does characterize the situation in which many HIV patients in clinical drug trials find themselves, especially now that better treatments are becoming available for opportunistic infections.

Given this assumption, the argument works in the following way: A patient with HIV or AIDS, considering participation in a clinical trial, might reason, "I am best off if everyone else (or enough others) participates in the clinical trials, but I am free to pursue the unproven drug on a parallel track since I have some information that makes it reasonable for me to want to try it (instead of a placebo or alternative, for instance); if others abandon the clinical trials in favor of expedited access, then I am still better off pursuing the unproven drug than I am restricting myself to waiting for the results of trials that cannot succeed." But if everyone reasons the same way, and all of us try to get the unproven drugs without regard to safeguarding clinical trials, we will each be worse off than if everyone abided by the restrictions and seek expedited access only when clinical trials were viable. We will each be worse off because we need the information about the outcome of such trials to make informed choices about our treatment. In short, if each of us who has HIV or AIDS pursues our own interest in this way, the effect will be that we all will be made worse off. Spelling out the argument like this makes the parallel to the Switching Dilemma explicit.

Under these conditions, clearly it is better to block self-interested behavior by putting in place a proviso like that in the FDA regulations concerning the parallel track. The proviso might work indirectly, defining eligibility for the parallel track in ways that protect the clinical trial. For example, in the actual regulations, access to the parallel track is possible only for those not medically suitable for the clinical trial, or for those outside its geographical area. Or the proviso could work directly, monitoring enrollments in the clinical trial and allowing the parallel track to be cut off if those enrollments are threatened.

This defense of the proviso is not paternalistic, at least not in the sense that it involves coercively restricting a behavior in the best interest of the restricted parties who are assumed incompetent or unfree to make prudent choices themselves. Still, it does protect each person's individual welfare (over the long run) against the collectively irrational effects of the unconstrained pursuit of self-interest.

Nor does the argument involve restricting a benefit to some people in order to produce greater aggregate benefits for others. If the argument holds up, each person is better off as long as the proviso is maintained (except for those facing probable death during a clinical trial). Because the argument is neither paternalistic nor merely utilitarian, it avoids the strain on commitment that plagued those arguments. All concerned can see the constraints imposed by the proviso as a protection for themselves. Expedited access, *subject to the proviso*, is fair treatment for all and works to make each better off than he or she would otherwise be. We can justify expedited access—but only if it does not undermine the scientific evaluation of drugs.

In Closing: A Qualification

Recent scientific developments reinforce belief in the importance of protecting sound clinical trials and therefore of the proviso that the availability of a parallel track is contingent on the adequate enrollment of subjects in the clinical trial. AIDS activists have pushed two strategies of reform in the drug-testing process. They have demanded wider, expedited access to unproven drugs, as we have seen. They have also argued, along with some scientists, for a quicker process of assessing the drugs. Each of these strategies deserves a qualifying comment.

To assess drugs more quickly, without having to wait for typical clinical outcomes (like reduced morbidity and mortality), requires selecting "surrogate markers" to measure the effectiveness of a drug. For example, in the testing of AZT, effects on certain cell levels (the CD4 marker) were used as an outcome measure. As a result of a major English and French study (the Concorde study) of clinical outcomes over a multiyear period, there seems to be no measurable effect of AZT on mortality—and only temporary effects on the quality of life (v. James, 1993). This suggests to many that the CD4 marker does not tell us much about the value of the drug after all—and that we may not yet know enough to place our confidence in surrogate markers. If this assessment is correct, it is bad news for the strategy of short-circuiting the approval process.

The bad news does not, however, altogether undermine the importance of granting expedited access to unproven drugs. Nevertheless, there is one troubling aspect of the "consumerism" that motivated the AIDS activists' pursuit of expedited access. The highly educated, politically aggressive, and well-connected gay men who spearheaded the drug-testing reforms could readily project themselves as the models of the informed consumer who wanted autonomy to use the knowledge they acquired. But the demographics of the epidemic have shifted; in the United States, the patient population is increasingly made up of drug abusers and their sexual partners and children, and this is a much less educated population. Many in this group are not in a position to use effectively the avenues available to gay men to procure unproven drugs.

The benefits of the expedited-access reform seem to fall largely on a shrinking proportion of the HIV patients. If the push by this same group for early approval and expedited access has the effect of producing worse information about drugs in the pipeline—AZT is the paradigm for this scenario—the costs of the reform may fall disproportionately on the poor, minority population that constitutes the new wave of HIV patients. I do not believe there is a serious or inequitable distributive effect so far, especially because the movement toward expedited access has left clinical trials intact, but the demographic shift in the patient population raises an issue of concern to which we need to be alert.

One last remark concerns the effort some may make to impose on third-party payers the costs of expedited access, such as the costs of diagnostic tests and other related medical procedures. In our system, there is always a temptation to "stick it to" the insurer, who is assumed to have deep pockets; physicians engage in deception to "game" coverage for their patients—and this is defended as "advocacy" even though it involves deception, for example about a patient's diagnosis. But, as I argued early in this chapter, there is a real question whether people who choose to take unproven drugs should be able to pass the costs of those decisions on to other people in the insurance pool. This is a complex issue, and disservice is done when we try to disguise the value judgments involved by hiding behind the concept of "medical necessity." Saying that an unproven drug is "medically necessary" because it is the only treatment that "might" work is a way of hiding important value judgments and assumptions behind a term we take to be one of medical expertise.

6

Justice and Access to High-Technology Home Care

Two Questions of Fairness

Home health care, and especially high-technology home care, is the fastest-growing area in health care services. For example, the market for equipment that allows infusion treatments, such as the intravenous administering of drugs or nutrients, to be done at home reached $575 million in 1991 for AIDS patients alone (Green, 1991:6). With the continued growth of the HIV-infected population, this market can be expected to expand significantly during the next decade. (Other high-tech home services enjoying spectacular growth include new ventilator and monitoring technologies, to permit assistance in respiration and in the electronic tracking of vital signs.) For this reason, looking at how we decide whether to make new treatments and technologies available to some or all AIDS and HIV patients is as good a way as there is to tackle the problem of when and how to ration scarce resources within the health care system.

Of necessity, this will mean looking at questions of distributive justice. In particular, we will need to look at two questions of fairness: Is it fair to allocate new resources to (sometimes experimental) home care technologies? Is it fair to provide high-tech home care services to only the socially best off of the patients who might benefit from them? In order to see why these questions are so central,

117

however, we need to look first at how we have arrived at the spot we find ourselves in.

Two forces propel the growth of home health care, one on the demand side, the other shaping supply (Melman and Youngner, 1991). First, many people would rather remain among their family and friends than have to stay in a hospital. Indeed, AIDS patients— given their compromised immune systems—are especially suscepti- ble to iatrogenic diseases (those that result from medical interven- tion); hospitals can be very dangerous places for them. More than that, the increasing demand for home health care is a result of other partial successes in our health care system. People with HIV infec- tion are living longer than they did only a very short time ago: This represents the much heralded conversion of an acute disease into a chronic one. The effect, however, is that they must be treated more intensively and more expensively. (Similarly, newborns who years ago would have died are now treated aggressively and a large propor- tion of those who survive are disabled and need long-term, intensive treatment. The rapid rise in the "old old" population, a trend pro- jected to last well into the next century, assures there will be a growing demand for these new technologies and services in the home.)

The second force informing the growth of home health care consists of measures aimed at cost containment and cost shifting. These measures shape or direct the supply of resources away from institutional services and toward home health services. Hospitals are very expensive hotels, at least for chronically ill patients. Get- ting seriously ill but relatively stable patients out of hospitals and into their homes can yield great savings, especially for third-party payers (recognition of this fact was largely what led to the decision to include a hospice benefit under Medicare).

Of course, there is some inevitable cost shifting here: Home expenses rise; families and friends contribute labor time, even when nursing care is also available, often at the expense of earnings. Costs such as these do not show up on the ledgers of public or private third-party payers; from a societal point of view, however, they con- stitute cost shifting rather than true cost savings. Furthermore, we do not have good information about how much of the provision of high-tech home care is a substitute for hospital-based technology and how much constitutes additional services that might have been forgone had they not been available in the home.

These demand and supply forces have produced the recent rapid growth of high-tech home care, and threaten to continue unabated.

As a result, we see huge quantities of health care resources drawn into a *new* area of expenditure at precisely the time we are becoming most aware that we cannot provide all medically beneficial or even "medically necessary" services, and that we must develop new ways of limiting or rationing care. Moreover, many of these services are aimed at people whose quality of life has been irreversibly compromised and who may in fact be dying. For some commentators, like Callahan (1987), who have urged that we substitute "high touch" care for high-tech care for those near the end of life or those for whom we can do little, the burgeoning high-tech home care industry looms as a perversion of their goal. They press the following sets of questions: Should we be developing these technologies on this scale? Aren't there better things we could do with our scarce medical resources? And perhaps above all: By expending resources on these new technologies, aren't we being unfair to others with more important needs elsewhere in the health care system—or even elsewhere in society (for example, the educationally underserved)? Even if reimbursements have flowed toward high-tech home care in part to save resources, shouldn't we bite the bullet harder and simply turn off the fiscal spigot that nourishes the high-tech home care market?

Other commentators worry about a different question of fairness. They are not concerned that we may be unfairly denying others access to the more beneficial services they may have forgone because home health care is provided. Rather, they worry that home services can be appropriately utilized by only a fortunate (and small) fraction of the patients who might benefit medically from them. Unless a family has personal and economic resources adequate to sustain a virtual home clinic, for instance, a patient is not well served by being sent home. Thus there are concerns both that some patients will be forced into homes incapable of receiving them, for cost-saving (and cost-shifting) reasons, and that other patients who lack an adequate home setting will be denied the benefits of home health care and be stuck in hospitals. For example, although a gay man with AIDS who is a member of the professional class may have friends or family able to provide the stable environment necessary to turn a home into a clinic, a poor African-American or Hispanic IV drug user—the fastest-growing group of patients with AIDS—is far less likely to have such personal resources and is therefore likely to be denied these benefits. Providing generously for a category of beneficial services that we know from the outset can be used by only *some* of the patients for whom they are medically suitable clearly raises questions of fairness. Strictly, one might want to argue, fairness requires that *all* the patients for whom a particular set of services is medically appropriate—including those for whom they are socially unsuitable—should get those services.

Both of these sets of concerns, as I pointed out, raise questions of distributive justice. Answering the question about deciding whether it is fair to allocate new resources to these technologies requires spelling out the conditions under which we should make the kinds of rationing decisions that allocating scarce resources necessitates. These conditions, I shall claim, are far from met in our health care system, and—as a result—precipitous rationing decisions are more likely to generate inequities than to eliminate them. But instead of defending the status quo, I believe we need to seek the reforms that make it acceptable to make this and other necessary rationing decisions. Addressing the question about the unfairness of giving a class of services only to the socially best-off patients who might benefit from them also requires considering broader reforms of our social system. The difficult issue here is how much we can or should use medical resources to redress broader societal injustices.

Prerequisites for Rationing Fairly

To see whether justice requires or permits the rationing of high-tech home care, we must consider what justice in general says about the rationing of health care. Here again I shall draw for specificity on the fair-equality-of-opportunity account that I explained in Chapter 1 and have been using throughout (v. Daniels, 1985, 1988), although many of the points I will make do not presuppose that account.

On this view, it will be recalled, the central principle of justice that should govern the design of health care institutions—including institutions and procedures for limiting beneficial services, when necessary—is a principle assuring fair equality of opportunity (v. Rawls, 1971, 1993). The rationale for invoking this principle is that the central aim of health care is to maintain and restore functioning that is normal or typical for our species. Disease and disability are construed as departures from normal functioning, and that as such they shrink the range of opportunities open to an individual. More precisely, an individual's fair share of the normal range is the array of life plans that an individual can reasonably choose, given his or her talents and skills. A person's fair share is reduced when disease or disability affects that individual; how serious the impairment is depends on the impact of the particular disease or disability. By aiming at preserving normal functioning, health care institutions make a very significant (if limited) contribution to the protection of equality of opportunity.

We cannot make much sense of all this, or understand why this so critically raises the specter of rationing, if we do not accept the fact that resources are limited. Rawls (1971:126–27) calls this moderate scarcity a "condition" of justice; if resources were abundant, we would not need principles to resolve conflicting claims on them. Although health care is specially important because of its impact on opportunity, it is of course by no means the only important good. Education, for example, competes with health care for resources that have a direct impact on fair equality of opportunity. Thus even when (perhaps *especially* when) fair equality of opportunity is at stake, we must expect there will be limits on health care resources; we will have to ration our resources, in small ways or large.

Specifically, the supply of resources is such that it does not permit everyone whose opportunities are diminished because of disease or disability to be restored to full functioning. We must pick and choose whose opportunities will be protected—and in what ways, and to what degree. Individual "entitlements" to health care are thus necessarily system-relative; they are the result of resource-allocation choices made in a system aiming to abide by the equal-opportunity principle (Daniels, 1985:54).

Justice requires, nevertheless, that we develop a *public, fair procedure* for deciding how health care (and other) institutions will allocate resources, given scarcity. In insisting on this requirement, I am in effect rejecting the suggestion made by Calabresi and Bobbitt (1978) that the costs of making *explicit* tragic choices are sometimes too high, and that we might better appeal to *implicit* procedures. I believe, on the contrary, that *publicity is a crucial requirement of justice.*

Ideally, the fair-equality-of-opportunity principle would itself tell us specifically how to determine the moral priority among competing services and claims on them. Unfortunately, it offers only general and indeterminate advice—and it shares this feature with comparable distributive principles that govern other kinds of good (for example, "equality before the law") (Daniels, 1993:225). We do learn from it, however, that it is more important to prevent or treat the diseases and disabilities that severely limit opportunities than to prevent or treat less-disabling conditions, and that those therapies which effectively correct greater degrees of impairment are more important than ones that provide less benefit. But this advice is inadequate as a basis for deciding crucial questions about rationing.

At least four important types of problem are left unsolved (Daniels, 1993:225–32); each has some impact on our decisions about high-tech home care. First, there is the unsolved Priorities Problem. Although the equal-opportunity principle gives some priority to treating the most seriously ill or impaired individuals, because their opportunity is most compromised, it does not tell us just how *much* priority. For example, it would be implausible to act as *maximiners*, i.e., give full priority to the worst-off cases, for that might require us to pour resources into those cases regardless of the size of the benefits (in opportunities) we are having to forgo for others. But in between giving no priority to the most seriously ill and giving full priority to them, there are myriad intermediary positions. We have no principled account of where on the middle ground to take our stand. Second, there is the Aggregation Problem. We want to be able to use our resources to protect opportunity in the system *as a whole*, which implies we should be able to aggregate more modest benefits to many people in ways that offset more significant benefits to few. But we are not straightforward sum-ranking *maximizers*, either; here, too, we have no clear, principled solution telling us where to stand in the middle ground. Third, we have the Fair Chances versus Best Outcomes Problem, which arises because we are not sure how to trade off giving more people the chance of obtaining *some* benefit against the importance of achieving the *best* outcome. We have no clear principle, in other words, that tells us when we must resist the temptation to put resources where they produce the greatest benefit in order to respect each individual person's claim on having a chance at some benefit. Depending on the relative benefits in question, we may give more or less weight to fair chances or best outcomes.

Finally, we are not sure how much confidence to put in the outcome of a democratic decision procedure. The deepest form of this Democracy Problem derives from the fact that we cannot tell whether a democratic procedure should count as an instance of *pure* or *imperfect* procedural justice. A fair spin of a roulette wheel determines a fair outcome: This is a case of pure procedural justice, since there is no prior notion of a fair outcome other than what the wheel determines. A criminal trial, however, is an imperfect procedure aimed at selecting all and only those who are guilty of committing the crime; that it is an imperfect procedure is made evident by the prevalence of miscarriages of justice (Rawls, 1971:89–90).

We have traditionally not been sure whether there are principled solutions to the first three of the rationing problems I have spelled out. If there are, democratic procedures must aim at satisfying them; failure to do so is grounds for criticizing the procedure, just as new evidence that someone is not guilty is grounds for criticizing the outcome of a trial. If there are no principled solutions to these problems, however, then *whatever* a fair democratic procedure yields will determine what counts as fair.

I shall look in the next section at how these unsolved problems bear on any decision regarding the use of high-tech home care, but I want here to continue elaborating the conditions under which *fair* rationing decisions may be made and implemented, regardless of whether they have to do with AIDS patients, high-tech home care, or something totally apart from the world of health care technologies. Thus far I have argued that justice involves—requires—rationing; we seek guidance from distributive principles, but we must at some level rely on a fair, democratic procedure to make the grounds for choice publicly accessible. I want to emphasize two additional, important conditions to making fair rationing decisions.

To make judgments about the relative importance—medical and moral—of high-tech home care services we must have reasonably *adequate information* about their costs and benefits, as well as about the costs and benefits of other kinds of services that are competing for resources. The decision to use one kind of service rather than another is a decision about *opportunity costs.* In the standard economic sense of "opportunity cost," in allocating resources for one kind of therapy we must compare the net benefits of alternative therapies, considering the benefits we forgo when we use one service rather than another—not merely whether one therapy has a net benefit considered by itself. There is a more specific sense of "opportunity cost" here as well, since we are considering alternative impacts on the normal opportunity range: The benefits some enjoy in improvement of their opportunity range is at a cost to others, who forgo improvements in their opportunities.

The remaining condition has a bearing on the design of the institutions in which rationing decisions will be carried out. Rationing choices should be made within what I shall (loosely) call a *closed system* (Daniels, 1986:1381–82). A system is closed if the resources relevant to decisions made within it are finite and the costs and benefits of the decisions about resource allocation made in it are internal to it. For example, if we decide to forgo one service in favor of another, then the cost of forgoing it is borne by those in the system; the benefits and the costs of the alternative are likewise borne by those in the system.

A closed system forces us to face the consequences of our deliberate choices to deny benefits to some who have reasonable claims on them. To see why this is important, consider two examples in which the system is *not* closed. Suppose we have a managed-care system, and that we agree we should not make certain high-tech home care services available because—compared to possible alternative uses of the resources—other services have a greater claim on being provided. Suppose further, however, that instead of putting resources into the preferred alternative we simply put them toward bonuses for the medical staff. The costs and benefits of what we actually do are not factored into our original decision: The closed system has leaked. Similarly, suppose we decide that Medicaid should not provide certain high-tech home services because adding them will increase the rate of growth of Medicaid budgets and because there are alternative uses of the resources that have greater benefits. Nevertheless, these services are then covered by private insurance or can be bought out of pocket by those wealthy enough. The system again has a leak: Our denial of the service on the grounds that the opportunity cost of offering it is too great has been superseded by a different rationing principle: availability by ability to pay. A judgment that might be sufficient to justify a rationing choice in a closed system, namely a comparison of opportunity costs, may not be sufficient if a different rationing principle operates by default in the "leaky" system as a whole.

Rationing High-Technology Home Care

On the face of it, our current situation meets none of the conditions that I have argued are prerequisite for rationing fairly. Any decision categorically to target high-tech home care for rationing seems unjustifiable. We have no public, fair, democratic procedure for deciding whether or how to ration these high-tech services any more than we do for any other services. In addition, any rationing choices we now make *fail to apply* within a closed system: We have a mixed public-private system of payments with no global budget to constrain resources. Furthermore, we lack adequate information about the costs and benefits of these technologies, and we lack comparable information about the technologies competing for the same resources. Each of these claims warrants further explanation; I will take them in reverse order.

As I noted earlier, one force driving growth of high-tech home care services is the belief that it is less expensive to deliver infusion therapy, for example, at home than in the hospital. Three key assumptions underlie this judgment: Similar medical benefits and risks obtain in both situations; delivering these technologies in the hospital means that reasonable overhead charges that come from maintaining a hospital facility will be included; the overhead costs of running a household clinic will not be chargeable to third-party payers. Let's look at each of these assumptions.

First, though I cannot give evidence for the claim, I think we know less than is assumed about the actual comparability of medical benefits and risks in the two settings. I doubt that anyone has run controlled trials comparing outcomes in a way that could lead to a precise calculation of comparable risks. Nevertheless, let the first assumption stand.

Second, hospital charges often reflect far more than the real costs of a service. For example, hospitals typically factor into their charges an allowance for future hospital expansion, for debt servicing of past (unrelated) capital investments, for investment in new technologies, and—in the case of for-profit institutions—even for profits that will be spent on non medical investments. Practically speaking, these are the charges (however inflated) that third-party payers must take into account. But charges like these clearly distort our view of the real costs of a service; they stack the deck in favor of funneling new resources into home care services.

Third, the costs of home delivery of these services are distorted in two different and opposing ways. On the one hand these costs are clearly underestimated. It may be reasonable from the perspective of a private third-party insurer to omit the true costs to a household of sustaining a patient at home—since these will not show up as charges—but they are real social costs and ought to play a role in rationing decisions. The costs to society and family may in fact be significant: lost earning power, cost of replacing trained workers, costs to children from having parents deeply enmeshed in providing home care, loss of family mobility. Ignoring these costs yields judgments that reflect the interests of the third-party payer without adequately capturing the perspective of society as a whole.

Since rationing decisions are matters of justice, I believe they should reflect societal concerns about how to meet obligations and should not be treated simply as a form of cost shifting—unless the principle behind the cost shifting has itself been publicly defended as a rationing principle. Another way to think about this point is to suggest that we have failed to close the system within which the calculation about costs and benefits is made; crucial costs fall outside the subsystem within which third-party payers make their decisions, yet the broader view captures facts necessary for a societal decision about rationing. Some problems of this sort are unavoidable in a decentralized system, but some are features we get because we fail to link the components of our system into a single, coherent system.

Other forces work to *overstate* the real costs of high-tech home care, namely the failures to force the reasonable pricing of these services either through regulation or through appropriate negotiation with a properly designed purchasing agent. Paralleling the distorting effects we noticed in the case of hospital charges, we observe the dramatic pricing effects documented by New York City Consumer Affairs Commissioner Mark Green (1991). Home care providers selling services to third-party payers in New York often refuse to detail their charges and the justification for them in advance; there are no standards for how such charges are made. For example, infusion companies typically charge for nursing care although many AIDS patients prefer self-administration and therefore do not use nursing care. The variations in charges from company to company are wide, so much so that there is no real relationship between charges and actual costs; markups can approach 600 percent.

The effect of these inflated charges is enormous, as one example shows. Green (1991:13) claims that costs for total parenteral nutrition (TPN), a balanced nutritional diet supplied by infusion, accounts for nearly one-third of the estimated $150,000 average lifetime cost of caring for an AIDS patient. In the face of such gross profiteering, made possible because the purchasing system fails to act as a unified buyer of services with the power to negotiate for uniform practices and reasonable charges, we really cannot say much about the relative savings that accrue from substituting high-tech home care for hospital-based services.

One last point bears on our knowledge about costs. We have no large-scale studies of the degree to which home services are acting as substitutes for hospital services and the degree to which they constitute additional utilization. For example, individuals who might reconcile themselves to dying at home without intensive therapies might accept treatments at home that they would refuse in a hospital setting. Without knowing whether this phenomenon is common or rare, we cannot say how much money home services save.

A proper rationing decision must rest on reasonably good information about relative costs and benefits of the services being compared. I have pointed out that we lack that information even about comparisons of home and hospital delivery of the same technologies—but that kind of comparison should not really be the basis for rationing categories of care in any case. Rather, rationing requires an appropriate comparison of *all* technologies competing for the limited resources. To target high-tech home care for rationing just because it is new is arbitrary from the perspective of fair rationing policy. Rather, we must compare both high-tech home care *and* hospital delivery of the same services with a broader set of services.

As soon as we see this point, it is obvious that we must distinguish the different types of benefits delivered by various high-tech home services. Some technologies—for instance, the infusion of antibiotics at home—may cure an acute episode of an infection. For some patients, this may produce a long life of high quality; for others, it may buy only a few months or weeks of life of diminished quality before death. Similar points may be made about total parenteral nutrition, which sometimes produces only palliation during a prolonged dying process, but which can also be part of a more beneficial curing process. Simply lumping all services together as "high-tech" or as "home-delivered" completely ignores many differences that are relevant for purposes of rationing decisions.

Once we sort out the relevant contrasts among uses of these technologies, whether delivered at home or in the hospital, we still have a task that involves unresolved moral issues of the sort I noted earlier. There will be patients who are very seriously ill, with terrible prognoses, for whom some high-technology home service (or hospital service) would yield only very modest benefit at very high cost. Should we simply seek to produce comparable or greater benefits at lower cost for patients who are initially less seriously ill? Or should we be so concerned about helping those whose prospects are worst that we forgo producing more cost-effective benefits elsewhere? Should we, for example, devote respirator technologies to patients in a persistent vegetative state (PVS), accepting that prolongation of their comatose state is a medical benefit, or should we be willing to aggregate to other patients benefits that fall well short of extending life and conclude that these apportioned benefits are more important to deliver than the benefit to the persistent-vegetative-state patient? We lack principled solutions to these and the other problems I noted above, yet nearly every comparison of a use of high-technology home care with uses of other services for other categories of patients will involve one or another of these unsolved rationing problems. I will return to this issue shortly, when I talk about why it is so important to rely on a fair democratic process for making rationing decisions.

The fact that we do not operate our health care system as a closed system for purposes of rationing has major implications for this discussion of rationing high-tech home care, and thus it is important that what is meant by a closed system is understood. I shall operationalize—and simplify—the idea of a closed system by considering a globally budgeted health care system and contrasting it with ours. Under a global budget, expenditures made for one type of service will not be available for others. In contrast, in our open system, leaks permit new resources to be added, when we think of the system as a whole, despite the decision made by one party or sector to restrict the use of a service. A critical feature of a leaky system is that *we do not really live with the consequences of our rationing decisions*. Though I have touched on some of these points already, let me emphasize three implications here.

A global budget forces decision-makers to face the consequences of their choices. One important use of high-tech home care services will be for seriously disabled infants who need respirator, infusion, or monitoring services. These services should be considered as the downstream costs of aggressive treatment of low-birthweight or otherwise seriously defective newborns. A decision to reduce the availability of these services should be factored into the related decisions on whether to use aggressive rescue efforts for newborns. A system in which the costs of these services are borne within different budgets, by different insurers, is one in which we are not really forced to face the consequences of decisions made separately within the different budgets. For example, if public budgets largely cover the costs of seriously disabled children, but aggressive rescue efforts are decided upon by those who must contend primarily with private insurers or even with different public budgets, then those who authorize aggressive rescue efforts can escape their consequences.

A closed system means that rationing decisions are not converted into cost-shifting exercises and that services forgone in order to direct resources into a more important service actually have that effect. I have already noted that the decision to favor home delivery of high-tech services over hospital delivery of those same services involves cost shifting to families. Suppose, however, that public insurance no longer included coverage for a broad range of high-tech home care services. It might even be the case that the basis for this decision was a reasonable one when the benefits and costs of certain uses of these services are compared to other uses of the same resources. Some of these services might still be covered by private insurers, and some would still be purchased out of pocket by some families. We will not have redirected resources in the way intended by the decision, at least not when we look at the system as a whole.

Finally, the lack of a global budget can mean that although an individual responsible for a rationing decision might make that decision on grounds that seem reasonable (given the opportunity costs of relevant competitors for the use of the resources), nonetheless in the system as a whole the operative rationing principle might be "ability to pay." For example, if some services were excluded from a "basic" benefit package in a managed-competition insurance scheme (but these services are available in more deluxe plans that cost more), then only those willing and able to afford the more deluxe package would be able to obtain the benefits. If only the best-off individuals can get these services, we might complain that there was an objectionable inequality—though some might argue it was not so serious. But if the worst-off groups are denied these services, while they are obtainable by most other individuals, then the *structure of inequality* that results from the rationing decision is objectionable (Daniels, 1986; 1991a:2233–34). Some effects of relying on ability to pay are worse than others.

The remaining condition for fair rationing—the requirement that there be a fair, democratic process for making rationing decisions—is not met in most health care systems. Even comprehensive, globally budgeted systems like the Canadian system lack an attempt to articulate publicly the grounds for key decisions bearing on the allocation of health care resources. Many European systems are struggling to articulate and justify principles that they can use to guide rationing choices (Government Committee on Choices in Health Care, 1992). I would like to illustrate the virtue of a public, democratic process by referring to Oregon's ongoing attempt to establish priorities among health care services.

When Oregon developed a list of 709 ranked pairs of conditions and treatments in 1991, considerable criticism was directed at the very low ranking given to the treatment of HIV infection for AIDS patients with less than six months to live. That ranking might be thought (incorrectly) to bear on the rationing of high-tech home services (like the infusion therapies so widely used by AIDS patients). Was Oregon simply denying those therapies to these patients?

According to the executive director of the Oregon Health Services Commission, Paige Sipes-Metzler (personal communication), many of the uses of these technologies would in fact be permitted. For example, infusion of antibiotics was really categorized as the treatment of a specific opportunistic infection, and use of high-tech home care was to have been covered by a condition-treatment pair ranked much higher on the list. Similarly, total parenteral nutrition for a terminally ill AIDS patient would have been covered as palliative care, and thus not rationed out of the system by the low ranking of item 709 either. In fact, all the Health Services Commission intended was that aggressive treatment of the HIV infection itself for late-stage HIV patients not be authorized, given that there was no effective treatment available.

The treatment-condition pair ranked 709 was eliminated from the version of Oregon's plan submitted in November of 1992 for Medicaid waiver (and approved in 1993). According to Sipes-Metzler, experts testified that there was little basis for singling out late-stage HIV infection as a well-defined stage of a disease. The point of having made a public, explicit decision of the sort made in 1991, in the context of an accountable, democratic process, was that further criticism was able to lead to a change. Because the grounds for the decision were public, they could be publicly challenged.

A public, democratic process that undertook to consider whether to ration certain high-tech home care services would have to defend its decisions along many of the dimensions I have articulated. It would have to show that the cost and benefit estimates were reasonable; that process might bring public scrutiny to bear on the kinds of abuses Green (1991) documented in the home care services industry. It would have to make appropriate comparisons of competitor services: Only a much more fine-grained assessment than one that uses such clumsy categories as "high-tech" and "home versus hospital" would survive scrutiny. Finally, the process would require taking a stand on the moral choices I earlier categorized as unsolved rationing problems. A stance would have to be adopted on how much priority should be given the sickest patients, as well as on how (whether, to what extent) we should distribute benefits. Either we would be forced to develop a principled defense of the stance we adopt on these issues, or we would simply fall back on the claim that—since there was no consensus on principle—it was sufficient to have democratic agreement. Either result would be ethically defensible.

I do not mean to imply that I endorse the Oregon strategy of trying to rank broadly construed treatment-condition pairs. There are many reasons to think that we might ultimately have to rely on gatekeeping decisions by clinicians who make much more precise assessments in light of information they have about their particular patients' conditions and prognoses. For example, Canadian practitioners appear to exclude some categories of patients—or patients sufficiently unlikely to derive benefit—from intensive care units more often than their United States counterparts do (Daniels and Sabin, unpublished research). They may have internalized a somewhat more restrictive approach to intensive-care utilization because they operate in a more restrictive, globally constrained environment; certainly their practice does not appear to be guided by adequate public discussion of the kinds of decisions they make. They lack a fair, democratic process—as do all systems, to date. But the approach— relying as it does on the internalized judgment of practitioners who have to negotiate how their patients are placed in a globally constrained setting—is in fact an alternative to the Oregon arrangement, an alternative that would be vastly improved with the assistance of a public democratic process.

Social Barriers to the Use of High-tech Home Care

Suppose for the sake of argument that we have met the conditions necessary for making a fair rationing decision, and we have decided that certain high-tech home care services ought to be reimbursable in our insurance scheme. We might in fact suppose that there is a strong justification for making the corresponding hospital versions of these services less (or even un-) available for those for whom the home version is medically suitable. For example, though the home versions are cost effective beyond some agreed-upon threshold, hospital delivery fails to meet the threshold; were there only hospital versions of these technologies, they would not be included in the system. The questions of fairness we now face concern those who are medically suitable for these services but whose home situation makes providing them with them inappropriate.

One way to deal with hard choices is to duck them by finding another alternative. If hospital-based versions of a therapy fail to meet some criterion for inclusion, whereas home versions should be included, then there may also be an intermediary format for delivering the service that might also warrant inclusion. Some group setting or low-overhead nursing home setting might meet the relevant criteria. Then the issue would be whether the health care system is designed in such a way that such settings will be made available.

Another alternative might be to provide additional nursing care in whatever home setting would otherwise be unsuitable. But this alternative might push the costs over the relevant threshold, or it might simply be unavailable because of serious (and insurmountable) inadequacies in the home setting.

Clearly there will be some cases we cannot avoid in this way. The general form of the problem is this: Reasonable rationing criteria mean that some medically suitable people, specifically those who are worst off economically or socially, will be left unprotected by the system in cases when economically or socially more fortunate individuals can be helped. In effect, we are allowing better-off individuals to use their extra resources to subsidize the delivery of a service they, too, would otherwise be denied since it is unavailable to anyone in a hospital.

How we should respond to this situation depends, I think, on the kind of benefit the service in question provides. If it has a significant effect on individuals, that is, if it protects the normal opportunity range in a significant way, then I think the tiering that results in the system is seriously objectionable; this simply becomes another instance of the objectionable nature of any multitiered health care system—that is, a system in which better-off individuals can buy benefit packages that protect opportunity significantly more than it is protected in the basic benefit package made available to the worst-off individuals (or to the majority). This is precisely the sort of tiering that is prohibited in the Dutch and German systems, where private and public insurance schemes rarely differ in anything but amenities and other services that are not medically necessary. If, however, the benefits of the high-tech home services are really this great, then it is less likely the original rationing criteria would have the consequences we are supposing. More likely, the benefits are modest or marginal—and in that case, we can better tolerate the structure of inequality that results from the hypothetical rationing.

A compromise outcome might be this: If the benefit is significant, but it is far more cost-effective to deliver that benefit at home, we might nevertheless provide hospital delivery for those for whom we can find no more cost-effective alternative (even though hospital delivery considered by itself would not have been included on reasonable rationing criteria). Under a global budget, this decision would have opportunity costs, and we would have to make sure we were not protecting equality of opportunity in this instance at the cost of a more serious sacrifice of it elsewhere. Alas, being precise at this point is difficult, because many of the judgments depend on what the alternative uses of resources might turn out to be. What counts as a "significant benefit," for instance, is a judgment we can make only when we are considering what options really are feasible alternatives under the circumstances.

In short, to the question of how we should react to the inequity that arises between patients for whom high-tech home care is suitable and those for whom it is not, we must respond: It depends. It depends on how significant the benefits are, what alternatives are available to us, and on whether reducing this inequity creates more significant inequities elsewhere. More specific answers are possible only when we have very specific cases and alternatives in mind—but these are precisely the kinds of issues we must always face as we make decisions about what and when and how to ration health care benefits.

7

Morality, Prevention, and Sex Education

Moral Disagreement and Prevention Strategies

Fair treatment in the HIV epidemic must involve protecting the uninfected, not simply providing help to those already infected. It is in the area of prevention more than treatment, however, that our sharpest social conflicts have emerged. Because HIV prevention entails changing the intimate behaviors of individuals, and because these behaviors are the focus of moral concerns for many, public measures aimed at both prevention and the protection of life and health rapidly become enmeshed in private concerns about morality.

The stability of fair arrangements depends on the willingness of those who hold competing moral and religious views to settle disputes about what goes on in the public sphere by reference to values and principles all can accept as reasonable and fair. The tension I seek to explore in this chapter is between the view that is shared by most people, namely that the protection of the health and lives of children (and adults) is a concern of paramount importance, and the views held by some that certain widely practiced sexual behaviors are immoral. To what extent should these special moral views influence deliberations about public policy? To what extent does appealing to them undermine the "overlapping consensus" (Rawls, 1993) on principles and public values that permits us to cooperate with one another on fair terms despite our other disagreements? These are the issues at the heart of liberalism raised by the advocates of abstinence-only sex education, who are opposed to comprehensive sex eduction programs being introduced into our schools.

A Cautionary Tale

The Newton (Massachusetts) School Committee members sat behind a horseshoe of Formica cafeteria tables covered with microphones. Several hundred parents—some with children present—filled every seat in the junior high school auditorium; others stood in the rear or sat on the steps in the aisles, in violation of the fire codes. Television cameras from several stations settled their crews in the aisles and behind the stage. A popular talk-show host, supporting a group of parents opposed to the program under consideration, had urged everyone in the area to attend the meeting. Anxious about a possible influx of "outside organizers" representing fundamentalist groups, devoutly liberal Newton parents pilgrimaged early, desperate to get in. The subject? Comprehensive sex education.

The acoustics were poor, and all strained to listen as one father gripped his notes and leaned tautly toward the microphone: "No teacher's going to shove a condom under my child's nose. We're her parents, and we're responsible for her morals." Two rows of parents applauded; others shifted impatiently in their seats.

"In our home," he went on in softer tones, "we believe sex must wait for marriage. Our daughters and our son have all been taught from their earliest years that they must respect the opposite sex, and that respect requires waiting for marriage. My daughters do not need detailed instructions on how to put a condom on their date—the situation will not arise." A few rows away someone whispered, for all to hear, "Wanna bet? How can he be so sure?"

"Why should they see adults, supposedly in positions of respect and responsibility—their teachers, no less, and the principal and the school committee—encourage and condone immoral sex? That would undercut everything we stand for in our home!"

The school committee chair interrupted: "Your time is up."

"I just want to add," the father went on, refusing to yield the floor, "that this is one case where doing the right thing clearly has its rewards. I don't want anyone undercutting my children's confidence in doing the right thing. I don't want anyone opening the door to immoral sex for my children and putting them at risk. I don't want anyone telling them a condom is safe, when it is not, when only

abstinence is truly safe. You do what's wrong, you pay the price."
The same whispering voice came louder this time: "Yeah, and God's
on your side."

The next speaker, a high school sophomore, read her remarks
nervously and quickly. "You," she said looking at the school committee, "cannot abandon us. You are sworn to educate us, and that
means giving us all the facts we need to live in this complex world.
Obviously, whether some parents want it or not, some of my fellow
students are having sex—unprotected, unsafe sex. Some of the parents here may think these kids will deserve what they get"—she
paused, looking briefly in the direction of the previous speaker, who
had just sat down among his approving friends—"but your job is not
to moralize about them, it is to educate them." She finished her text
and turned to leave the microphone, but hesitated, and—again looking at the previous speaker—summoned her most intense disap-
proval for a closing remark: "I, for one, cannot understand how
anyone could think that someone deserves AIDS just because they
fall in love and have sex."

Resounding applause foreshadowed the results of the evening,
the unanimous passage of the new sex education curriculum, a pilot
version of which was to begin the next year. In 1993, Newton was
joining a growing wave of cities in Massachusetts, California, Ohio,
Georgia, North Carolina, Kentucky, and elsewhere that have insti-
tuted some form of explicit, comprehensive sex education. Three
years earlier, Cambridge Rindge and Latin High School had become
the first school in Massachusetts to make condoms available on the
school grounds. At the time the Newton controversy surfaced, Cambridge was able to say that there had been no increase in sexual
activity, though there was a 43 percent increase in condom use by
sexually active students (Nealon, 1993). By 1993, only 6 percent of
the high schools in Massachusetts were distributing condoms,
though most had some form of AIDS education program in place.
New York City had approved condom distribution and comprehensive sex education for middle and high school students in 1991, in a
decision bitterly contested around the same issues as those raised in
Newton. In July 1993, New Haven approved a program that included
distributing condoms to fifth-graders.

The record shows that concern about early sex is not exaggerated. A 1991 "Survey of Risky Behaviors" undertaken by the Centers
for Disease Control showed that 40 percent of ninth-graders are
sexually active, with 75 percent active by the senior year of high
school. A National Public Radio report (August 6, 1993) on New

Haven suggested considerable evidence of multiple-partner sexual activity among young teens, noting a twelve-year-old with nine reported partners. The chairperson of New Haven's school board said, "Any time that you have children at risk of dying, then I can't imagine anything more urgent than that. If there's anything you can do to prevent that, then that is your moral obligation to do so" (Levy, 1993).

Nationwide, opponents of comprehensive sex education clearly disagree, believing the moral obligations of school boards fall elsewhere. Nor have all Massachusetts communities voted the way Newton did. Braintree, a more conservative town with much better-organized opposition, voted down a comprehensive sex education proposal during the spring of 1993. And in Kingston, Massachusetts, a local clergyman—urging an abstinence-only program—insisted that explicit instruction and condom distribution "says that we're legitimizing your involvement sexually and creates the impression that using a condom will make the sexual act physically safe" (Bass, 1993:24).

Where these opponents hold sway, many towns have adopted abstinence-only curricula, like "Teen AID" and "Sex Respect." Those who support Teen AID argue that "people are the solution, not technology," and focus on the negative consequences of premarital sex. No instruction is given on birth control devices, and the school systems that adopt these programs usually do not have the devices available through school clinics. Similarly, Sex Respect drills students in slogans such as "Pet Your Dog, Not Your Date" or "Save Your Urgin', Stay a Virgin." Its supporters insist that it "reinforces, not undermines, the positive things taught at home." In an NBC documentary on sex education produced by Jeanne Blake (Spring 1993), enthusiastic Sex Respect teachers emphasized that even saliva could transmit the HIV virus. The young people picked up on this quickly. Being safe really meant no kissing "except chicken pecks," as one of the terrified, yet skeptical, youngsters put it. Asked if she thought she would avoid "deep kissing" until she was married, the child giggled, "I don't think so."

Because schools and their curricula are controlled locally in this country, community views about the appropriateness of different kinds of sex education will no doubt continue to produce votes like the one in Newton *and* the one in Braintree—and all along the spectrum in between. What the distribution of such choices about programs is nationwide is not yet clear (the CDC is trying to improve on the results of an early survey that proved inadequate [Deborah Rugg, CDC, personal communication, August 1993]), but even without knowing the distribution we can see that serious questions about fair treatment are bound to arise.

If sex education is a primary defense against HIV transmission, and if abstinence-only and comprehensive programs differ in their effectiveness in reducing the risks of HIV transmission, is it *fair* that young people in some towns are better protected than those in other towns? Reducing risky sexual behavior may be the only way now available to protect adolescents from HIV. If so, providing methods that will effect that reduction is one requirement of the fair-equality-of-opportunity account of just health care that I have described and on which I have been relying throughout. Is it fair treatment of children and young people in, say, a New Orleans school for the majority to provide them with nothing more than an abstinence-only approach? What happens to those who nonetheless do not abstain? Is it fair to appeal to general "community values" about sexual morality in this way, when individual lives are at stake? Can we compromise societal protection of fundamentally important goods, like health or life or opportunity, because some fraction of the population—never mind whether minority or majority—believes that the steps we must take to afford that protection involve us in "legitimizing" what they consider immoral behavior?

The questions about fairness arise on both sides of the controversy. Is imposing an explicit sex-education curriculum fair to those who believe in abstinence before marriage, whether for secular or for religious reasons? Is sex education like vaccination—something we may insist parents cannot deny their children even for religious reasons? Or must school systems that offer comprehensive sex education also provide parents opposed to it with an option of withdrawing their offspring from the class sessions devoted to that part of the school curriculum? Such an option exists in New York City and Newton, for example; it appears to be fairly common wherever comprehensive sex education programs have been implemented (Rugg, 1993).

These questions about fairness take us deep into the heart of liberalism as a political philosophy. So do some other controversies about HIV prevention in which morality has been invoked—for example, the needle exchange programs attempted in a few American cities. Communities threatened by drug users may resist steps that appear to condone drug-abusing behavior in the very neighborhoods where the greatest effort must be made to reduce these activities. Community activists will argue for drug treatment programs instead, inveighing against anything that they feel legitimizes the drug behaviors destroying their young people. Proponents can now point to considerable success with these treatment programs, especially where they were implemented early in the AIDS epidemic and where they are coupled with programs that respect confidentiality (GAO, 1993). The points I will make about sex education could be generalized to the case of needle exchange programs (as well as to other programs having to do with behaviors that arouse moral aversion). I will, however, focus my discussion on sex education because in that arena, even more than in matters having to do with, for instance, drug use, the special concern parents have about controlling the moral upbringing of their children moves onto center stage.

The "Immorality" of Premarital Sex

The tense Newton father, like the Kingston minister, believes that premarital sex is immoral because it fails to show adequate respect for the opposite sex; sex must wait for marriage. Other people who claim premarital sex is immoral may do so for different reasons. Some, thinking primarily of adolescents, believe it is immoral because of its consequences. They are concerned that these practices are harmful, medically or psychologically: Girls in their early teens may be more vulnerable to sexually transmitted diseases than more mature women; adolescents may be incapable of managing the intimacy that sex involves.

But many others—perhaps most of those who favor abstinence-only programs—think premarital sex is immoral because of what it *is*, not what it *does*. They may say it is "intrinsically wrong" or "wrong regardless of its effects." Some may offer reasons rooted in religious views about the "natural" or divinely approved procreative role of sex and marriage in our lives. Still others offer nontheological reasons, perhaps insisting that only certain kinds of publicly sanctioned relationships built around avowals of commitment exhibit virtues we must strive for in our lives. (The Newton father seems to belong here.)

Nothing in the arguments that follow depends on the nature of the reasons people give for their view that pre- or extramarital sex is wrong, however, for I am not at all interested in debating the rightness or wrongness of such sexual activity. I am concerned only with the role that claims about the morality of sexual activity should play in our deliberations about health protection. I am going to assume (following Rawls, 1993) that reasonable people will develop comprehensive philosophical, moral, and religious views that involve different conclusions about the morality of certain behaviors. Further, I will assume that arguments made from within these comprehensive views may be resistant to arguments based on other views.

Making these assumptions about conflicting, comprehensive moral views—all of which may be reasonable (even if only one is true and the others are false)—does not commit me to moral skepticism. The fact that many reasonable comprehensive views may arise is explained by what Rawls (1993:56) calls the "burdens of judgment": The evidence for a view is sometimes conflicting and complex, and we may disagree about what weight to give it; our concepts are often vague and fuzzy; our total experience may shape our response to evidence; and it is difficult to make an overall assessment of the normative elements in a view (especially when every view must be selective about what it includes).

The result of the "burdens of judgment" and our freedom to develop competing comprehensive views is that *pluralism* is an inescapable fact about the context in which we must seek to cooperate with one another in ways we can agree are fair (v. Rawls, 1993, for an extended discussion of this assumption and its implications).

"Immoral Because Unsafe" versus "Immoral Even if Safer"

Parents who oppose comprehensive explicit sex education often say that such programs are wrong or immoral because they encourage or condone or legitimize immoral sexual behavior. Almost in the same breath, however, opponents say these programs are immoral because they will lead children away from the only completely safe course of behavior—sexual abstinence before marriage. Of course, both of these points might be true, and the Newton father and Kingston minister no doubt believe they are. Nevertheless, they are very different and as such require different responses from society. The crux of the issue is how much weight we should give to the first point about immorality if the second one, about safety or efficacy, is false. The fact that opponents of comprehensive sex education often make the efficacy argument suggests that they place some weight on it for purposes of public policy deliberation. Either they honestly believe it is the relevant issue, or they know that most people think it is and simply want to win allies where they can. We need to see what happens if they lose the efficacy argument.

Suppose we have very strong evidence that comprehensive sex education programs do not lead to earlier or more sexual activity. Suppose also that these programs decrease unsafe sexual practices among sexually active adolescents. And suppose further that comparative studies show abstinence-only programs are considerably less effective than comprehensive ones at discouraging early and unsafe sex. In other words, we are supposing that comprehensive sex education programs function like vaccinations: Children exposed to them avoid transmission better than unprotected children or those protected by abstinence only programs. I will shortly consider what evidence we actually have about all these suppositions, but I first want to see what impact they should have on the argument.

Some proponents of abstinence-only programs would agree—if we could give them such (hypothetical, for now) evidence—that comprehensive sex education programs should be adopted in the schools, even if those programs are immoral in the sense that they legitimize immoral behavior. They might be willing to adopt this policy for different reasons. Some might think that protecting the health of children is more important than getting "dirty hands" by legitimizing immoral sex (such a priority might be part of their own comprehensive moral view). Others might believe that for purposes of public policy, where groups with diverse views about sexual morality must agree on a course of action, it is inappropriate for them to insist that everyone avoid what they consider dirty hands (though in their own religious and other private groups, such as community youth clubs, these advocates of abstinence-only would of course be free to—and no doubt would—adhere to their own values, avoiding legitimizing immoral sex in any way). In their different ways, both these responses take seriously the evidence—which I am still supposing, for the sake of argument, is very clear-cut—about the effects of the alternative programs on the health of children in the public schools.

Some opponents of comprehensive sex education, on the other hand, might have a much more disturbing response. They might say that we should not adopt such programs, despite the strong evidence of their greater effectiveness, because it is always immoral to legitimize immoral behavior. For them, although adhering to abstinence-only programs exacts a price in health, lives, and opportunity, immoral public policies must be avoided at *all* costs. Dirty hands must be avoided, even if significant harms result.

Reasonable people may develop a comprehensive moral or religious view that contains just such a position, and they may even

defend it against powerful opposing arguments. Nevertheless, accepting greater risks to children is a hard pill even for purists to swallow,
and one that is harder yet to persuade others to swallow. But purists
may refuse to take steps to avoid harms that are significant even on
their own comprehensive moral view if those steps require deviating
from the straight and narrow as they see it. In such instances—not
least because they know that others consider the harms overriding—
there is a strain on the commitment to principle within such a view.

Two common palliatives are available to ease this strain in the
present context. The first is to believe that the additional disease
and death that accompany abstinence-only programs (again, I am
still assuming they are less effective) are "just deserts" or even "just
punishment" for immoral or sinful behavior. The second is to insist
that the *intention* is only to promote moral behavior, not to produce
the foreseen but unwanted result that some children will fail to
abstain and will practice unsafe sex (with bad consequences). By
following this route, the purists can claim we are responsible and
culpable only for the intended effects of our actions, not the foreseen
but unintended ones. (This distinction is traditionally called the
Principle or Doctrine of Double Effect. Used for various purposes in
Catholic doctrine, it makes possible, for instance, the justification of
killing innocents in war or allowing a mother to die in order to save
the fetus in childbirth.) Neither palliative is likely to persuade the
nonpurist public in a pluralist community, and each faces further
objections if the abstinence-only programs lose the argument about
effectiveness. I shall return to these points shortly.

Although purists advance an argument for the effectiveness of
abstinence-only programs, they would not abandon their policy if
they lost that argument; it does not follow, however, that they are
being disingenuous. They may be acknowledging that the public in a
pluralist community will be unresponsive to their purist position;
they are aware that the public as a whole will not ignore the consequences of a policy and will not be satisfied with arguments about
its "intrinsic" wrongness. They will therefore advance the view—
which they also believe—that only abstinence is a safe course of
action. Their position may be something like this: "We want
abstinence-only programs for reasons that may not persuade you,
but we are happy to have you join us in supporting them because you
believe (with us) that they work more effectively."

Especially in light of the fact that none of us actually has evidence
as strong as the suppositions I made earlier in my attempt to uncover
the purist view, we must grant that the purists are much more likely

wrong or confused about what will be effective than they are dishonest. The Newton father and the Kingston minister insist, for example, that abstinence is safer than using a condom. They are no doubt correct, and no one disagrees, but this is not what is at issue. They have subtly changed the subject: The real issue is whether school-based programs focusing on abstinence only—*operating in our diverse culture*—will actually produce such a strong and widespread commitment to abstinence that they will protect children and young people to a greater degree overall than comprehensive sex education programs will. The confidence that abstinence-only advocates place in their programs derives, I will suggest, from an unrealistic confidence in the power of the wish, the will, and the influence of school authorities. First, however, we should see what we actually know about the efficacy of alternative sex education programs.

The Effects of Sex Education Programs

A central charge of the opponents of comprehensive sex education programs is that they will entice young people into having early sex, increasing the risks they face, since we can hardly count on all that early sex being engaged in with appropriate safeguards. This central charge has, however, no evidence in favor of it. A review of nineteen sex education studies (fifteen of them American), which was sponsored by the World Health Organization, found that not a single study gave any evidence that sex education programs led to earlier or increased sexual activity by the young people who did engage in sex (Baldo et al., 1993). Nor did access to counseling and contraceptive services encourage or increase early sexual activity, according to two of the studies reviewed. The experience in a Cambridge, Massachusetts, high school noted earlier corroborates that result. Six American studies showed that sex education either delayed the onset of sexual activity or decreased it, and a majority of the studies showed that sex education increased the adoption of safer practices by sexually active adolescents.

Most important for our purposes is the clear evidence that comprehensive programs, which promote postponement of sexual activity and provide explicit instruction about how to practice safer sex, do have a definite effect—delaying the onset of sexual activity and decreasing unsafe sex practices among those who are sexually active. We have *no* such evidence about abstinence-only programs, primarily because the studies of these programs fail to look directly at behavior and focus instead on knowledge and attitude. Positive effects on knowledge and attitude do not necessarily translate into the relevant behavior changes. Some researchers have even explicitly concluded that abstinence-only programs are less effective than comprehensive ones (Baldo et al., 1993; v. also Bass, 1993), but more definitive negative conclusions about such programs may have to wait for better studies (Rugg, 1993). We do have good evidence that programs emphasizing actual behavior and social norms are more effective than those focusing only on knowledge. Finally, some studies suggest the most effective comprehensive programs are those that involve role playing, where young people have an opportunity to practice actually responding concretely to situations where the pressure to engage in sex, or to engage in unsafe sex, is presented in real-life terms (Bass, 1993:24). One such comprehensive program ("Postponing Sexual Involvement") produced lasting effects on middle and high school students in Atlanta when compared to students who were not given the chance to participate in the program (Bass, 1993:24). In the NBC documentary cited above, there was some evidence that abstinence-only programs also produced *mis*information (e.g., about the risks of kissing) and inculcated fearful, negative attitudes about sex. (There was no discussion of these points in the studies reviewed by Baldo et al., 1993.)

All this evidence falls short of the much stronger claims contained in the suppositions I made earlier, largely because of the weaknesses in the key studies of abstinence-only programs. The most we can claim is that there is no demonstrated effect of abstinence-only programs on behavior, but that there is a demonstrated positive effect of comprehensive programs—especially those that develop skills through role playing and other devices. Someone firmly committed to the belief that premarital sex is immoral might still be skeptical about the comparisons we have made so far, on the grounds that all the studies examined *aggregate* effects. The fact that in the *aggregate* teens exposed to explicit sex education do not engage in earlier sex does not show that some who engaged in early sex would not have not done so if they had been confronted with abstinence-only programs; a good result in the aggregate does not tell enough about the distribution of the effects. (This is another reason the Newton father need not be considered disingenuous for refusing to surrender the safety argument to advocates of comprehensive sex education programs. He can claim there is wiggle room for reasonable doubts and that all the evidence is not in.)

Nevertheless, it would be surprising if comprehensive programs did not produce considerably better results in the aggregate than abstinence-only programs. Abstinence-only programs fail to address the widespread needs of youths who do not abstain from premarital sex (the 40 percent of ninth-graders and 75 percent of twelfth-graders reported in the CDC's "Survey of Risky Behavior" to be sexually active). Even in conservative communities, such programs thus fail to speak to a relevant part of the audience. I am reminded of Krista Blake, of Columbiana, Ohio, living as she put it "in basic, white-bread America," who found out at eighteen that she had been infected with HIV at age sixteen by an older boy—a hemophiliac who knew he was infected but did not tell her (*Newsweek*, 1992:49). In typical American cities, it appears, abstinence-only programs are likely to prove no more effective against teen sex than Nancy Reagan's "Just Say No" campaign was for abstinence from drugs.

Cultural Prerequisites for Sexual Chastity

I believe a deeper problem faces the safety claims of programs that moralize about sexual behavior in the way abstinence-only programs do. These claims overestimate the degree to which a school-based appeal to morality, even one backed by (sometimes misinformed) threats about the consequences of deviations, will really promote chastity *in our culture*. Why the claims are likely to prove exaggerated becomes more clear if we think honestly about the conditions that would have to obtain for our communities and institutions to sustain a commitment—reflected in practice—to sexual chastity (including a commitment to no premarital sex).

Historical precedents are somewhat frightening. Virginity—especially among females—was enforced: Rigid rules restricted contact between youths prior to marriage, and severe punishments (including death) were meted out for violations of rules on chastity. Marriages were arranged in many cultures, and a culture of romantic love often did not exist or was suppressed by the authorities. In any case, the period of opportunity for temptation was short: Marriage often took place shortly after puberty. Very strong family institutions, in which parental authority was backed by power over the transmission of property, status, and opportunity, all worked to sustain sexual moral codes—which, in turn, worked to uphold these forms of power and authority.

Of course strong cultural regard for sexual abstinence has not existed *only* under these conditions, but some combination of them has generally accompanied—and been necessary to sustain—commitment to rigid sexual codes. Religious sects or communities in the United States, for example, must invoke important elements of these conditions to sustain their sexual mores within the larger culture. In the absence of these conditions—and they *are* clearly absent in the society as a whole—sexual abstinence and ideals of chastity wane, despite the urgings of parents and churches. Simply adding school teachers to the chorus proclaiming the message is unlikely to tip the balance in the other direction.

School-based abstinence-only programs cannot substitute for all the other cultural supports that have generally been needed to sustain a commitment to chastity. That no study has demonstrated such programs measurably delay sexual activity or decrease unsafe sex practices is not surprising; they are a finger in the dike that cannot possibly hold back the floodwaters of a larger culture where every medium is inundated with a variety of messages and incentives regarding sex and marriage. I said earlier that belief in the effectiveness of abstinence-only programs rested on an unrealistic faith in the power of the wish and the will; never has implementation of rigid sexual codes rested on such slender institutional support. For better, for worse, there is little or no reason to believe abstinence-only programs can be relied on to produce the moral commitment they seek in our culture.

I also said earlier that purist proponents of abstinence-only programs—those who support them even while acknowledging they are less effective—face a real strain on personal commitment: They must accept more death and disease as the price of sustaining their sexual morality. To ease their strain, I pointed out, purists might claim that the death and disease are the just deserts of immoral acts, or they might insist they do not *intend* the death and disease and so are not culpable for it. Neither way of easing the strain survives my suggestion that abstinence-only advocates have unrealistically overestimated the power of their policy to produce widespread commitment to abstinence, however. To be responsible for abiding by an abstinence-only sexual morality, and to be culpable if we fail, requires that we can *standardly be expected* to abide by it in the conditions we are likely to face. But it must be feasible for us to adhere to this morality, given the institutional supports and the culture that surround us; otherwise, acting as a moral agent requires herculean effort and commitment. Surely it is wrong to hold people morally responsible and punishable for falling short of some standard achievable only though extraordinary effort and commitment. Morality must be possible for most of us in the real world.

If I am right that elaborate cultural and institutional supports are necessary to sustain a commitment to the kind of sexual code advocated by the abstinence-only proponents, then the view that AIDS is just desert or punishment for immoral behavior or sin is untenable in our culture. At least it is untenable by reference to the criteria for ascribing responsibility to which we ordinarily adhere. Perhaps certain theological doctrines might hold people accountable for sins that they cannot standardly be expected to avoid committing. For example, some people believe in a god who holds us to a higher standard than we can reasonably hold ourselves to in everyday life or for judicial purposes in society. But such special beliefs should not be invoked in determining public policy, especially where it affects matters as important as the protection of health and life. *Public policy should rest on publicly accessible reasons and reasoning.* The proponents of "abstinence only" cannot appeal to the idea of just punishment for immorality as a way to persuade the public as a whole to accept greater risks to young people.

The second way I identified that purists might seek to ease the strain on commitment that they face is via the Doctrine of Double Effect. Claiming they do not intend the extra cases of AIDS that will result from implementing their policy, they insist rather that their intent is only to produce commitment to moral behavior through these programs. But if my argument is correct, that these programs do not provide the causal conditions required for sustaining a commitment to the chaste sexual behavior they espouse, then this intention flies in the face of reasonable expectations. Simply adding abstinence-only instruction in the schools, as I indicated above, cannot reasonably be expected to counteract the many cultural forces pushing our children and young people toward other behaviors; the moral authority of the schools *cannot* substitute for all the institutions that have historically proven necessary to support a commitment to chastity (and then not always with complete success). The proponents may *wish* or *hope* that such programs will have the effect that they desire, but they cannot reasonably *expect* or *intend* them to.

Public Reason and Sex Education

One implication of the fair-equality-of-opportunity account I have relied on throughout is that we have a social obligation to protect those who are uninfected with HIV. The public-policy debate about how to discharge that obligation in the educational setting thus looks as if it should be a debate about the most effective form of such protection and about the resources that we must devote to it. Some advocates of abstinence-only programs accept these ground rules for the debate, but others—harboring a purist view—would require us to trade greater protection for moral purity (as they see it). Once we strip away from this position the support that comes from those who think abstinence-only programs are *safer*, it will turn out to be a much less appealing position, even for the purists themselves. If it is also true that a moral commitment to chastity cannot be sustained in our culture by the slender device of an abstinence-only program, then the appeal of the purist view is further diminished, because it is no longer possible—without changing our concepts of culpability and intention—to dismiss extra death and disease as just deserts for immorality or to claim the intention was to produce moral behavior.

The effect of my argument so far, as I have hinted, is to say that advocates of abstinence-only programs who lose the effectiveness argument *have no publicly recognizable, reasonable grounds for persuading most people in a pluralist culture to accept their view.* In some—perhaps many—small communities, by sheer weight of numbers or by virtue of the very effective organization or generous support of religious groups, they may be able to produce a majority vote that establishes an abstinence-only program. But when the evidence shows—as almost certainly will be the case when all of it is in—that comprehensive programs are significantly more effective ways to reduce risky behavior, then these majoritarian appeals to a community's views about sexual morality should not dominate public policy where goods of fundamental importance are at stake.

Nevertheless, my claim about the possible desirability of imposing limits on majority rule is controversial; it suggests that a standard way we have for adjudicating disputes about value in communities—namely, majority rule—may not yield morally acceptable results in this case. We standardly restrict majority rule when it conflicts with various rights, of course—especially fundamental ones of the sort that are laid out in our Constitution. But in a case like the one we are discussing here, it is not always obvious whether the right or entitlement at issue here is constitutionally protected. We cannot claim it is obvious there is a "right" to the most effective form of education against risky behaviors, though I have suggested that our moral right to fair equality of opportunity may govern this instance. Thus it might seem acceptable simply to let the majority decide. Moreover, the purist view need not be characterized in theological or religious terms: Nonreligious views about morality may be involved, making it impossible to argue against the purist view that it violates constitutional restrictions on the establishment of religion through the public schools.

My analysis of the argument—at least of the purist advocate of abstinence-only—makes the simple power of the majority seem problematic, however, and for reasons that resemble the constitutional objections to establishment of religion. Imagine that a local majority of such purists rejects the kind of reasoning that sustains fair cooperation in the society as a whole and invokes instead special reasons that derive from comprehensive moral views not shared in the society as a whole (though, by hypothesis, dominant locally); the result would be that some children whose education is left to the responsibility of the public sphere would be put at increased risk for reasons not relevant to debate about relationships in the public sphere.

I conclude it is wrong for a local majority to insist—for reasons that violate the spirit and content of cooperation in a liberal pluralist society—on abstinence-only programs in public schools, *once those programs are shown to be less effective than alternative programs.*[1]

Respecting Parental Claims of Conscience

Though there are strong reasons for not letting proponents of abstinence-only deny children more effective sex education programs, these reasons do not entail that parents who strongly believe in the sexual morality underlying sexual abstinence should be forced to have their offspring participate in comprehensive, explicit sex education programs. A sound public policy that is fair to all should respect parental claims of conscience—unless these lead to certain kinds of harms to children. In many communities that have implemented comprehensive sex education programs (including, again, Newton and New York), parents opposed to them have been given the option of exempting their children from the curriculum. This option *should* be the general rule, despite the administrative complexity it introduces.

One of our deep moral commitments in a pluralist society is to allow people to pursue their conception of a good life, provided their doing so respects the rights, opportunities, and well-being of others. One element of that liberty is the right to raise one's children according to one's conception of a good life, including deeply held views about values and morality. Our constitutional protections in the

United States for "free exercise" of religion touch on a central aspect of this broader moral commitment.

At the risk of oversimplifying a very complex issue, let me note some parameters the courts have recognized in their rulings on free exercise of religion. One crucial case is *Wisconsin v. Yoder*, 406 U.S. 205 (1972). The Supreme Court ruled that the state of Wisconsin could not compel Amish children over the age of thirteen to attend school, despite state laws requiring most children to attend school until age sixteen. The Amish way of life, as the Court discovered in its thorough inquiry, aims at preparing children for the virtues of a rural, agricultural community, and public schooling beyond age thirteen unduly interfered with that religious goal. The Court was clearly aware that children thus prepared are at a disadvantage compared to other children if they choose to leave their communities, and that the ruling thus did not protect their equality of opportunity under all foreseeable circumstances. But the Court insisted, despite this cost in terms of a good most of the rest of society would consider extremely valuable, that it is not the prerogative of society as a whole to insist its values should take precedence over those held by a particular group (in this case, the Amish).

Free exercise of religious beliefs do have limits, however. Despite the religious objections of parents, for example, children may be vaccinated and subjected to other crucial public health measures and life-extending treatments (*Jehovah's Witnesses v. King County Hospital*, 390 U.S. 598 [1968]; *In re Green*, 448 Pa. 338, 292 A.2nd 387 [1972]). Where there is a direct and significant harm to health or life, free exercise of religion is circumscribed by society's interest in protecting life and health, at least for minor children.

Earlier, for the sake of argument, I asked what we should do if comprehensive sex education programs worked as effectively as foolproof vaccinations in reducing the risks to children and young people from unsafe sex. I had wanted to flush out the purist from the thicket of advocates of abstinence-only programs. But sex education programs are not like vaccinations for several reasons. First, *agency* is involved in sex education programs. Risk comes from acting in certain ways; safety comes from other actions. In contrast, without vaccination, people are at risk regardless of what they do. Thus the effectiveness of sex education programs is mediated by individual agency; hence, they are a very indirect way of protecting people. If parents argue that their children will not behave in risky ways, or are much less likely to than the population at large, there is little evidence to controvert their claim.

A second difference has to do with efficacy: Sex education is far less effective than vaccinations. Parents who are concerned about the immorality of early sex are being asked to forgo their concern in return for a very modest promise of protection. Indeed, they might claim, as I earlier noted, that the risks for their children are being potentially increased in order to reduce the risks to others. Finally, since agency is involved in sexual transmission, the argument that is sometimes made about vaccinations for children—namely that there is a risk these children will infect others if they are not vaccinated—is much more indirect in the case of HIV protection. The child who is exempted from explicit sex education is not necessarily a greater threat to others than one who has sat through such a course. (I should note that the "threat to others" argument is not as persuasive as it seems, since the unvaccinated are not threats to those who are vaccinated, and exemptions can be granted without risk to third parties (v. Tribe, 1978).

Public Reason: Toleration and Compromise in Public Policy

Two elements of a defensible public policy concerning sex education emerge from these considerations. First, the primary grounds for deciding between comprehensive sex education and abstinence only programs should be their relative effectiveness in lowering the risks for the children exposed to them. This is largely an empirical matter: We must see what the effects on behavior are of the different programs. If there is adequate evidence to show that abstinence-only programs have limited effectiveness compared to comprehensive programs which also argue for postponement of sexual activity, then concerns about the immorality of comprehensive programs should not be allowed to interfere with their implementation.

There is a compromise here. Those who think premarital sex is immoral are being asked to allow public institutions, schools and their authorities, to teach material that appears (to them) to condone such behavior. They are being asked to place a concern for the health of children above these moral views—for public-policy purposes. The basis for asking for them to agree to this compromise must be a commitment on everyone's part to avoid intruding certain kinds of personal reasons into the public debate; without such a commitment, the overlapping consensus on the terms of fair cooperation that all share is undercut.

The second element of our public policy involves fairness to those who hold comprehensive moral views. In the face of the HIV epidemic, many are willing and prepared to break long-standing social and moral taboos, believing that only explicit, comprehensive sex education will adequately protect children. But this enthusiasm for taking action (not to say panic about the need to do so) must not lead us to ignore the legitimate concerns of parents who want to control the moral education of their offspring.

Here, too, compromise comes into play. We may have good evidence that comprehensive programs supply all children with needed skills and attitudes necessary to avoiding risky behaviors. Allowing some parents to exempt their children on moral grounds means leaving those children at what we believe is greater risk. Unless we have evidence that sex education works as effectively as vaccination, however, we are not in a position to insist that our public concern about those risks outweighs parental rights to shape the moral upbringing of their children.

Comprehensive moral views can encourage moral aversion to a broad range of behaviors, as we know: pre- and extramarital sex, homosexual sex, reliance on alcohol or other drugs, etc. The history of the HIV epidemic in particular is a history in which such attitudes have frequently surfaced and interfered with the fair treatment of groups at risk (regardless of whether they are infected). But ours is a society in which people with diverse views have elaborated a basis for fair cooperation in the distribution of fundamental rights, powers, and goods. These include health care and health protection. Allowing moral views about sex or other lifestyle issues to intrude into the domain of fair cooperation threatens the stability of our basic institutions. A plea for toleration and compromise of the sort I have made here is a plea for the importance of liberal virtues.

8

Fairness and National Health Care Reform

HIV and National Health Care Reform

HIV patients suffer special forms of discrimination. Nevertheless, the main obstacles to the fair treatment of HIV patients are obstacles any of us might have to overcome because of the way our health care system is designed. All of us potentially face exclusion from insurance because of risk, loss of insurance coverage with job loss or job change, maldistribution of appropriate providers, and inadequate coverage for home care, mental health care, and other services, including drugs. A system that corrected these and other problems we all risk having to confront would also go a long way toward ensuring fair treatment for HIV patients. The most effective way to achieve this would be to enact a comprehensive national health care reform that met key criteria for justice or fairness.

But what *does* a just or fair system require? What criteria of fairness should it be judged by? Specifically, in a climate in which many seek to reform the system, what criteria should we use to assess the fairness of health care reform proposals?

Some important hints about these criteria are offered in earlier chapters along with reminders about the ways in which decisions we make in the context of the HIV/AIDS epidemic inform our decisions about health care (and health care reform) more generally. In our discussion of the duty to treat HIV patients, we noted that their access to appropriate, willing physicians and other providers is a requirement of justice. Society has the obligation to ensure that there are adequate practitioners to meet the health care needs of HIV patients, and that professional and individual practitioner obligations and prerogatives are compatible with the requirements of justice. In my discussion of the insurability of HIV patients, I suggested that the exclusionary practices of health care insurers employing standard underwriting procedures violate considerations of justice. Health care insurance must be governed by different criteria of fairness than some other forms of insurance against risk, because its primary goal is to assure access to services that play a central role in assuring fair equality of opportunity. Demanding significantly higher premiums from those at higher risk, I concluded, violates requirements about the fair sharing of the burdens of meeting health care needs. In my discussion of access to high-technology home care, I argued that fair treatment involves careful consideration of the kinds of services that should be included in an insurance benefits package. I argued that we should not deny access to a new technology simply because it is high-cost or because it falls into a particular category of services, such as long-term care rather than acute care. Rather, we should limit access to a beneficial service only if we can show it is less important to offer it—because of its opportunity cost—than other services we should be offering. If we are to impose fair limits on services we must develop reasonable criteria and fair procedures for making such decisions.

Introducing Design Principles

The time has now come to consider more systematically what all of us should consider fair treatment in health care reform. Of course, there is no uniquely just health care system. A variety of institutional designs may exhibit the crucial features and functions that principles of justice require. A just system might be purely public (as in Canada) or mixed (as in Germany)—or a just system might involve a national health service (as in Great Britain) or national health insurance (as in most countries). When we fashion institutions, our goal must be to reconcile political feasibility and efficiency with the requirements of justice without violating the principles that inform those requirements. As we shall see, comparing the fairness or justice of competing reform proposals is a complex and multidimensional task.

To bring my views about justice to bear on the proposals, I shall use a series of what I will call "design principles," which are intended to highlight morally important properties and functions of just health care institutions. Design principles—though they are not themselves principles of morality—are reasonable requirements to impose, given the views about justice and health care I have sketched (see Chapter 1) and given our knowledge of how the delivery of health care actually works. Any list of design principles could be expanded or contracted, practically at will (depending in part on the degree of rigor with which one wished to evaluate the institutions or proposals in question); I have chosen to work with some dozen and a half of what seem to me the most salient of the many principles one might wish to apply. Among these are efficacy, compulsory coverage, comprehensive benefits, universal coverage, portability, nonexclusion, community rating, explicit rationing, and financing by ability to pay.

What these design principles do is help specify appropriate answers to such critical questions as these: How universal is insurance coverage? How portable are insurance benefits? How comprehensive are the benefits provided? They also provide a multidimensional matrix that can be used to assess the fairness or justice of a broad range of competing reform proposals (not only the ones considered here)[1] as they emerge at either the federal or state levels. To show how the matrix of design principles can help us assess the fairness of a health care system, I shall apply it to four comprehensive proposals presented to the 103rd Congress. Though none of these reforms was enacted, they represent a spectrum of central ideas about the design of a broadly reformed system. Even modest, incremental reform, if that is all that is possible in a political climate opposed to "big government" interventions, will draw on key elements of these proposals.

A Spectrum of Reform Proposals

The Clinton "Health Security Act" dominated the debate, calling for a combination of market forces—"managed competition"—and robust government regulation (and mandates) to guarantee universal coverage and cost controls. To its left stood Senator Paul Wellstone's (D-MN) and Representative Jim McDermott's (D-WA) versions of a Canadian-style "single-payer" system; its tax-based system would eliminate private insurance companies and join everyone in a uniform public health care insurance scheme. To its right stood plans—like Senator John Chafee's (R-RI) "Health Equity and Access Reform

Today" (HEART) and Representative Jim Cooper's (D-IN) plan—that called for more reliance on market forces and less on government involvement. The health care reform that is enacted—whether it is a federal or ultimately state-by-state reform—will embody some elements of these proposals. Before fully developing the matrix of design principles, however, I want to describe very briefly the central features of the representative plans to which I will apply it. This description cannot of course be complete, since the plans are complex. But seeing how the matrix allows us to analyze and evaluate the fairness of these proposals will illustrate its value in assessing actual reforms. I will comment on other features of each as I apply the matrix to them in subsequent sections.

I shall begin this sketch of typical reform proposals with the most radical, the effort to adopt a Canadian-style single-payer system. The Wellstone-McDermott proposal, backed by nearly ninety members of the 103rd Congress, called for eliminating all private insurers. This is a highly popular move because many people believe health insurers have diverted a significant proportion of health care dollars into administrative costs and profits, thus contributing greatly to the relatively high cost of the current health care system in the United States. Since it eliminates the "hassle factor" involved in negotiating reimbursements for treatment from insurers with different rules and procedures, it is popular with patients as well as with many practitioners.

Instead of myriad private insurers, the single-payer proposal would make the government a public insurer—negotiating fees and payments to hospitals, physicians, and other providers who would offer services to all citizens on presentation of a health care card. Funding would require that a payroll tax replace the complex system of general tax revenues, employer contributions, and individual payments of premiums and out-of-pocket payments that we currently have—making the funding mechanism relatively progressive (though for many whose employee benefits are now "invisible," a payroll tax will seem to be a new tax).

Benefits are not fully detailed in the existing proposals, but the advocates of this style of reform intend to make them comprehensive—aiming for parity between mental and physical health, and between acute and chronic or long-term care. The uniform health plan would not involve "tiering." Since there would be no competing insurers trying to avoid adverse selection by high-risk patients, there would be no risk exclusions. Coverage would be completely portable. Tax revenues would constitute a global budget for health care expenditures. Cost containment would result from several factors: The global budget would force careful consideration of investment in new technologies and apply pressure against overutilization of many services; large-scale fee and hospital-charge negotiation, under budget constraints, would markedly slow the rate of growth of these costs.

The Clinton Health Security Act attempted to seize a political middle ground between such a single-payer ("big government"), public insurance scheme, on the one hand, and proposals that rely almost entirely on "managed" market forces (and weak or absent government mandates), on the other. One option open to the states under the Clinton proposal was for them each individually to adopt a single-payer system. This option seemed necessary, because competition among health plans is feasible only in large population areas that can sustain stable noncolluding competitors, while more than 30 percent of the population lives in areas where competition is unfeasible (Kronick et al., 1993). But the primary focus of Clinton's reform incorporated an idea that is shared with various plans to its political right, namely managed competition.

No one should confuse managed competition with managed care. The latter is an insurance plan that tries to control cost and quality through the selection of providers and the regulation of services. Managed competition, in contrast, provides for a "sponsor" to act on behalf of large numbers of insurees to negotiate favorable prices from competing "qualified" health plans, many of which will be managed-care plans. The sponsor may be a public agency, like the "health alliances" under Clinton's plan, or a large employer. Purchasers, whether individuals or employers, would buy insurance at the managed (that is, negotiated) rates—but they would be made conscious of costs by the way employee tax benefits for health care premiums would be reduced or eliminated. For example, the Clinton plan mandated employers to provide insurance, but they would pay at most 80 percent of the premium of a "basic" plan, while employees would pay the remaining 20 percent as well as any additional cost of a more generous insurance plan. Unemployed or self-employed individuals buy insurance through health alliances; subsidies to low-income individuals help them purchase insurance. All health plans would have to offer a comprehensive package of benefits, defined by the Clinton legislation. (We shall look later at what is meant by comprehensive benefits.)

Though Clinton, Chafee, and Cooper all incorporate elements of managed competition, Clinton's plan would give the managers—his public health alliances—a stronger set of powers than their counterparts in the other plans would have. In addition, the Clinton plan called for a National Health Board to be empowered to set "premium caps" that limit the increase in premiums by tying increases to growth in the Gross National Product. This regulatory mechanism was denounced as a form of "price controls" by those touting more market-based plans. Without question, it gives the Clinton plan a feature that resembles the single-payer budget as a form of social control over health care expenditures.

The Clinton plan also involved more powerful mandates to assure universal coverage—for example, its mandate to all employers. Although the Chafee plan required individuals (as opposed to employers) to purchase insurance, the phase-in of universal coverage was expected to take many years and would depend on the availability of savings produced by competition among health plans. The Cooper plan, stripping away even more of the possible government control, eliminated any mandate for universal coverage and depended very heavily on market forces to make insurance more affordable. All plans agreed that private insurers should no longer exclude people on the basis of risk but they disagreed or remained vague about how to adjust reimbursements to make taking on higher-risk patients affordable. Plans also differed on how comprehensive the covered benefits should be in a basic plan eligible for subsidies and on who should make the determinations. Those who support more reliance on market forces and "consumer choice" of course want less government regulation of benefits.

Applying Design Principles to National Health Care Reform Proposals

What are the important design principles and how is one to apply them? In Chapter 1, I argued that the central, unifying purpose of health care is to promote "normal functioning"—functioning that is typical or normal for our species. By impairing normal functioning, disease and disability deny us our fair share of opportunity. Health care—be it preventive, acute, long-term, or palliative—thus protects equality of opportunity. Because we have a general social obligation to assure people fair equality of opportunity, we have specific obligations to provide health care services that promote normal function. These obligations require that there be no financial or other barriers to a level of care that promotes normal functioning, given reasonable or necessary limits on resources. My design principles spell out the implications of this view; they capture features and functions of a health care system that are important from the point of view of justice.

I will use these design principles to assess the answers to five central questions: Who is covered? What is covered? How are costs contained and efficiency assured? How are costs shared? What choices do consumers have? (These headings disguise points of overlap, and so some of the principles will appear or come up for discussion more than once.) I will first discuss what seem to me the relevant design principles under each question, and I will then summarize my analysis of the salient points made about the principles governing each question in table form (one table per question). In the tables, I have used symbols to indicate qualitative differences in the way the proposals comply (or do not) with the principles. The rationale for most of the judgments will have been provided in the text.[2]

As the debate about health care reform progresses, legislation may emerge that combines features from various proposals. For example, the Clinton Health Care Task Force originally recommended full parity between mental and physical health care. When the Health Security Act was presented, however, parity was eliminated in favor of a *promise* of parity by the year 2001. Other reform proposals weaken mental health benefits still further. But although the matrix of design principles will help us track the implications for fairness of these changes if legislation is passed and implemented, it is not exhaustive; it is a tool that begs for refinement.

Who Is Covered?

To protect equality of opportunity, health care institutions must provide appropriate, effective services to everyone, regardless of such facts about them as their race, economic status, geographical location, or health risks. Several of the design principles address aspects of this question.

Ideally, no one should be excluded from coverage; the Universal Coverage Principle makes that a requirement. Leaving significant "gaps" in insurance coverage violates this design principle. The Cooper plan, for instance, imposed no mandate on either employers or individuals to provide or purchase insurance. The result is that though it would be easier for some people to acquire insurance under this proposal, serious gaps are left, and universal coverage is but a distant goal.

Insurance gaps can arise for a variety of reasons, some of which might initially seem justified. Therefore, although strictly speaking I need only one design principle governing access to insurance and services in order to evaluate proposals, it will be useful—for analytic purposes—to look at more than one in order to focus attention on several of the ways universality can fail. For example, in a mixed public-private system in which the purchase of insurance is voluntary, people who "choose" not to buy coverage, though they can afford it, are responsible for their lack of coverage. If we as a society then provide needed medical services to these imprudent people, feeling an obligation to assist those in need, we encourage free-riders. Similarly, private insurers fearing adverse selection will identify and exclude high-risk insurees, even claiming they are obliged to do so because it is actuarially unfair and therefore unjust to force those at low risk to subsidize those at higher risk (a point I reviewed in detail in Chapter 4). Risk selection also traps people in jobs where *they do* have coverage; they dare not switch jobs for fear of losing the coverage.

Several design principles work to close these specific gaps in access. In a mixed system, a Compulsory Coverage Principle requires people to purchase private insurance. In a purely public, tax-financed system (such as Canada's), the principle is trivially satisfied because taxes are compulsory and coverage is therefore automatic. In a mixed public-private system, where employers or individuals must purchase insurance, the Compulsory Coverage Principle does away with free-riders. Requiring people to buy insurance makes their premiums function like a tax, but it also eliminates adverse selection, making it easier to require insurers to cover all people regardless of risk. Clinton's Health Security Act included provisions requiring any who are uninsured to enroll in a health plan at the time they apply for treatment; the problem would primarily involve the unemployed and self-employed, because of the universal employer mandate. Chafee's HEART proposal mandated individual purchase of insurance, quite probably making the problem of free-riders more widespread. HEART relied on the IRS and Department of Health and Human Services to track nonpurchasers through tax and medical records. The Cooper plan failed to alter the status quo, for it neither mandated coverage nor provided any mechanism for eliminating free-riders.

The Nonexclusion Principle closes the gap caused by insurance underwriting practices and by the latitude allowed under current legislation (called ERISA) to self-insuring employers. This principle prohibits the exclusion of people from coverage because of existing conditions or anticipated health risks. (Such a principle governs private German insurers.) As I showed in my earlier discussion of HIV and insurability, those who most need insurance in our current system—people with "prior conditions" and people at high risk—are denied coverage or given only reduced coverage at higher premiums.

In the popular mind, these exclusions undermine the whole point of insurance, which is to protect people by sharing risks as widely as possible. Insurers, however, view health insurance as another commodity in the risk-management market: People buy insurance to manage their health risks (which insurers like to imply are just like any other risks), and they should be charged a price that reasonably reflects only their own risks. The "product" should remain attractive or marketable to those who know they are at less than average risk, and adverse selection must be avoided. Sharing risks, however intuitively appealing, is no longer a marketable idea to those with low risk, once they know their risk is low.

The public's intuitive view about sharing risks can be supported by assigning a different social function to health insurance, as I argued in Chapter 4. In buying health insurance people are not simply buying economic security at an actuarially fair price; they are assuring themselves access to needed medical services. This is the function assigned to health insurance by the fair-equality-of-opportunity account. Because we have a shared, social obligation to protect people's opportunity against the effects of disease and disability, low-risk individuals cannot disavow an obligation to subsidize those at higher risk. That obligation is part of the cost of protecting opportunity for all—including in the end those who at present *appear* to be at low risk.

There is no room for actuarial fairness in a just health care system. Not only *must* those at higher risk be given coverage, they *must not* be made to bear the extra financial burden of their risks. The burden must be shared. Specifically, the Community Rating Principle requires that people pay a common price for insurance regardless of their level of risk.

In a single-payer system like Canada's, the whole population forms a single risk pool. No standard underwriting practices are possible. Nonexclusion is clearly satisfied, but community rating is not applicable since people pay their share of insurance costs through progressive taxes rather than insurance premiums.

The Clinton, Chafee, and Cooper proposals would have prohibited risk-based exclusions or reductions in coverage. Clinton's health alliances were required to sell insurance at community rates, while adjusting reimbursement rates of health plans that take on higher risk patients. Community rating can be protected in the Clinton plan if employers who "opt out" of health alliances pay a surcharge to the alliances whenever their employees form a lower-risk pool than health alliance insurees do. The Chafee and Cooper plans were less explicit than Clinton's about how nonexclusion and community rating might be accomplished. All of these plans, however, depended on developing a mechanism for "risk adjustment," so that health plans can be reimbursed in ways that compensate them for taking on higher-risk patients. Unfortunately, it is controversial whether the technology for risk adjustment can be developed and refined enough to enable full compliance with the principle. Some reform proposals—less comprehensive than the plans we are comparing—call for insurance market reform, including the elimination of risk exclusion and risk rating. If universal coverage is not mandated and made feasible, however, it is difficult to see what form the legislation could take that would enable it to accomplish its stated aims.

Protection of equality of opportunity through health insurance should not be left to the vagaries of employment status. According to the Portability Principle, coverage must persist outside one's home region; it must form a seamless web among all employed persons regardless of whether they are working full- or part-time, in a large or a small company, and so on. Portability promotes efficiency and security: People should not be chained to jobs because of their health status (or that of their dependents).

The Canadian Medicare card offers a paradigm of portability, assuring all who carry it access to any provider in the country. The McDermott-Wellstone proposal similarly complied fully with the Portability Principle. Clinton's plan boasted such a card, symbolizing access, but the existence of many different health plans would make portability a matter for negotiation among plans and for enforcement by health alliances. In addition, employees of large companies (with more than five thousand employees) that opted out of the health alliances might have to change plans and doctors if they change or lose jobs. If the Clinton proposal allowed smaller employers to act as "corporate alliances," then portability would be compromised further. The Chafee plan was set up in a way that made it difficult to assess issues of portability: Individuals would be able to buy plans that are not tied to their employment status or employer's choices, but many employers would still provide coverage. The Cooper plan also left many of the portability problems in the current

Table 1
Who Is Covered?

Design Principle	Current U.S.	Cooper Plan	Chafee Plan	Clinton Plan	Wellstone-McDermott (Single-Payer) Plan
Universal Coverage	V	PC	PC	C*	C*
Compulsory Coverage	V	V	C	C	C
Nonexclusion	V	PC·	PC●	C*	C
Community Rating	V	PC−	PC+	C++	C (DNA)
Portability	V	V	PC>	PC>>	C

V = Violates or maintains status quo
PC = Partial compliance or some improvement over status quo
C = Compliance or significant improvement over status quo
*   Except for nonlegal residents
·   Difficult without univeral coverage
● Risk adjustment more difficult without powerful health alliances
− Unclear how assured
+ Ideal only if risk adjustment works
++ Provided large employers who opt out subsidize premiums for alliance plans
> Some gain, some do not
>> Large employer opt-out reduces portability

system unaddressed. Still, to the extent that all three reform proposals eliminated risk exclusion, at least some of the barriers to portability were diminished.

Justice requires that nonfinancial barriers to access also be reduced. These barriers are diverse: lack of primary-care providers in rural and inner-city areas, cultural and educational barriers to utilization, physical barriers to the disabled. No one feature of design can address them all. The Clinton plan specifically confronted the issue of increasing the number of primary-care practitioners by changing the rules about medical education. The less comprehensive Chafee and Cooper proposals did not undertake to deal with these issues.

What Is Covered?

According to the fair-equality-of-opportunity account, we have social obligations to provide those services that most effectively and efficiently protect our fair shares of the normal opportunity range once reasonable or necessary limits on resources are taken into consideration. This includes preventive, curative, restorative, chronic, compensatory, and palliative services. But because scarcity is unavoidable—in part because health care is not the only important good people seek in a society—we cannot provide everyone with *all* beneficial services. Where we withhold services, however, we must assess their effect on protecting opportunity rather than arbitrarily limiting whole categories of service (as insurers now do with regard to preventive, mental-health, and long-term-care services, for instance). The fair-equality-of-opportunity account also of course rejects restrictions on beneficial services when they apply only to the poorest sectors of society.

The Comprehensive Benefits Principle comes into play here, telling us that all categories of service which meet health care needs will be included and that the judgments we make about including some services rather than others must be based on the effects of these services on the range of opportunities we enjoy. Such judgments will cut across the traditional categorical distinctions—like mental versus physical, preventive versus acute, and acute versus long-term—that have led to underprovision of many important services by both public and private insurers. In effect, comprehensive benefits are what is promised but not delivered when legislative or contract language assures us that insurance provides all "medically necessary" services (v. Sabin, Forrow, and Daniels, 1991b; Sabin and Daniels, 1994). Adherence to the principle would mean parity between mental and physical health, and an end to the bias in favor of acute-care services that we have now.

Our current system clearly violates the Comprehensive Benefits Principle. The Clinton plan appealed to the notion of a comprehensive, mandated benefits package, but recognized the principle without achieving full compliance with it. Although it added many preventive services and went some way toward establishing parity of benefits between mental and physical health, it made only incremental improvements in long-term care. The Chafee and Cooper plans left the full content of the benefits package unspecified, and the Chafee plan even left the door open to *reducing* the benefit package in unspecified ways if savings from reform are inadequate to fund subsidies needed to move the system toward universal coverage. The McDermott-Wellstone plan included a benefits package more comprehensive than the Clinton package, adding a more robust long-term-care benefit.

Our obligations to assure access to needed health care services extend only to providing efficacious services. We are obliged to provide what we have reasonable evidence to believe *works*. We are *not* obliged to provide unproven or unnecessary treatments. The Efficacy Principle emphasizes the need to fund research about health outcomes and to develop practice guidelines: We are woefully un-derinformed about which of our medical practices actually meet reasonable standards of efficacy. We do, however, have extensive evidence that much unnecessary treatment is given; regional varia-tions in utilization rates imply that utilization is supply-driven rather than need-driven (Hadorn, 1992; Kolata, 1994). This all means that we must develop not only information but incentives, regula-tion, and training for producing compliance with practice protocols. The Efficacy Principle implies we should cover proven therapies but not experimental ones, which means we need a fair process for decid-ing how to draw the distinction; it also requires distinguishing treat-ments of disease and disability from services that merely enhance function (or appearance) that is already normal for our species. (I do not undertake to comment here on this very particular application of my account, since I have done so elsewhere, and it does not in any case bear centrally on the issue at hand [v. Daniels, 1992; Sabin and Daniels, 1994]).

All the reform proposals criticize the current system for not com-plying with the Efficacy Principle and note the importance of mea-sures aimed at improving compliance. The Clinton proposal, with its premium caps and the expanded powers of the health alliances to provide consumers with information, put more pressure on health plans to induce providers to comply with the Efficacy Principle. It also emphasized improving consumer information about outcome measures of the different health plans. Still, it did not specify just what federal support will be given to outcomes research. The Chafee proposal also called for setting up an information system adequate to telling us more about outcomes and appropriate practice guidelines. The details of the system were not fully developed, however, and—like the Clinton plan—it failed to specify funding for outcomes re-search. The Cooper plan was silent on many of these matters. Finally, there is nothing about a single-payer system that makes it intrinsi-cally better than the Clinton proposal at complying with the Efficacy Principle. In the Canadian system, as in some managed-care plans, physicians internalize restraints on ineffective utilization because they must retain credibility with other professionals who control limited resources under global budgets. But all professionals still need hard information about what does and does not work.

Some people believe that rigid adherence to the Efficacy Princi-ple would make it unnecessary to engage in the rationing of benefi-cial services. Squeezing all the waste out of the system would suf-fice to make available resources adequate to meet other needs. This was the stance taken by the Clinton administration when members of the Ethics Working Group of its Health Care Task Force requested that the proposal pay careful attention to the need to limit the use of beneficial services—the need to ration. Those of us on the Ethics Working Group were told that there should be no mention of rationing in our writing about the plan, that rationing would not be necessary; the Clinton administration feared appearing to condone rationing. Despite this attempt to shield the plan from this type of criticism, advocates of other reforms attacked the Clinton plan anyway for opening the door to rationing, on the grounds that its premium cap and the powers it gives to a National Health Board to monitor the benefit package over time amounts to rationing. And so it does. These attacks were, however, highly disingenuous. The current system already rations care at many levels—by excluding people from both public and private insurance and by making many decisions about what services and technologies to cover. All reform proposals that fail to establish a fair mechanism for addressing rationing decisions will thus perpetuate the highly inconsistent and capricious set of decision-making processes we now employ—which themselves result in rationing. Given the rapid growth of new medical technologies—the prime force affecting the rate at which health care costs are increasing worldwide—we simply have to be prepared to make decisions about withholding some beneficial treatments whose costs are not worth their benefits (v. Schwartz, 1987; Newhouse, 1993).

When we ration beneficial services, we make choices about whose opportunities we will protect. Calabresi and Bobbitt (1978) argue that the social cost of publicly and explicitly making such "tragic choices" is high, and that sometimes we should sacrifice the legitimacy such openness brings in favor of less visible methods. Where rationing affects the fundamental life prospects of people, I believe the requirements of publicity are stringent, as I argued in Chapter 6. We need a publicly accountable process for making these decisions. The Explicit Rationing Principle says that the grounds or principles for establishing priorities among services must be publicly available and open to democratic criticism, and that rationing decisions must result from a fair process.

The fair-equality-of-opportunity principle, like other general distributive-justice principles, falls short of telling us precisely *how* to make certain rationing choices, as I noted in Chapter 6 (v. also Daniels, 1993). For example, although the equal-opportunity principle implies that we should give *some* priority to those whose opportunities are most seriously restricted, it does not tell us how much. Similarly, it allows us to sum up or aggregate the effects on the opportunities of various individuals, so that modest benefits to many people can sometimes outweigh more significant benefits to a few—but it does not tell us what principle of aggregation to employ. Again, it does not tell us how to weigh "getting the best outcome" from some service against "giving people a fair chance" at getting some benefit from it. Since we do not have principled solutions to these rationing problems, I will interpret the Explicit Rationing Principle to require a fair procedure that includes *making public* the grounds for all choices.

None of the reform proposals clearly complied with the Explicit Rationing Principle. The Clinton proposal assigned the National Health Board the task of deciding what treatments to include in the comprehensive benefits package, but it did not (for reasons explained above) mention rationing health care or even consider how to take costs explicitly into account when thinking about coverage decisions or quality of care. Clinton's plan included a mechanism for a "grievance procedure" within health plans to address complaints about benefits from both patients and doctors. Of course, an after-the-fact fair procedure for addressing complaints is better than nothing, but a fair procedure for making decisions about limits to care would be better yet. Other proposals did not specify anything that pertains to a public process for making rationing decisions. Moreover, it should be noted that single-payer systems are not immune from arranging to keep public scrutiny away from rationing decisions; the Canadian system has little provision for a public, democratic process in decisions about limitations on services.

The Structure of Inequality Principle says that restrictions on access to beneficial services must not apply primarily to the worst-off or poorest groups. Suppose that budget limitations mean we cannot include certain (significant) beneficial services in the only plan low-income people can afford. If these benefits are then available to most other people—who can afford to buy better insurance—the structure of inequality is unacceptable. In contrast, if these benefits are available only to the richest groups in society, and the great majority—including the poor—cannot afford them, then the structure of inequality is more acceptable. Fair equality of opportunity proscribes leaving the poor well behind the rest of society, but it does not mean that strict equality is a requirement in health care rationing. Whether the extra advantages enjoyed by the rich are acceptable will further depend on how significant those advantages are judged to be (and on whether the income distribution is itself just, overall).

Our current system fails to comply with the Structure of Inequality Principle; at the other extreme, the McDermott-Wellstone single-payer system would. We have contemporary examples in other countries as well. Consider how the Canadian system works: The best-off Canadians avoid queues and purchase some services in the United States, but the great majority of persons are all affected roughly alike by rationing decisions. Similarly, in Germany and the Netherlands, the wealthiest third of the population may enjoy more amenities in its private insurance, but the rich receive no treatments offering *significant* benefits that are unavailable through public schemes.

The Clinton proposal tried to limit violation of this principle within a managed-competition system by setting a 20 percent limit on the degree to which health plans can exceed the benchmark price for health plans. The goal was to limit both the degree to which more expensive plans could portray themselves as vastly superior in quality and the degree to which low-cost plans would be labeled as low-quality, with the result that low-income people dependent on subsidies would be locked in to the lowest tier of plans. If the only differences between plans are in amenities, market segmentation would not clearly violate the Structure of Inequality Principle. Richer plans, however, can also "buy" more or better specialists, or introduce cutting-edge technologies more quickly. Where significant effects on health outcomes result, the Structure of Inequality principle is violated; regulatory restrictions prohibiting such inequalities, e.g., restricting the range of premiums charged or offering more generous subsidies, would go some distance toward satisfying it.

The other proposals, which emphasized their appeal to market forces, did not impose any restrictions on the emergence of such tiering and inequality. To some extent, this problem is obscured by the claim that a basic, uniform benefits package will be described by an appropriate commission, both in the Chafee and Cooper plans. The basic package may turn out to be thin; even if it is not, plans that charge more, selling themselves on quality, may develop different coverage patterns despite the apparent uniformity of benefits. Medicaid offers broad benefits, like many other insurers, for instance. But it offers (or is typically perceived to offer) a distinctly lower quality of care. Replicating the inequalities between Medicaid and the best private insurance plans would certainly violate the Structure of Inequality Principle.

Table 2
What Is Covered?

Design Principle	Current U.S.	Cooper Plan	Chafee Plan	Clinton Plan	Wellstone-McDermott (Single Payer) Plan
Comprehensive Benefits	V	V+	PC++	PC+++	PC+++
Efficacy	V	PC	PC>	PC>	PC?
Explicit Rationing	V	V??	V??	PC??	PC??
Structure of Inequality	V	·V&	V&	PC&	C

V   = Violates or maintains status quo
PC = Partial compliance or some improvement over status quo
C   = Compliance or significant improvement over status quo
+   Does not provide adequate details on benefits
++ Covers only serious mental illness; no long-term care
+++ Clinton plan promises full parity of mental and physical in 2001, offers extensive preventive services and some expansion of long-term care; details on McDermott-Wellstone plan to be provided
>   All reform proposals talk about using outcomes research, but Clinton and Chafee plans propose information systems that would support such research efforts
?   Advocates of single-payer systems say less about outcomes research, relying more on the global budget, but this is short-sighted
?? Cooper and Chafee plans allow benefits to vary by tier according to ability to pay; Clinton plan's task force was instructed to avoid public talk about rationing, though the National Health Board might have the task within its powers; rationing by queuing, as in Canada, is itself explicit, but there is not enough attention to fair public processes for deciding what queues should exist
&   Clinton plan allows only 20 percent gap between benchmark and high-cost plants, reducing tiering; Chafee and Cooper plans do not counter tiering

How Are Costs Contained and Efficiency Assured?

Efficiency is often thought to compete with justice: Fairness can be costly, and efficiency may be unfair (to some). Nevertheless, promoting efficiency within a just system by avoiding wasteful use of resources will enhance its fairness in crucial ways. A wasteful system puts too many health care dollars into administrative costs, or into treatments that do not work, or into services that provide very little benefit relative to the cost involved. As a result, such wasteful systems force the rationing of useful services that less wasteful systems can afford to deliver. A wasteful system thus leaves some individuals and groups at risk, while a less wasteful system better protects them. Justice requires we meet our health care obligations with as little waste as possible.

By raising the overall costs of delivering reasonable medical benefits, a wasteful system can drain resources into the health care sector that could be better spent elsewhere. Promoting health—however important—is not our only important social goal, a point to which I have already drawn attention. For example, a larger investment in education or job training might actually protect the range of opportunities open to people more than the investment we make in low-benefit medical services.

Some people object to restricting what we spend on health care, claiming that there is no one spending level that justice requires or permits. People "vote" with their dollars; if people vote in this manner for more health insurance, then that is the democracy of the market in action. To sing such a refrain is to ignore the degree to which corporations and professionals control this vote; it also ignores the fact that other social goods do not compete with health care on a level playing field in our system. We determine expenditures for many other socially important programs—like education, crime protection, social welfare, and defense—when our representatives pass government budgets. But our largely private "votes" to buy health care services are what determine our collective health care expenditures, including those in entitlement programs.

Several design principles aim at reducing waste within the health care sector and at preventing us from spending too much on health care. The Comparability Principle requires that demand for health care services should compete with the demand for other comparably important social goods through mechanisms that control supply in similar ways. We express our demand for educational services, police and fire protection, national defense, public health, transportation, and social welfare programs largely through our tax dollars; we weigh their relative importance through public-budget decisions. In contrast, we express our demand for health services largely through tax-sheltered employee benefits, while professionals who act as our agents tell us what we need and spend our dollars for us. At best, these agents "pull out all the stops" and do "everything possible" for us; at worst, they manage the demand for a good they have a vested interest in promoting. Both "best" *and* "worst" inflate demand in this instance.

Two market strategies aim at improving comparability. Some conservative economists recommend "privatizing" other government functions, but they have failed to persuade us that our social obligations can be met that way. We will continue to make public-budget choices, not merely private ones, for other important goods. Comparability must therefore be sought another way. Managed competition tries to eliminate the distorting influence of public (tax) subsidies on private decisions, for example, by reducing tax sheltering for employee benefits. But raising private "cost consciousness" in this way will not force the same discipline that we show in the public sphere, where the goods directly compete with one another. In any case, cost consciousness also erects significant barriers to access based on ability to pay. Comparability must be sought in the public sphere.

The global budgeting of health care expenditures achieves comparability in the public sphere. I shall operationalize the Comparability Principle by substituting a Global Budgeting Principle for it. The broader the scope of a global budget (that is, the more health care expenditures it captures) and the "harder" (or more enforceable) it is, the more effectively the public can act on its choices about the importance of health care.

The Global Budgeting Principle is clearly violated by the current system, while it is satisfied by a Canadian-style single-payer system like the McDermott-Wellstone proposal. The Clinton plan proposed that a National Health Board set a premium cap on the growth of health care expenditures in a given year. States would be accountable for staying within the cap. To control cost increases, a global budget must prevent cost shifting. This is most straightforwardly done when all existing insurance sectors—Medicaid, Medicare, veterans, Department of Defense, workmen's compensation, and all supplementary insurance—are integrated under one budget, and there is a specified agency accountable for translating the budget into component budgets for different elements in the health care system. The Clinton proposal would likely be in partial compliance with the Global Budgeting Principle, since it left some room for health expenditures not captured by a premium cap. Neither the Chafee nor the Cooper plan called for any kind of budget cap, relying instead solely on market forces to contain health care costs.

The Global Budgeting Principle seeks comparability between health care and other social goods, but global budgeting also aims at reducing wasteful services within the health care sector. Canada uses its global budget to force decentralized decisions about the priorities that should be followed in delivering other health care services. Physicians who do not follow reasonable priorities in, say, pursuing CT scans or home health services for their own patients (claiming their patients are urgent cases when they are not), are soon seen as uncooperative. Doctors of necessity learn to internalize a sense of restraint—even though they work on a fee-for-service basis—which encourages less wasteful use of resources. Some of these effects are possible within the global budgets of well-run managed-care plans.

Global budgeting and competition need not be mutually exclusive: They may be combined in various ways and at different levels in a health care system. The Clinton proposal incorporated competition among health plans within a globally budgeted system, gambling that competition would generate highly efficient delivery systems once cost shifting were eliminated by the force of a global budget. The gamble is that gains in efficiency will outweigh the higher administrative costs of a more complex system. The proposal also gambled that competition would not push costs up if "upscale" tiers created a demand for enriching the lower tiers. But managed-care systems also reformulate ratios between specialists and primary-care generalists without invoking the heavy hand of the government. Simply introducing a single-payer system like Canada's in the United States would not bring with it parallel savings unless we also established their more favorable ratio of generalists to specialists.

In light of these remarks, we must be tentative in assessing compliance with the Efficient Management Principle, which seeks the delivery of effective health care with low administrative costs in a system that is easy for doctors and patients to use. The current system clearly fails to comply; its private insurance sector has high administrative costs and imposes a serious hassle factor on both doctors and patients through complex re-imbursement procedures and micromanagement of clinical decision-making. In contrast, the Canadian single-payer system has remarkably low administrative costs and imposes little bureaucratic burden on either patient or doctor. The Chafee and Cooper plans promised little to reduce the complexity and administrative inefficiency of the current system. Both plans in effect gambled that competition among managed-care plans would produce administrative savings, despite increased complexity—but it should be noted that little in the experience of managed care in the United States to date gives us reason to be optimistic on that score. The Clinton proposal made the same gamble, but it also sought to simplify medical reporting requirements and reimbursement processing. If increased competition under a global budget drives many insurers out of the market, some complexity would be eliminated. Putting more information in the hands of consumers about the performance of different plans would also create pressure to simplify administration, since consumer satisfaction is likely to be lower in plans that have a high hassle factor. Still, how well the Clinton proposal would perform in this arena is a matter of speculation: The competitive forces have an unknown effect, while the complexity of the system is a familiar worry for practitioners.

Physicians accept a role as gatekeepers if they see that role as deriving from their own sense of what competent medicine requires under fair and reasonable resource constraints. Professionally generated practice guidelines, internalized through good training in environments that support those guidelines and backed up by profiling of physicians, are far more likely to promote efficiency than microregulation of case-by-case clinical decisions by insurance bureaucrats. In the best HMOs, providers are involved in the process of developing practice guidelines, believe in their content, and accept the constraints of managed care with little gaming of the system. Whether more intense competition will support or undercut such successful management practices is unclear.

A focus on primary care is a key to controlling costs in the Canadian system, in many European systems, and within managed-care plans. Compliance with the Primary Care Principle, which calls for needs-based distribution of generalists and specialists, would mean that fewer specialists would have incentives to overutilize and overdisseminate specialized technologies. The principle is clearly violated in the United States as a whole, while it is satisfied in Canada. The Chafee and Cooper proposals relied on each health plan to define its own ratio. In theory, this puts pressure on specialists to undertake more primary-care work and creates a long-term incentive to reduce the number of specialists being trained. The Clinton proposal added to these pressures by refocusing training funds on primary-care physicians, and in so doing more clearly aimed at compliance than did the other reform proposals (which said little or nothing about the matter).

One design principle that simultaneously addresses cost containment and the allocation of personnel is the Negotiated Fee Principle. Canadian provinces negotiate directly with the provincial medical association to establish a fee structure for a whole region. The fee structure keeps physician costs within the constraints of a global budget and creates incentives to alter primary-care to specialist ratios. None of the reform proposals except single payer comply with this design principle, though it will be available under the Clinton plan to states that choose a single-payer plan. The Clinton plan—like the Chafee and Cooper plans—relied mainly on negotiation with individual managed-care plans to contain fee increases and incorporate incentives to alter the composition of the health care

Table 3
How Are Costs Contained and Efficiency Assured?

Design Principle	Current U.S.	Cooper Plan	Chafee Plan	Clinton Plan	Wellstone-McDermott (Single Payer) Plan
Global Budgeting (Comparability)	V	V	V	PC	C
Efficient Management	V	V	PC?	PC?	C?
Primary Care	V	V>	V>	PC>	PC>
Negotiated Fee	V	V	V	V	C
Tort Litigation Reduction	V	PC*	PC*	PC*	PC*

V   = Violates or maintains status quo
PC = Partial compliance or some improvement over status quo
C   = Compliance or significant improvement over status quo
?   Managed competition gambles that competition will produce delivery efficien-
      cies that offset the complexity lacking in low-administrative-cost single-payer
      systems
>   Managed-care plans redefine generalist to specialist ratios within the plans, but it
      is unclear what effect they have on overall ratios; Clinton plan refocuses training
      and incentives on primary care; introducing single-payer in U.S. has no short-
      term solution to unfavorable ratios unless explicit measures to redefine ratios are
      undertaken.
*   All reform proposals talk about some malpractice reform; this row is a
      placeholder for a more detailed evaluation not provided here

workforce. Whether these mechanisms are as effective at achieving what is done through regionally negotiated fees is unknown.

Compliance with the Tort Litigation Reduction Principle would also reduce waste in the system. Any reform would have to reduce the defensive overutilization of services by physicians and the costs of liability insurance, while retaining a fair procedure for compensatory justice. I do not evaluate the reform proposals for compliance with this principle in my next table, but I include the principle to indicate that it will need to be part of any final, complete assessment of the fairness of a reform proposal.

How Are Costs Shared?

Although our obligation to provide access to needed health care services is a social one, the fair-equality-of-opportunity account itself does not have anything to say about the fair distribution of income and wealth or about fair patterns of taxation or subsidization. Earlier, when I defended the Community Rating Principle, I argued that those at low risk cannot disavow an obligation to subsidize the costs of those at high risk; this falls short of telling us how to finance our general obligation to provide health care services, however—an issue that deserves at least a brief discussion.

One main option is to retain health insurance premiums and to subsidize their purchase for people who cannot afford them. Financing for such a subsidy can itself be funded through more progressive or less progressive forms of taxation. By relying on the Financing by Ability to Pay Principle, this option captures one crucial element of fair sharing: No one shall be denied coverage because of the *lack* of ability to pay. Compared to our current system, it involves the least redistribution of income even though families will vary enormously in their ability to pay for health insurance premiums. The second main option is to finance purchase of insurance through a more progressive tax, a move that itself divides into more progressive and less progressive alternatives— depending on which kind of tax is chosen. A fixed-percentage payroll tax would be more progressive than a premium-based contribution, but it would be less progressive than a graduated income tax (especially one that included, as taxable, unearned income). For my purposes here—where I am concerned primarily with introducing the *idea* of these design principles—it will suffice to assume that the more progressive the tax base, the more fairly costs are shared (a more exhaustive account would of course have to defend this assumption); I have, accordingly, constructed Table 4 on the strength of that assumption. The table also repeats the assessment of the Community Rating Principle because that also captures a critical feature of the fair sharing of costs.

What Choices Do Consumers Have?

A health care system defines a set of choices for both consumers (patients, purchasers of insurance) and practitioners. The fair-equality-of-opportunity account says little about choice: To say that whatever arrangements best promote equal opportunity without violating anyone's basic liberties are acceptable does not suffice; more must be said about choice from the perspective of justice and fair treatment. Specifically, I urge a Consumer Choice Principle, which requires that a health care system facilitate making effective and informed choices about providers, health care plans, and treatments. Choice in each of these areas is affected by the range of options open to us, the information we have about them, and the number of people who can exercise these choices; there may *be* no "best" pro-

Table 4
How Are Costs Shared?

Design Principle	Current U.S.	Cooper Plan	Chafee Plan	Clinton Plan	Wellstone-McDermott (Single Payer) Plan
Financing by Ability to Pay	V	PC?	PC??	PC???	C&
Community Rating	V	PC−	PC+	C++	C (DNA)

V = Violates or maintains status quo
PC = Partial compliance or some improvement over status quo
C = Compliance or significant improvement over status quo
? Increased subsidization for people who cannot now buy insurance, so plan is somewhat more progressive than current system
?? No progressive taxation in the plan; improvement comes from a more generous subsidy to individuals with incomes well above federal poverty level, but funds for subsidies must come from savings elsewhere in the system
??? Regressive tobacco tax is proposed, plus a mandate for employer contributions, with subsidies for small employers; no new progressive tax base is proposed
& Payroll tax is proposed
− Unclear how assured
+ Ideal only if risk adjustment works
++ Provided large employers who opt out subsidize

posal for promoting consumer choice, since enhancing choice in one area may require trade-offs with choices in another. Consumer choice is important for the health of the system and not just for individuals: Informed, effective choice is a powerful engine of reform, driving concerns about quality and cost.

Today it is widely recognized that patients have the right to give informed, voluntary consent to the treatments they undergo. Though this is sometimes cast simply as a right to refuse certain treatments, it has broader implications for the process of deciding about treatments. Physicians must invest the time to discuss alternative, *available* treatments with patients so they can make informed choices that reflect their own values and preferences. Reimbursements to plans and providers must therefore provide incentives to give that time. Moreover, good information about outcomes must be available, or the physician cannot properly inform patients; this kind of information, too, has costs associated with it.

The choice of health plans is complex, since plans differ in the services they cover, in the quality of their services, in their amenities, and in their price. In the system current in the United States, consumers have poor information about the performance of health plans; they may have some information about coverage (though it is often not detailed), and they have access to information about costs (though it is often confusing because of co-payment and deductible requirements). To empower consumer choices about health plans, a significant investment must be made in providing information about both outcomes and consumer satisfaction in various areas of treatment. Without such information, consumer choice in health care is far less informed than the choices made by those same consumers when they buy cars or plumbing fixtures (which at least are reviewed in *Consumer Reports*). Provision of the information cannot be left to the health plans: There must be an independent agency responsible for making information about plan performance readily available (and helping to assure that it can be understood). The effective range of choices open to people is also important. If tiering occurs, because health plans compete on price and there are significant premium differences among health plans, then the choice range for low-income individuals will be reduced.

"Choice" for most people means choice of physician. Proponents of managed competition argue that Americans overvalue having a choice of physicians, since these choices are generally not well informed. For example, people typically turn for recommendations to friends or relatives who have little hard information even about their own physicians. The alternative may not be to replace choice of physician with choice of health plan, but rather to provide better information about the performance of physicians. In any case, it will be particularly important to devise a system that does not require interfering with the satisfactory, long-term relationships with physicians that many people have—and fear losing. This may be an especially critical issue for people with disabilities or other special medical problems, but a good relationship with a specialist *or* a primary-care physician cannot always be easily replicated.

Evaluating the various proposals for their effect on consumer choice is particularly difficult because there are so many different dimensions of choice. The current health care system in the United States clearly fails to protect (or even in some instances to offer) consumer choice, in several important ways. Though some people can (at great cost) retain a choice of physician, many others lose those choices because of the power employers have to select and impose health plans (which in turn restrict physician choice). For many people, whether they realize it or not, the status quo is actually on course to reduce significantly their choices of physician. In addition, there is little provision at present for adequate information about physicians, plans, *or* treatments. We may be better at informing patients about treatments than many other countries, but we know no more than others about what works.

The Cooper plan would put the power of choice in the hands of employers rather than consumers in many cases and it did not address the problem of information. Aside from providing some more people with coverage—people who now have no choice of plan or physician—there is no clear gain over the status quo. The Chafee plan mandated individuals to purchase insurance; to the extent that some or many employers would stop providing insurance, there could be an unanticipated gain in individual choice. The availability of a comprehensive information system could be used to increase choice of plans, but the Chafee proposal did not pursue this idea as far as the Clinton plan—which emphasized developing "report cards" to provide information about plan performance. The Clinton plan, like the Chafee and Cooper plans, would drive more people into managed care, costing some people their existing choice of physicians; however, the plan reduces employer control over choice of plans, except for very large employers. Moreover, the Clinton proposal mandated that all alliances—corporate and public—offer an indemnity plan with full choice of physicians. (The cost of the plan might have put these choices out of reach of most people, however.)

A single-payer system could leave people with a much broader choice of physicians, even if it eliminated the choice of plans. Proponents of the Canadian system argue that no one cares about choice of *plans* as long as a choice of physician and hospital is still available. Information about the performance of physicians and hospitals is no better in Canada than it is here, however, and thus we are faced with the choice between the known satisfaction expressed about the choice available in the Canadian system and the promise of benefits that will result if we give ourselves effective choices among competing health plans.

Fairness, Reform, and the Needs of HIV Patients

Since many of the problems of fair treatment faced by HIV patients are *systemic* problems that affect everyone, comprehensive health care reform is the single most important step we can take to enhance fair treatment. In the debate about health care reform, fairness is usually not a prominent issue: We hear instead about costs, efficiency, and political feasibility. I have here developed a framework—a matrix—for assessing the fairness or justice of competing reform

Table 5
What Choices Do Consumers Have

Consumer Choice Principle		Current U.S.	Cooper Plan	Chafee Plan	Clinton Plan	Wellstone-McDermott (Single Payer) Plan
Physicians	R	PC*	PC*	PC*	PC*	C
	I	V	V	V	V	V
Plans	R	PC**	PC**	PC**	PC**	DNA
	I	V	V	PC?	C	DNA
Treatments	R	PC−	PC−	PC−	PC+	C
	I	PC−	PC−	PC−	PC+	PC

R = Range of choices
I = Steps taken to provide adequate information
V = Violates or maintains status quo
PC = Partial compliance or some improvment over status quo
C = Compliance
* Partial compliance varies in these cases; current system has little choice for uninsured, decreasing choice for many, considerable choice for some; Cooper plan has decreasing choice as managed care increases, leaving employers with control of plan choices in many cases; Chafee plan may reduce employer provision, and some buying through alliances may leave some employees with more choice; Clinton plan promises every health alliance retains plan giving full physician choice, but decreases in choice for those in managed care, while decreased control by employer increases choices
** Current system has myriad plans in some areas, few in others, control of range by employers, recent growth of PPOs (some with options to increase choice of specialist); Cooper plan will not change current forces except that more individuals will have some choice of plan because of more subsidy for insurance; Chafee plan may reduce somewhat employer choice of plans and increase individual choice, but not by design; Clinton plan reduces employer choice of plans significantly (except for large employers) and mandates health alliances to offer options including full-choice plan; Clinton plan may lead to fewer overall plans
? Unclear whether extra effort to provide good consumer info
−/+ Negative/positive interference with doctor/patient decisions by insurers, except for Clinton plan promise to simplify microregulation; improved information on what works in Clinton plan and possibly in Chafee plan

proposals. Drawing on my fair-equality-of-opportunity account of justice and health care, I have articulated a set of design principles that describe essential features and functions of a just health care system.

The application of this matrix to recent reform proposals yields the conclusion that the Canadian-style single-payer plan complied better with the design principles than any of the alternatives, though all plans offered some improvement over the status quo. The Clinton proposal, which gave states a choice of a single-payer or a modified version of managed competition, did almost as well; the Chafee and Cooper plans fell off sharply in their fair treatment of everyone in the system. The crucial issue of political feasibility—which I have not discussed at all—of course has to be faced at some point. Clearly, many design features of the Clinton plan were aimed at making it politically more acceptable than a pure single-payer plan, might be. Whether Clinton underestimated the public acceptability of the single-payer plan, or overestimated public willingness to accept government regulation is hard to assess. He clearly underestimated the power of the lobbies representing insurers and other vested interests to confuse the public with expensive advertising campaigns. I only hope that the sudden collapse of Congressional support for comprehensive reform at the end of 1993 is the result of such disinformation and the confusion it produced rather than the result of the public and its representatives deliberately refusing to meet a social obligation they had begun to articulate and understand. I will leave further exploration of these matters to others, however, because *my* goal is ethical rather than political analysis.

Let me return, therefore, to my starting point: What issues of fair treatment for HIV patients are not addressed by national health care reform? In many instances, the shortfall for HIV patients will be a shortfall for everyone. This is because the needs of HIV patients are similar to the needs of many other patients; there is, after all, in one sense little that is unique about HIV—even if the seriousness of the AIDS epidemic has brought every aspect of the health system *as it affects HIV patients* into sharp relief.

Consider some of the most important health care needs of HIV patients and how there may be a shortfall for them even after national health care reform has been accomplished. If the mental health benefits are not given parity with physical health benefits, this will affect the treatment of HIV patients along with others. If the adequacy of coverage for drugs leaves HIV patients at some risk, it will probably affect people with other conditions as well. We can be sure that the reforms on the table now will not solve the problems of long-term care faced by HIV patients—for example, the coverage of adequate home care and social support services; but then, neither will they address in a serious way the problems all of us face in this area of health care. Similarly, HIV patients have problems finding primary and specialty care in many regions of the country—and it is unlikely that recent reform proposals have adequately addressed this problem (though it at least received serious attention in the Clinton plan). Another example is the growing problem for some HIV patients with the inadequacy of drug-abuse treatment programs—a problem hardly confined to those infected with HIV. The Clinton and Wellstone-McDermott plans, for instance, improved coverage in this area—but others did not. There was also some provision in the Clinton plan for support for clinical trials, which is of great interest to HIV patients, but here, too, the comprehensiveness of the benefit package is an obvious target for compromise.

Indeed, the comprehensiveness of the benefits package is one of the central areas of disagreement among reform proposals. Those who oppose large-scale reform see too generous a package as one of their prime targets. This is a strong hint that until we as a society are prepared to acknowledge more generally the societal obligation to provide a fair equality of opportunity to all, we are unlikely to achieve justice in our health care system.

The HIV/AIDS epidemic has taught us many lessons about the shortcomings of our health care system. More than that, it has brought into sharp relief the larger issues of our rights and responsibilities in health care. If we take these seriously, and have the political courage to reform our system, we will all live better lives. Fair treatment is a unifying idea: The issue is not how "we" treat "them," how the uninfected treat those with HIV. The real issue is how we all treat one another. But how we treat one another in our health care system is a metaphor for how we treat one another in all the dimensions of our social life. Or so I hope I have shown.

Notes

Chapter 1: AIDS & The Moral Fabric of Society

1. When Rawls (1971) developed his arguments for a principle assuring fair equality of opportunity, he had simplified his theory by assuming people functioned normally over the whole course of their lives. My account suggests how Rawls's theory can be extended (an approach he endorses [Rawls, 1993]) and shows how to reconcile Rawls and Sen (1992); cf. Daniels, 1990. My account does not presuppose Rawls's theory, however, but rests only on a general principle guaranteeing fair equality of opportunity.

Chapter 2: The Duty to Treat

1. Though I will not comment further on it, it is worth noting that this account faces a common objection raised against virtue ethic accounts in general: Someone can fall short of carrying out some ideal of virtuous behavior without being subject to public sanction for having failed in his duty.

2. It is worth noting the converse problem for those who emphasize the consensual nature of acquired obligations: We seem to acquire some duties, such as filial duties, even though we did not consent to be children (v. Daniels, 1988:Chs. 2 and 7, for an attempt at a contractarian view of filial obligations).

3. Some hospitals in high-incidence areas are reluctant to "force" the issue. Informal understandings arise about which physicians will accept HIV referrals and which will not; some institutions allow this to become explicit, setting up a formal division of labor. Where cumulative risks are

182

estimated to exceed the standard, any of these methods involves a way for physicians (less so for other staff!) to accept or refuse the extra risks. Where risks are within the standard level, however, not reaffirming the duty to treat and tolerating systematic violation of it are tantamount to renegotiating the extent to which it is a duty.

Chapter 3: HIV-Infected Surgeons and Dentists

1. The suggestion that biomedical ethics and public health considerations represent conflicting moral frameworks with conflicting standards was suggested to me by Ronald Bayer. The point developed here is a variation on that theme.

Chapter 4: AIDS and Insurability

1. The Office of Technology Assessment (1988:3) Survey showed that 86 percent of commercial insurers screen for HIV infection, with about 50 percent using tests for HIV either for all applicants or for selected applicants; 73 percent of Blue Cross/Blue Shield plans screened for HIV with personal history questionnaires, and 60 percent sometimes used an attending physician's statement (APS) to help determine risk for AIDS, but none used tests for HIV; 53 percent of responding HMOs screen for AIDS (20 percent of respondents are prohibited by state law from screening), 40 percent use attending physician's statements, and 13 percent use tests for HIV.

2. It might be thought that I have confused cause and effect, and that social insurance *must* be mandatory simply because it is actuarially unfair. People who are being treated unfairly would not voluntarily become members of the scheme (Dan McGill, personal communication, 1990). This objection begs the question, however, because it assumes that what is actuarially fair *is* thereby fair—precisely what I am endeavoring to demonstrate is not true. To be sure, social insurance keeps individuals from pursuing the economic advantage that might result from having low risks in an actuarially fair system; but what is at issue here is whether it is *unfair* to deny them that chance to pursue their self-interest. If we have social obligations to protect fair equality of opportunity by guaranteeing access to health care insurance, then—as I have attempted to explain already—it is not unfair to set up a system that is actuarially unfair.

Chapter 7: Morality. Prevention, and Sex Education

1. Although I draw on Rawls (1993) for the philosophical framework of my remarks about public reason, he is careful to restrict the role of public reason to deliberation about matters that affect the basic terms of social cooperation—the principles of justice and their embodiment in constitutional law. Where policy touches on the distribution of basic goods, like

health protection or education, in nonconstitutional settings, I believe some extension of Rawls's argument is needed; I may have gone beyond where he would.

Chapter 8: Fairness and National Health Care Perform

1. In March 1993, I presented a paper articulating design principles for assessing health care reform at a conference at the Dana-Farber Institute. Also that month I began participating as a member of the Ethics Working Group of the White House Health Care Task Force. The Dana-Farber paper influenced the work of the Ethics Working Group. Specifically, when Dan Brock and I formulated a set of "Ethical Principles and Values for the New Health Care System," we drew on ideas in the original draft. Further discussion within the Ethics Working Group, and especially with Dan Brock (Brown University), with whom I co-authored Brock and Daniels (1994), as well as comments by Robert Baker (Union College) and Donald Light (Rutgers), have led me to modify somewhat the design principles originally discussed in March 1993, adding a few and modifying the description of others. The articulation of this matrix of design principles is part of a larger project Donald Light and I have worked on, supported by the Robert Wood Johnson Foundation. In that work, the design principles, considerably modified, have evolved into benchmarks that can be used to score reform proposals on a numerical scale (v. Daniels, Light, and Caplan 1994).

2. It should be noted that the evaluations the tables contain—as I have included them here—are only qualitative, sometimes involving judgments about the degree of compliance or improvement over the status quo; it is possible, however, to develop more refined criteria for the application of these principles and to score compliance with them numerically (for numerically scoreable "benchmarks of fairness," v. Daniels, Light, and Caplan, 1994). Given that my goal in this context is to illustrate how we can assess the fairness of health care reforms, however, it is not necessary to pursue here the complications such a scoring system involves.

References

Allen, James R. 1988. "Health Care Workers and the Risk of HIV Transmission." in *Hastings Center Report* 18 (suppl.): 2–5.

Altman, L.K. 1991a. "An AIDS Puzzle: What Went Wrong in the Dentist's Office." *New York Times* (July 30):C3.

———1991b. "Medical Units Lag on AIDS Guidelines." *New York Times* (August 30):A1, A19.

———. 1991c. "Dentists' Group Offers No List for AIDS Risk." *New York Times* (October 11):A12.

———. 1991d. "Agency Faulted on List to Show AIDS Risks." *New York Times* (November 5):C2.

———. 1991e. "U.S. Backs Off on Plan to Restrict Health Workers with AIDS Virus." *New York Times* (December 4):A1, C19.

American Medical Association 1987. Council on Ethical and Judicial Affairs. "Ethical Issues Involved in the Growing AIDS Crisis." December (cited in Freedman 1988).

———. 1988. Council on Ethical and Judicial Affairs. "Ethical Issues Involved in the Growing AIDS Crisis." in *JAMA* 259(9):1360.

———. 1991. "Statement on HIV Infected Physicians." January 17, Chicago.

American Nurses' Association 1986. Committee on Ethics. "Statements Regarding Risk v. Responsibility in Providing Nursing Care." (cited in Freedman 1988).

Annas, George J. 1988. "Legal Risks and Responsibilities of Physicians in the AIDS Epidemic." *Hastings Center Report* 18 (suppl.):26–32.

Antonarakis, S.E. 1989. "Diagnosis of Genetic Disorders at the DNA Level." *New England Journal of Medicine* 320(3):153–61.

Applebome, P. 1987. "Doctor in Texas with AIDS Virus Closes His Practice Amid a Furor." *New York Times* (October 1):B8 (cited in Barnes et al. 1990: 311).

Arras, J. 1988. "The Fragile Web of Responsibility: AIDS and the Duty to Treat." *Hastings Center Report* 18(suppl.):10–20.

Baldo, M., Aggleton, P., Slutkin, G. 1993. "Does Sex Education Lead to Earlier or Increased Sexual Activity in Youth?" WHO Global Programme on AIDS. Abstracts from Berlin AIDS Conference. June 1993.

Barnes, M., Rango, N.A., Burke, G.R., and Chiarello, L. 1990. "The HIV-Infected Health Care Professional: Employment Policies and Public Health." *Law, Medicine, and Health Care* 18:4:311–30.

Barr, Stephen 1994. "What if the Dentist Didn't Do It?" *New York Times* (April 16):A21.

Barry, B. 1989. *Theories of Justice*. Berkeley: University of California Press.

Bass, A. 1991. "Health Chief: AIDS Shouldn't Bar Doctors." *Boston Globe* (October 12):25, 27.

———. 1993. "AIDS Prevention Plans Work Elsewhere, Data Say." *Boston Globe* (March 5):21, 24.

Berwick, D. 1991. "The Double Edge of Knowledge." *JAMA* 266(6):841–42.

Blake, J. 1993. NBC Documentary. Boston.

Blendon, R.J., and Donelan, K. 1990. "The Public and the Emerging Debate over National Health Insurance." *New England Journal of Medicine* 323 (3):208–12.

Boyd, C. 1991. "Florida AIDS Mystery: How Dentist Infected His Patients May Never Be Known." *Boston Globe* 240(Aug 26):3.

Brock, D., and Daniels, N. 1994. "Ethical Foundations of the Clinton Administration's Proposed Health Care System." *JAMA* 271:15:1189–96.

Buchanan, A. 1989. "Public and Private Responsibilities in the U.S. Health Care System." (Unpublished ms, Blue Cross/Blue Shield Association.)

Calabresi, G., Bobbitt, P. 1978. *Tragic Choices*. New York: W.W. Norton.

Callahan, D. 1987. 1987. *Setting Limits: Medical Goals in an Aging Society*. New York: Simon and Schuster.

Centers for Disease Control (CDC) 1989. "Guidelines for Prevention of Transmission of Human Immunodeficiency Virus and Hepatitis B Virus to Health-Care and Public Safety Workers. *Morbidity and Mortality Weekly Report* (June 23, supp. 6):5–6.

———. 1991a. "Estimates of the Risk of Endemic Transmission of Hepatitis B Virus and Human Immunodeficiency Virus to Patients by the Percutaneous Route During Invasive Surgical and Dental Procedures." January 30 (draft) (cited in Gostin 1991: 141).

———. 1991b. "Recommendations for Preventing Transmission of Human Immunodeficiency Virus and Hepatitis B Virus to Patients During Exposure-Prone Invasive Procedures. *Morbidity and Mortality Weekly Report* 40(no. RR-8):1–9.

———. 1991c. "Revised Recommendations for Preventing Transmission of

Human Immunodeficiency Virus and Hepatitis B Virus to Patients During Invasive Procedures." November 27 (draft).

———. 1993. "HIV AIDS Surveillance Report." 3rd quarter edition 5:3(October):13.

Chafee, Senator John. 1994. "Health Equity and Access Reform Today." S 1770, 103rd Congress, 1st Session.

Chapter 458 of Acts of 1993, An Act Providing Coverage for Bone Marrow Transplants for Certain Patients with Breast Cancer.

Charen, M. 1989. "My Brother, the Doctor, Is in Danger." *New York Doctor* 2:7:17.

Clifford, K.A., and Iuculano, R.P. 1987. "AIDS and Insurance: The Rationale for AIDS-Related Testing." *Harvard Law Review* 100:1806–24.

Clinton Administration 1994. Health Security Act.

Cohen, J. 1989. "Democratic Equality." *Ethics* 99:4:727–51.

Coleman, B. 1991. "Medical Groups Balking at AIDS Rules." *Boston Globe* 140(Aug. 31):3.

Congressional Budget Office (CBO) 1993. *Managed Competition and Its Potential to Reduce Health Spending.* Washington, D.C.: U.S. Government Printing Office.

Cooper, Representative Jim. 1993. The Managed Competition Act of 1993. HR3222, 103rd Congress, 1st Session.

Cowan, D., et al. 1988. "HIV Prevalence in Military Reservists Employed in Health Care." Abstract, 5th International Conference on AIDS: 63.

Daniels, N. 1985. *Just Health Care.* Cambridge: Cambridge University Press.

———. 1986. "Why Saying No to Patients in the United States Is So Hard: Cost Containment, Justice, and Provider Autonomy." *New England Journal of Medicine* 314(May 22):1381–83.

———. 1988. *Am I My Parents' Keeper? An Essay on Justice Between the Young and the Old.* New York: Oxford University Press.

———. 1990. "Equality of What: Welfare, Resources, or Capabilities?" *Philosophy and Phenomenological Research* 50(supp.):273–96.

———. 1991a. "Is the Oregon Rationing Plan Fair?" *JAMA* 265:17(May 1):2232–35.

———. 1991b. "Duty to Treat or Right to Refuse?" *Hastings Center Report* 21(2):36–46.

———. 1992. "Growth Hormone Therapy for Short Stature: Can We Support the Treatment/Enhancement Distinction," *Growth & Growth Hormone* 8 (May Supp. 1):46–48.

———. 1993. "Rationing Fairly: Programmatic Considerations." *Bioethics* 7:2–3:224–33.

Daniels, N., Light, D., and Caplan, R. 1994. "Assessing the Fairness of National Health Care Reform." Robert Wood Johnson Foundation Report (under review).

Delaney, Martin 1989. "The Case for Patient Access to Experimental Therapy." *Journal of Infectious Diseases* 159:3(March):416–19.

DHHS, FDA 1987. "Investigational New Drug, Antibiotic, and Biological Drug Product Regulations; Treatment Use and Sale." *Fed Reg* 52 (May 22): 19466–77, codified at 21 C.F.R. 312.34 (1988).

Dickey, N. 1991. "Statement of the American Medical Association to the Centers for Disease Control." Chicago. February 21.

Dworkin, R. 1982. "What Is Equality? Part I: Equality of Welfare." *Philosophy and Public Affairs* 10:3:185–246; "Part II: Equality of Resources." *Philosophy and Public Affairs* 10:4:283–345.

Eckholm, E. 1993. "$89 million Awarded to Family Who Sued H.M.O." *New York Times* (December 30): A1, A12.

Emanuel, E. 1988. "Do Physicians Have an Obligation to Treat Patients with AIDS?" *New England Journal of Medicine* 318:25:1686–90.

Engelhardt, H. T. 1986. *The Foundations of Bioethics*. New York: Oxford University Press.

Enthoven, A.C. 1978. "Consumer Choice Health Plan: A National Health Insurance Proposal Based on Regulated Competition in the Private Sector." *New England Journal of Medicine* (March) 298(12) and 298(13): 650–58, 709–20.

Enthoven, A.C., and Kronick, R. 1989. "A Consumer Choice Health Plan for the 1990's: Universal Health Insurance in a System Designed to Promote Quality and Economy." *New England Journal of Medicine* 320(1) and 320(2):29–37, 94–101.

Enthoven, A.C., and Kronick, R. 1991. "Universal Health Insurance Through Incentives Reform." *Journal of the American Medical Association* 265 (18):2532–36.

Evans, R. 1989. "Controlling Health Expenditures: The Canadian Reality." *New England Journal of Medicine* 320:9:571–77.

Fahey, B.J., et al. 1989. "HIV-1 Infection After Occupational Exposure." Abstract, 5th International Conference on AIDS:725.

FDA 1992. "First AIDS Drug Tested Under Parallel Track Policy." Press release "Talk Paper." Food and Drug Administration, DHHS, October, 5, 1992.

Feldblum, C. 1991. "A Response to Gostin, 'The HIV-Infected Health Care Professional: Public Policy, Discrimination, and Patient Safety.' " *Law, Medicine, and Health Care.* 19:1-2:134–39.

Ferguson, J.H., Dubinsky, M., and Kirsch, P.J. 1993. "Court-Ordered Reimbursement for Unproven Medical Technology: Circumventing Technology Assessment." *JAMA* 269:2116–21.

Fill, G. 1991. "Dentist Faces Fine over AIDS Patient." *New York Times* (August 7):A14.

Flegenheimer, W.V., et al. 1989. "A Model for Facilitating Physician's Acceptance of Risk When Treating Patients with AIDS." Abstract, 5th International Conference on AIDS:960.

Foreman, J. 1990. "Researchers Say Heredity Plays a Key Role in Lung Cancer." *Boston Globe* (August 1):11.

Fox, Daniel M. 1988. "The Politics of Physicians' Responsibility in Epidemics: A Note on History." *Hastings Center Report* 18 (Supp.):5–10.

Freedman, Benjamin 1978, "A Meta-Ethics for Professional Morality" *Ethics* 89:1:1–19.

———. 1988. "Health Professions, Codes, and the Right to Refuse to Treat HIV-Infectious Patients." *Hastings Center Report* 18 (Supp.):20–25.

Freudenheim, M. 1990. "Health Insurers, to Reduce Losses, Blacklist Dozens of Occupations." *New York Times* (February 5):A1, D5.

Fuchs, V., and Hahn, J. 1990. "How Does Canada Do It?: A Comparison of Expenditures for Physician Services in the United States and Canada." *New England Journal of Medicine* 323:13:884–90.

Garamendi, J. 1992. *California Health Care in the 21st Century: A Vision for Reform.* Sacramento: State of California.

Gauthier, D. 1986. *Morals by Agreement.* Oxford: Oxford University Press.

General Accounting Office (GAO) 1993. "Needle Exchange Programs: Research Suggests Promise as an AIDS Prevention Strategy." GAO-HRD-93–60. Washington, D.C.

Gerberding, J.L., et al. 1987. "Risk of Transmitting the Human Immunodeficiency Virus, Cytomegalovirus, and Hepatitis B Virus to Health-Care Workers Exposed to Patients with AIDS and AIDS-Related Conditions." *Journal of Infectious Diseases* 156:1–8.

Gerbert, B., Macguire, B.T., and Coates, T.J. 1989. "Physicians and Acquired Immunodeficiency Syndrome: What Patients Think About Human Immunodeficiency Virus in Medical Practice." *JAMA* 262(14):1869–72.

Goodman, Ellen 1988. "For Doctors, an AIDS Dilemma That's Spreading with the Disease." *Boston Globe*, February 25.

Gostin, L. 1989. "HIV-Infected Physicians and the Practice of Seriously Invasive Procedures." *Hastings Center Report* 19(1):32–39.

———. 1991a. "The HIV-Infected Health Care Professional: Public Policy, Discrimination and Patient Safety." *Law, Medicine and Health Care* 18(4):303–10.

———. 1991b. "CDC Guidelines on HIV or HBV-Positive Health Care Professionals Performing Exposure-Prone Invasive Procedures." *Law, Medicine and Health Care* 19(1–2):140–43.

Government Committee on Choices in Health Care. 1992. *Choices in Health Care,* The Netherlands.

Green, M. 1991. "Making a Killing on AIDS: Home Health Care and Pentamidine." City of New York: Department of Consumer Affairs.

Gross, J. 1991. "Many Doctors Infected with AIDS Don't Follow New U.S. Guidelines." *New York Times* (August 18):A1, A20.

Hadorn, D.C., 1992. "Necessary Care Guidelines," in *Basic Benefits and Clinical Guidelines,* ed. D. C. Hadorn. Boulder, CO: Westview Press.

Hagen, M.D., Meyer, K.B., and Pauker, S.G. 1988. "Routine Preoperative Screening for HIV: Does the Risk to the Surgeon Outweigh the Risk to the Patient?" *JAMA* 259(9):1357–59.

Hammond, J.D., and Shapiro, A.F. 1986. "AIDS and the Limits of Insurability." *Milbank Quarterly* 64(supp.1):413.

Health Affairs 1993 "Managed Competition: Health Reform American Style." Supplement.

Henderson, D.K., et al. 1990. "Risk for Occupational Transmission of Human Immunodeficiency Virus Type 1 (HIV-1) Associated with Clinical Exposures: A Prospective Evaluation." *Annals of Internal Medicine* 113:740–46.

Hilts, P. 1989. "How the AIDS Crisis Made Drug Regulators Speed Up." *New York Times*, "Week in Review" (September 24):5.

———. 1991. "Congress Urges That Doctors Be Tested for AIDS." *New York Times* (October 4):A18.

Himmelstein, D., and Woolhandler, S. 1994. *The National Health Program Book: A Source Guide for Advocates.* Monroe, ME: Common Courage Press.

James, John 1993. "Berlin: Concorde Trial Questions Early AZT Use—Wide Implications." *AIDS Treatment News* 177(June 18):3–4.

Kantrowitz, B. 1991. "Doctors with AIDS: The Right to Know." *Newsweek* (July 1):48–57 (cover story).

Kavka, Gregory 1986. *Hobbesian Moral and Political Theory.* Princeton: Princeton University Press.

Kinsley, M. 1991. "Red Peril." *New Republic* 205(7):4,42.

Kolata, G. 1994. "Their Treatment, Their Lives, Their Decisions." *New York Times Magazine* (April 24):66, 100, 105.

Kronick, R., et al. 1993 "The Marketplace in Health Care Reform: The Demographic Limits of Managed Competition." *New England Journal of Medicine* (14 January):148–53.

Landesman, S. 1991. "The HIV-Positive Health Professional: Policy Options for Individuals, Institutions, and States: Public Policy and the Public— Observations from the Front Line." *Archives of Internal Medicine* 151(April):655–57.

Leary, W. 1991. "AMA Backs Off on an AIDS Risk List." *New York Times* (December 15):A38.

Levy, C. 1993. "Fifth Graders Get Condoms in New Haven." *New York Times* (July 28):B1.

Lowenfels, A.B., and Wormser, G. 1991. "Risk of Transmission of HIV from Surgeon to Patient." Letter. *New England Journal of Medicine* 325:888–89.

Lyall, S. 1991. "AIDS Tests Find No Link to L.I. Dentist." *New York Times* (August 10):A21–A22.

Macklin, R. 1990. "HIV Infection and Mouth-to-Mouth Resuscitation" (unpublished ms).

Marcus, R., and CDC Cooperative Needlestick Study Group 1988. "Surveillance of Health-Care Workers Exposed to Blood from Patients Infected with the Human Immunodeficiency Virus." *New England Journal of Medicine* 319(17):1118–23.

Marcus, R., et al. 1988. "HIV-1 Infection After Single Blood Exposure." Abstract, 5th International Conference on AIDS:63.

Mariner, Wendy K. 1990. "New FDA Drug Approval Policies and HIV Vaccine Development." *American Journal of Public Health* 80:3:336–41.

McGill, D. 1990. Personal communication.

Melman, M., and Youngner, S.J. 1991. *Delivering High Technology Home Care*. New York: Springer Publishing.

Meyer, J., Silow-Carroll, S., and Wicks, E. 1993. *Managed Competition in Health Care: Can It Work?* Reston, VA: Economic and Social Research Institute.

Muro, M. 1991. "Dark Days for Dentists." *Boston Globe* (August 1):61, 66.

National Commission 1990. National Commission on Acquired Immune Deficiency Syndrome, Report No. 3, "Personnel and Workforce." (pp. 1–13) Washington, D.C.

Navarro, M. 1991. "Health Workers Learn to Fight HIV Fears." *New York Times* (August 2):B1.

Nealon, P. 1993. "Condoms a Fact of Life in Many Massachusetts Schools." *Boston Globe* (March 5):21, 24.

Newhouse, J.P. 1993. "An Iconoclastic View of Health Cost Containment." *Health Affairs* (supp.) 12:152–71.

Newsweek. 1993. "Teenagers and AIDS" (August 3):45, 49.

Nozick, R. 1974. *Anarchy, State, and Utopia*. New York: Basic Books.

O'Connor, G.T., et al. 1991. "A Regional Prospective Study of In-Hospital Mortality Associated with Coronary Artery Bypass Grafting." *JAMA* 266(6):803–9.

Office of Technology Assessment 1988. "AIDS and Health Insurance: An OTA Survey." Congress of the United States.

Parmet, W.E. 1990. "Discrimination and Disability: The Challenges of the ADA." *Law, Medicine and Health Care* 18(4):331–44.

Pollock, E.J. 1993. "HMO Held Liable for Refusing Coverage." *Wall Street Journal* (December 28):B5.

Public Health Service, DHHS 1992. "Expanded Availability of Investigational New Drugs Through a Parallel Track Mechanism for People with AIDS and Other HIV-Related Disease." Fed. Reg. 57:73(April 15): 13250–59.

Rawls, J. 1971. *A Theory of Justice*. Cambridge: Harvard University Press.

———. 1980. "Kantian Constructivism in Moral Theory." *Journal of Philosophy* 77:9:515–72.

———. 1993. *Political Liberalism*. New York: Columbia University Press.

Reuters 1991. "California Groups Rebuff AIDS-Risk List Request." *New York Times* (October 19):A8.

Rockefeller, J.D. 1991. "A Call for Action: The Pepper Commission's Blueprint for Health Care Reform," *JAMA* 265:19 265(19):2507–10.

Rosenthal, E. 1991a. "Angry Doctors Condemn Plans to Test Them for AIDS." *New York Times* (August 20):C1, C5.

――――. 1991b. "Study Sees Moves on HIV Infection Backfiring." *New York Times* (September 10):C5.

Rugg, D. 1993. Centers for Disease Control. Personal communication.

Sabin, J., and Daniels, N. 1994. "Determining 'Medical Necessity' in Mental Health Practice: A Study of Clinical Reasoning and a Proposal for Insurance Policy." *Hastings Center Report* 24(6): 5–13.

Sabin, J., Forrow, L., and Daniels, N. 1991a. "When Is Home Care Medically Necessary?" *Hastings Center Report* 21(4):36–38.

Sabin, J.E., Forrow, L., and Daniels, N. 1991b. "Clarifying the Concept of Medical Necessity." Group Health Association of America. *Group Health Institute Proceedings*:693–708.

Sack, K. 1991. "Albany Plans to Allow Surgery by Doctors with the AIDS Virus." *New York Times* (October 9):A1, B6.

Schatz, B. 1987. "The AIDS Insurance Crisis: Underwriting or Overreaching?" *Harvard Law Review* 100:1782–1805.

Schwartz, W.B. 1987. "The Inevitable Failure of Current Cost Control Strategies: Why They Can Provide Only Temporary Relief." *JAMA* 257:220–24.

Sen, A. 1992. *Inequality Reexamined*. Cambridge: Harvard University Press.

Sipes-Metzler, P. 1993. Executive Director, Oregon Health Services Commission. Personal communication.

Slovic, P. 1987. "Perception of Risk." *Science* 236(April 17):280–85.

Slovic, P., Fischhoff, B., and Lichtenstein, S., 1979. "Rating the Risks." *Environment* 21(3):14–29.

Smith, D.D. 1990. "Physicians and the Acquired Immunodeficiency Syndrome." *JAMA* 264(4):452.

Starr, P. 1992. *The Logic of Health Care Reform*. Knoxville, TN: Whittle Direct Books.

Sullivan, J.F. 1989. "Should a Hospital Tell Patients if a Surgeon Has AIDS?" *New York Times* (December 12):B1 (cited in Barnes et al., 1990:311).

Tokors, J., et al. 1993. "Surveillance of HIV-Infection and AZT (Zidovudine) Use in Health Care Workers After Occupational Exposure to HIV-Infected Patients." *Annals of Internal Medicine* 118:12(June 15):913–19.

Tribe, L. 1978. *American Constitutional Law*. Mineola, NY: Foundation Press.

Wilkerson, I. 1991. "A.M.A. Approves AIDS Testing for Doctors and Health Workers." *New York Times* (June 27):A7.

Wilson, R. 1979. "Analyzing the Daily Risks of Life." *Technology Review* (February):41–46.

Wolff, C. 1991a. "New Rules on AIDS Produce First Resignation of a Doctor." *New York Times* (July 27):A1, A10.

――――. 1991b. "Doctor with AIDS Virus Evokes Anger and Pathos." *New York Times* (July 29):B1–B2.

Zuger, A., and Miles, S.M. 1987. "Physicians, AIDS, and Occupational Risk." *JAMA* 258(14):1924–28.

Index